ARTFUL SENTENCES:

Syntax as Style

ARTFUL SENTENCES:
Syntax as Style

Virginia Tufte

ACKNOWLEDGMENTS

M y thanks go, first of all, to the authors of more than a thousand sentences quoted in *Artful Sentences: Syntax as Style*. Each author's name and the title of the work appear at the end of the quotation and again in a bibliography-index that includes publisher and date. I hope readers will enjoy these wonderful examples as much as I do and will be inspired by them.

Artful Sentences grows out of my 1971 book, *Grammar as Style*. Garrett Stewart assisted with *Grammar as Style*, and his insights, especially on syntactic symbolism, still inform this new book. I am grateful for his encouragement and cheery emails.

My friend Dawn Finley provided expert editorial assistance, subtle criticism, and even some computer repairs. My friend Wendy Furman-Adams read the manuscript with care and made extremely helpful comments.

When I was writing my previous books, it was my good fortune to have the companionship and perceptive observations of Edward E. Tufte, my late husband. During work on *Artful Sentences*, I have greatly appreciated the interest and unique suggestions of Edward Rolf Tufte, our son. From the day of his birth, he has added to my life immeasurable wonder and joy.

PUBLISHED BY GRAPHICS PRESS LLC
POST OFFICE BOX 430
CHESHIRE, CONNECTICUT 06410
UNITED STATES
WWW.EDWARDTUFTE.COM

Third printing, May 2010

CONTENTS

The streets were calm with Sunday.
Aimee Bender

War remains the decisive human failure.
John Kenneth Galbraith

Autos honked. Trees rustled. People passed. Arnie went out.
Langston Hughes

Everyone has someone. Except me.
Carolyn See

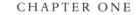 CHAPTER ONE

Short Sentences

And the words slide into the slots ordained by syntax,
and glitter as with atmospheric dust with those impurities
which we call meaning.
Anthony Burgess, *Enderby*, 406

Anthony burgess is right: it is the words that shine and sparkle and glitter, sometimes radiant with an author's inspired choice. But it is syntax that gives words the power to relate to each other in a sequence, to create rhythms and emphasis, to carry meaning–of whatever kind–as well as glow individually in just the right place.

The basic unit of English syntax is the clause. Its "slots ordained by syntax" are a subject and a predicate. What traditional grammarians call a "simple" sentence consists of an independent clause, independent in that it makes sense without being attached to anything: *Time flies*. Without losing its nature as a basic sentence, however, a "simple" sentence may include optional added slots such as spaces for modifiers, complements, objects.

Professional writers frequently use for particular effects these short sentences, their very length making effective juxtaposition with longer more complicated sentences. Often also, in creating a long sentence, good writers construct a short independent clause and attach free modifiers loosely around it. It is as if a short sentence serves as nucleus inside a long sentence.

Short basic sentences may be divided into four main types, depending on what is said about the subject's state of existence or activity. The types are distinguished by different kinds of predicates, arranged here according to increasing verbal activity:

Type one: equations with be. Some form of *be* with a noun, adjective, or adverb:
> This is a novel.
> James Michener, *The Source*, opening line

Type two: equations with linking verbs. A linking verb such as *seems, feels, remains, becomes* with a noun or an adjective:
> He feels empty.
> Alan Lightman, *Einstein's Dreams*, 179

Type three: intransitives. An intransitive verb, which may or may not be followed by an adverbial modifier:
> So the story creeps to an end.
> Grace Paley, *Goodbye and Good Luck*, 10

Type four: transitives. A transitive verb with a noun phrase as direct object:
> I constructed a triangle in my head.
> Steve Martin, *The Pleasure of My Company*, 157

Any of the basic patterns can include an adverb or other adverbial, for example, a prepositional phrase such as *to an end* or *in my head*, in the previous two quotations. The transitive pattern can include, besides the direct object, an indirect object or an objective complement. These basic patterns, in addition to their utility as sentences, also serve a vital generative role, well described by Noam Chomsky: he called them "kernels" and remarked on their "important intuitive significance."[1] Their incredible versatility as a creative resource can be seen in the examples that follow.

---

[1] *Syntactic Structures* (The Hague: Mouton, 1957), 80, and *Aspects of the Theory of Syntax* (Cambridge: Harvard University Press, 1965), 17, 18.

Type one: equations with be

The simplest form of the *be*-pattern is the exact equating of two noun phrases:

> Nat was Nat.
>> Bernard Malamud, *The Assistant*, 130

> So *that was that.*
>> Eric Ambler, *Intrigue*, 300

> "A Pangolin is a Pangolin."
>> Willie Ley, *Another Look at Atlantis*, 8

> *Unfair's unfair.*
>> Brooks Atkinson, *Brief Chronicles*, 176

Although such an assertion may seem minimal, it can provide a telling emphasis. Sometimes it is repeated to create an insistence:

> Among the poorest people on the continent, they were freely loading me up with provisions. I offered my watch in trade. He refused (not altogether convincingly), saying "*A gift is a gift.*"…His seven children followed along behind me…When I got to the edge of the forest, I took off my watch and handed it to the oldest boy. "This is for your father. Tell him I said *a gift is a gift.*"
>> Mark Plotkin, *Tales of a Shaman's Apprentice*, 198

Below, an equative clause reinforces an argument:

> As I was saying, *fair's fair.*
>> Katha Pollitt, *Subject to Debate*, 38

Variations abound. Inserting a prepositional phrase as modifier, on each side of the equation, enlarges meaning:

> The *reality* of art is the *reality* of imagination.
>> Jeanette Winterson, *Art Objects*, 151

In the next example, the author uses adjective modifiers in a pair of
sentences to create a persuasive finale:

> The individual *voice* is the communal *voice*. The regional
> *voice* is the universal *voice*.
>   Joyce Carol Oates, *The Faith of a Writer*, 1

Next, the rhythm of a repeated noun itself measures the intervals
of time the author is describing in the remarkable sentence italicized
below:

> And beyond any particular clock, a vast scaffold of time,
> stretching across the universe, lays down the law of time
> equally for all. *In this world, a second is a second is a second.*
>   Alan Lightman, *Einstein's Dreams*, 34

Lightman demonstrates his point by imaginatively extending a basic
syntactic pattern, as appropriate in its context as the well-known words
of Gertrude Stein:

> Rose is a rose is a rose is a rose.
> *Sacred Emily*, 187

Much more frequent among equative clauses are those that have
different nouns as subject and complement. Often they give an aphoristic effect:

> Work was his life.
>   Carlos Baker, *Ernest Hemingway–A Life Story*, 562

> Creators are workaholics.
>   Ellen Winter, *Gifted Children*, 293

> Music was my refuge.
>   Maya Angelou, *Singin' and Swingin' and Gettin' Merry Like
>   Christmas*, 1

> Space was the real problem.
>   Aimee Bender, *An Invisible Sign of My Own*, 1

> All four of Richard Wright's grandparents were former slaves.
>   David Markson, *Vanishing Point*, 9

The predicate noun can be repeated and redefined, as in the following example. Here the conjunction *yet* introduces the repetition:

> This is nonsense, of course; yet, useful nonsense.
> Donald Davie, *Articulate Energy*, 96

Below, the *be*-pattern shapes the rhetorical figure *synecdoche*, where the part stands for the whole. In order, the personal subject of each clause is equated with the virtue it embodies, the annoyance it inflicts, and the school it attended:

> I was all humility.
> Rupert Brooke, *The Prose of Rupert Brooke*, 3

> She was exasperation, she was torture.
> Vladimir Nabokov, *Ada*, 199

> He was Princeton, his daughter was Vassar,
> and I was College of One.
> Sheilah Graham, *The College of One*, 77

Adjectives stand as nouns in an equative pattern:

> The longest is the loveliest.
> Truman Capote, *Local Color*, 72

The next equative forms are metaphors, each in one of the several syntactic shapes that metaphorical statement may take:

> Her spine is a denial.
> William Gibson, *A Mass for the Dead*, 14

> Chaos was yawn.
> Samuel Beckett, *Murphy*, 175

> Dress is the frontier between the self and the not-self.
> Elizabeth Wilson, *Adorned in Dreams*, 3

> Stieglitz was a chameleon in his affections.
> Edward Dahlberg, *Alms for Oblivion*, 6

> The church was a bare, weather-beaten ghost of a building...
> Alice Walker, "A Sudden Trip Home in the Spring," 299

Her answer was ice.
　　Bernard Malamud, *The Assistant*, 130

I read my words. They were mirrors.
　　bell hooks, *Remembered Rapture*, 7

　　Metaphor is a powerful element of style. In addition to equative forms with noun complements that lend themselves to pointed metaphorical statements, *be*-sentences that direct their subjects toward a predicate adjective in the third slot can also be metaphoric:

The brooks are unlocked at last.
　　Kingsley was wrong-footed.
　　Fred Hoyle, *The Black Cloud*, 66

Here a past participle, *unlocked*, serves as an adjectival to describe the spring thaw, although one might also think of it as a passive verb:

The brooks are unlocked at last.
　　May Sarton, *Journal of a Solitude*, 128

A prepositional phrase, serving adverbially, can often present a metaphor:

He was in a fog.
　　John O'Hara, *Assembly*, 231

When a *like*-phrase fills this third slot, the metaphor, of course, becomes explicitly a simile:

Sincerity is like sleep.
　　W. H. Auden, *The Dryer's Hand and Other Essays*, 17

The following simile with *as … as* uses *winter* as an adjective:

The moose is as winter a creature as just about any.
　　Trudy Dittmar, *Fauna and Flora, Earth and Sky*, 33

　　Adjectival complements in *be*-sentences are common, useful, and sometimes metaphorical:

The streets were calm with Sunday.
　　Aimee Bender, *An Invisible Sign of My Own*, 69

The world was newborn.
　　Jonathan Franzen, *The Corrections*, 329

The heart attack was strange – fear is strange.
James Baldwin, *Tell Me How Long the Train's Been Gone*,
opening line

Again, the complement can be an adverb or an adverbial phrase:

Change was everywhere.
John Steinbeck, *Sweet Thursday*, 2

Nothing was out of place.
Margaret Atwood, *Surfacing*, 40

Type two: equations with linking verbs

Like the *be*-pattern, linking verbs may take nouns as complements.
Some of the linking verbs have a little more acute verbal action than
the *be*-equations:

Everything became a mist.
C. S. Lewis, *That Hideous Strength*, 380

He became a castaway in broad daylight.
William Golding, *Pincher Martin*, 56

A simple syntactic structure – a linking verb with a noun and two adjectives – here makes an urgent point:

War remains the decisive human failure.
John Kenneth Galbraith, *The Economics of Innocent Fraud*, 62

As predicate complements, adjectives that follow linking verbs often
carry the new information and draw the stress:

Argument remains inescapable.
Julie Thompson Klein, *Crossing Boundaries*, 211

She looked new and fresh.
Carolyn See, *The Handyman*, 173

The maid looked doubtful.
Dorothy Parker, "Big Blonde," 250

His mind turned opaque at the word.
John Knowles, *Indian Summer*, 152

This gets tricky.
  Joan Didion, *Where I Was From*, 177

I kept dumb about my home life.
  Janet Frame, *The Reservoir*, 55

Hasna remained hairless in a society of thick dark manes.
  Frances Khirallah Noble, *The Situe Stories*, 5

Her narrative grew less coherent here...
  John Barth, *Giles Goat-Boy*, 491

In these linking examples, the major emphasis tends to fall on the predicate complement or, sometimes, whatever word or structure is at the end of the sentence (unless the word is a pronoun or has a pronoun as headword), giving added weight to what tends, anyway, to be the most important information, the real news of the sentence. Opening the sentence, the subject is likely to be a character or thing we already know or an idea that has been under discussion, sometimes a pronoun that refers backward. Often it is a person or a thing or an idea carried over to receive some new predication: the chief interest is likely to be found in the second half of the sentence.

Below, a linking verb, *remains*, has as complement a noun phrase, here a metaphor expressing a potent opinion:

[Otto Jespersen] did not formulate the problem of designing an explicit linguistic theory. But his work remains a mine of perceptive and useful observations and insights.
  Noam Chomsky, *On Language*, 157

Type three: intransitives

Varying degrees of activity can be produced by the versatile intransitive. Reading the following sentences aloud, one can hear the differing effects depending on what kind of word receives strongest stress and what its position is in the pattern:

Ida reddened.
  Bernard Malamud, *The Assistant*, 34

She blushed under her clothes.
  Malamud, 15

The nothingness continued.
Tennessee Williams, *The Roman Spring of Mrs. Stone*, 147

The tables have turned.
Daren Fonda, "Revenge of the Bean Counters," 38

Autos honked. Trees rustled. People passed. Arnie went out.
Langston Hughes, *The Ways of White Folks*, 155

His insides were shaking.
Charles Johnson, *Dreamer*, 217

Harmony settled over the kitchen.
Norman Mailer, *Advertisements for Myself*, 127

A humidifier steamed at her feet.
J. F. Powers, *Morte d'Urban*, 116

Blame rests always.
Janet Frame, *Scented Gardens for the Blind*, 26

It began so unrecognizably.
John Wyndham, *Out of the Deep*, 6

His eyes gleamed angrily.
P. G. Wodehouse, *The Man Who Disliked Cats*, 97

A face looked in the spy-hole.
Brendan Behan, *Confessions of an Irish Rebel*, 11

The stairs trembled under his feet.
Johnson, 140

Time stretched on, indifferently.
William Golding, *Pincher Martin*, 182

John Hurston, however, ached with ambition.
Valerie Boyd, *Wrapped in Rainbows*, 15

Her eyebrows lifted like antennae.
Margaret Atwood, *Surfacing*, 125

The clouds were sitting on the land.
William Golding, *Lord of the Flies*, 70

Type four: transitives

Maximum activity often finds expression in the transitive, where the action of the verb crosses over to an object. Personal pronouns as direct objects, however, convey little or no new information but refer back to some person mentioned in a previous sentence. In transitive sentences ending in personal pronouns, the main emphasis usually remains on the verb:

> The room alarmed him.
> Brian Moore, *The Luck of Ginger Coffey*, 182

> Birdsong wakes me.
> Margaret Atwood, *Surfacing*, 47

When a multi-syllable pronoun serves as object, however, it may or may not draw the stress, or may share about equal stress with the verb:

> She read everything.
> Virginia Woolf, *The Common Reader*, 169

When a noun phrase is the direct object in final position, it brings new information and thus draws the stress:

> I felt anger.
> Erlene Stetson, *Silence: Access and Aspiration*, 241

> Marlborough swallowed the bait.
> Fred Hoyle, *The Black Cloud*, 63

> Veterans send ball-point pens. Banks send memo books.
> E. B. White, *The Points of My Compass*, 126

> That meant ash; ash meant burning; burning must mean cigarettes.
> Kingsley Amis, *Lucky Jim*, 64

In these transitive examples, an adverb or a prepositional phrase occupies the terminal slot and thus receives a strong share of attention:

> She changes the subject immediately.
> F. Scott Fitzgerald, *This Side of Paradise*, 143

> They peel the morning like a fruit.
> Lawrence Durrell, *Justine*, xxx

Here an adjective *numb* as an objective complement draws the stress:

> Enough pain makes people numb.
> Naomi Wolf, *The Beauty Myth*, 249

An effective and distinctive positioning of a prepositional phrase adds emphasis to both "someone" and the phrase because the latter is punctuated as a fragment:

> Everyone has someone. Except me.
> Carolyn See, *The Handyman*, 206

Although transitive patterns usually incorporate more verbal energy than the other patterns, this is not always the case, even though the transitive involves one more participant, the object. "The rocket exploded," or "I came, I saw, I conquered," both intransitives, are considerably more energetic than a transitive like:

> Two stripes ornamented the sleeve.
> Wyndham Lewis, *Blasting and Bombardiering*, 75

No real action is performed, and the verb itself is created from a noun, but Lewis's sentence is more energetic than "Two stripes were on the sleeve," or "There were two stripes on the sleeve."

Short, unadorned sentences, and short clauses within a sentence, are resources that can serve admirably in well-chosen locations. They are important also as a basic structure that can be transformed in a variety of ways and as the host for embedding or attaching new material.

The dynamics of the basic patterns in context

Four types of basic sentences have now been illustrated with isolated sentences. Reading some sentences in context will help to see whether a scale of verbal activity has any validity in actual practice, and whether a particular type has a specialized utility:

> Somebody sighed, from the heart; he looked up; it was Hannah. They were looking downward and sidelong. His sister's face had altered strangely among this silence; it had become thin, shy and somehow almost bridal. He remembered her wedding in Panama; yes, it was much the same face. He looked away.
> James Agee, *A Death in the Family*, 150

This scene of looking and recognition, of description, identification, and the transitive act of memory, is written with a prevalence of intransitives but a mix of all four types. Most of us usually write this way. Few ideas demand the services of only one kind of structure. But sometimes the innate qualities of a particular structure can contribute to a planned effect. In the next excerpts, for instance, the *be*-pattern, both its equative and its descriptive forms, is exactly suited to the terse, epigrammatic expression. The *be*-predicates are italicized:

> There *is* a radicalism in all getting, and conservatism in all keeping. Lovemaking *is* radical while marriage *is* conservative. So, too, the get-rich-quick capitalism *is* radical, while a capitalism intent solely on keeping what it already has *is* conservative.
> Eric Hoffer, *The Passionate State of Mind*, 12

> Religion *is* not a matter of God, church, holy cause, etc. These *are* but accessories. The source of religious preoccupation *is* in the self, or rather the rejection of self. Dedication *is* the obverse side of self-rejection.
> Hoffer, 33

Parallel patterns of the *be*-phrases are useful in the set of descriptive examples below, two recounting a dull, dreary routine and the third a scene of evacuation or absence:

> Casualties *were very few*, and supply *was regular*...
> It *was dreary*. There *was danger*, but it *was remote*; there *was diversion*, but it *was rare*. For the most part it *was work* and work of the most distasteful character, work which *was mean and long*.
> Norman Mailer, *Advertisements for Myself*, 133

> My classes *were dull*, my masters with a few exceptions *were dull*, the school-life in general, apart from the sports, *was dull*.
> John Drinkwater, *Inheritance*, 235

> The big sycamore by the creek *was gone*. The willow tangle *was gone*. The little tangle of untrodden bluegrass *was gone*. The clump of dogwood on the little rise across the creek– now that, too, *was gone*.
> Robert Penn Warren, *Flood*, 4

In vivid contrast to the above is the convening of intransitives and transitives, with limited expansion, to portray a frenzy of violent action. The whole paragraph is guided by a parallelism of subject-opened, brief declarative forms, sometimes compounded:

> He began to curse. He scrambled down the rock, found a too heavy stone, moved it about a yard and then let go. He threw himself over the stone and went cursing to the water. But there was nothing visible within reach that he could handle. He went quickly to the top again and stood looking at the headless dwarf in terror. He scrambled back to the too heavy stone and fought with it. He moved it, end over end. He built steps to the top of a wall and worked the great stone up. He drew from his body more strength than he had got. He bled. He stood sweating among the papers at last. He dismantled the dwarf and rebuilt him on the stone that after all was not too heavy for education and intelligence and will.
>
> William Golding, *Pincher Martin*, 80

Repetition of *he* as opener in the examples above and below intensifies the focus on the person performing the series of violent actions. Parallel, subject-opened, active sentences offer a mixture of transitives and intransitives. The following passage places in emphatic positions a series of forceful, violent verbs that contribute to the loud excess:

> He thought that he was god and that he could stop everything from moving. He thought that since he could, he had got to. He cried out loud. He swore at the top of his voice. He fired off a gun and made the people listen. He roared and he boasted and made himself known. He blew back into the wind and stamped on the rolling earth and swore up and down he could make it all stop with his invention. He got up in the teeth of the storm and made a loud speech which everybody heard.
>
> Thomas Merton, *The Behavior of Titans*, 31

Unlike the actions in the past tense in the preceding examples, the exciting moments described below are set forth in the present tense, mostly in a series of short action clauses of varying types. The confusion described is emphasized by the use of different persons as subjects of the sentences and several kinds of predicates with mostly action verbs; in the quieter scene at the end, *be*-predicates prevail:

> Suddenly she sits bolt upright. She is wide awake and lucid. "You have to ring that bell now," she says. "This baby is being born."
>
> A. clearly doesn't believe her. "I can feel it, I can feel the head," she says. A. pushes the button for the call bell. A nurse appears and checks, and now everything is happening too soon, nobody is ready. They set off down the hall, the nurse wheeling. Jeannie feels fine. She watches the corridors, the edges of everything shadowy because she doesn't have her glasses on. She hopes A. will remember to bring them. They pass another doctor... "Don't push," the nurse says. "What do you mean?" Jeannie says. Why should she wait? Why should the baby wait for them because they are late? ...
>
> She can see the baby... As for the vision, there wasn't one. Jeannie is conscious of no special knowledge; already she's forgetting what it was like. She's tired and very cold; she is shaking, and asks for another blanket. A. comes back to the room with her; her clothes are still there. Everything is quiet.
> Margaret Atwood, *Giving Birth*, 146-147

The variety of effects that *be*-clauses can bring in context is exemplified in some of the examples that follow. First, a series of descriptive *be*-clauses is jolted by an abrupt intransitive conclusion:

> Her ringlets are dark, her skin very fair. She is not mourning deeply. Her smile is smug, her fine eyes inviting and she did not wait long for a second husband.
> Evelyn Waugh, *A Little Learning*, 3

A *be*-pattern sets forth a basic quality of Hebrew poetry below, and transitive forms then take over to describe, actively, the rhythm supplied and the effect given:

> In other words, in Hebrew poetry the number of syllables is nothing; the accented words are everything. They alone supply the rhythm, and they alone give the effect.
> Mary Ellen Chase, *The Bible and the Common Reader*, 76

Even more in the following excerpts, the contrast in forms is appropriate to the contrast between things in themselves static and things essentially active. Linking patterns are mixed with others to describe a changing scene:

> The air became gray and opalescent; a solitary light suddenly outlined a window over the way; then another light; then a hundred more danced and glimmered into vision. Under his feet a thick, iron-studded skylight turned yellow; in the streets the lamps of the taxi-cabs sent out glistening sheens along the already black pavement.
>
> F. Scott Fitzgerald, *This Side of Paradise*, 254

Next, abruptly, a terminal action (intransitive) closes in stasis (*be*-pattern):

> His world is blowing over, his day is done.
>
> James Thurber, *Let Your Mind Alone*, 230

Here, in two short paragraphs, is a termination, with two static sentences followed by a final intransitive:

> It is over, then. Our good friend is no more.
> An era ends.
>
> Garson Kanin, *Remembering Mr. Maugham*, 3

Short sentences as topic sentences and as syntactic punctuation of a paragraph

Since the kind of idea that is compressed into minimal shape (or that naturally assumes it) tends to be rudimentary, short sentences of this sort often serve well as introductory sentences in a paragraph. As the writer moves into a new topic, in fiction or nonfiction, the *be*-sentence defines and introduces, singly or in pairs or triplets:

> In the morning *it was all over. The fiesta was finished.* I woke about nine o'clock, had a bath, dressed, and went downstairs. The square was empty and there were no people on the streets. A few children were picking up rocket-sticks in the square. The cafés were just opening and the waiters were carrying out the comfortable white wicker chairs and arranging them around the marble-topped tables in the shade of the arcade. They were sweeping the streets and sprinkling them with a hose.
>
> Ernest Hemingway, *The Sun Also Rises*, 227

The walls are white. The rug is white. The furnishings are white.
A ceiling of white gauze diffuses the lights glaring overhead.
A long traveling shot through the corridors of *The April Fools*
penthouse set finally discloses Catherine Deneuve, sitting in
a white fur-covered chair, in a white lace dress, the long
blond hair pulled back to reveal a face with outrageously
perfect features.
    Mary Most, *Une Créature du Cinéma*, 10

Ideas about the building of paragraphs from sentences usually concern "topic sentences" and the ordering of "subordinate ideas." Yet accomplished writers usually seem to have something else in mind when deciding how to put sentences together: the better the writers, of fiction and nonfiction alike, the more they tend to vary their sentence lengths. And they do it as dramatically as possible. Time and again the shortest sentence in a professional paragraph is brought up against the longest, or at least lodges among some much longer. This smallest sentence is often a basic sentence both grammatically *and* semantically, stating in simplest terms the central idea of the paragraph. Thus, as already seen, syntax, taking a minimal shape, often marks the topic sentence of the paragraph. This is true primarily in expository prose, more likely than any other to have a straightforward and orderly topic that can go, by way of summary, into a single sentence. Narrative prose may be fashioned on a somewhat different principle, a more dramatic one. It is still disposed into paragraphs most of the time, but short sentences when they do appear are less often a condensation of the topic than some narrowed, relaxed point of departure or a slamming start, a later point of rest, an abrupt turn or climax, or a simple close. Either way, however, as a topic sentence or as a kind of syntactic punctuation, a very short sentence can be effective.

A simple flat statement can also appear in the middle of a paragraph. Here, in an essay, it serves as a kind of pivotal assertion aided by the conjunction that starts the sentence:

The lack of structure in Italian universities made it possible
for individual scholars to produce original research, a
scarcely noticed form of Renaissance individualism. *And they
did.* The list of their accomplishments in law, medicine, philosophy, mathematics, and the humanities is very long.
    Paul F. Grendler, *The Universities of the Renaissance and
    Reformation*, 12

An equative sentence can also stand by itself as a paragraph to summarize the preceding three:

> If you stop Ted in the street and ask him the way he is always eager to direct you... He will rescue children in distress separated from their mothers in a crowd. At the scene of an accident he is among the first to restore calm, to comfort people, ring for ambulances, distribute hot tea.
>
> He will reprimand or report to the police anyone making himself a public nuisance or breaking the law. Ted has deep respect for the law.
>
> If you say good morning to him he returns your greeting with a cheerful smile.
>
> *That is Ted.*
> Janet Frame, *The Reservoir*, 117

Here action closes down to finish in a static *be*-sentence:

> The silence of the theater behind him ended with a curious snapping sound, followed by the heavy roaring of a rising crowd and the interlaced clatter of many voices. *The matinee was over.*
> F. Scott Fitzgerald, *This Side of Paradise*, 254-255

The same sort of sentence is used twice in the next paragraph, for a doubled emphasis, an insistent finality:

> He jumped to feel Ann's clasp upon his arm. She had been saying something to him. *It was all over.* He had seen the coffin awkwardly descend into the watery pit and heard the earth upon it. *It was all over.*
> Iris Murdoch, *An Unofficial Rose*, 11

Finally, there is a special kind of paired formula that, for the simple contrast of its thought, finds short equative sentences very useful. This is the contrastive pattern, which may be negative-positive, or positive-negative. Here are some, in separate sentences and in an internal combination:

> The life of his body, illclad, illfed, louse-eaten, made him close his eyelids in a sudden spasm of despair: and in the darkness he saw the brittle bright bodies of lice falling from

the air and turning often as they fell. Yes; and *it was not dark-*
ness that fell from the air. *It was brightness.*
James Joyce, *A Portrait of the Artist as a Young Man*, 234

Character, in my opinion, *is always the starting point, but not*
necessarily the end, of biography.
Carol Brightman, *Character in Biography*, 325

In addition to the *be*-patterns of all kinds, patterns with linking
verbs are sometimes used in many of these same ways to punctuate a
longer passage. In this use, as everywhere, they are less common than
the other three types. When they are appropriate, however, these linking arrangements can be very effective, as in the example below:

> Perhaps people think *A Man for All Seasons* is so great
> because unlike the usual movie which is aimed at twelve
> year-olds, this one is aimed at twelve-year-old intellectuals
> and idealists. And if they're grown into compromising and
> unprincipled people, can hail *A Man for All Seasons* as a mas-
> terpiece: heroism so remote, so totally the property of a
> superhuman figure, absolves them of human weakness. .
> *It becomes romantic.*
> Pauline Kael, *Kiss Kiss Bang Bang*, 154-55

Now and then a linking pattern, or more often an intransitive or a
transitive, joins a *be*-pattern as final punctuation for paragraph or novel:

> And now I realized that I couldn't return to Mary's, or to
> any part of my old life. I could approach it only from the
> outside, and I had been as invisible to Mary as I had been to
> the Brotherhood. No, I couldn't return to Mary's, only move
> ahead or stay here, underground. So I would stay here until I
> was chased out. Here, at least, I could try to think things out
> in peace, or, if not in peace, in quiet. *I would take up residence*
> *underground. The end was in the beginning.*
> Ralph Ellison, *Invisible Man*, 494

Intransitives are often used to set off or break up long stretches of
dialogue or description – for emphasis, for interruption, for transition,
for the introduction of a new speaker. It is the intransitive that pro-

vides also the simplest pattern introducing the speaking act itself: *the poet said, he vociferated, she announced, they bellowed, I interrupt*, and so on. Here, from a daydream:

> I remember myself as that girl sitting on a tram, an older gentleman with a butterfly net across from me. Although he appears to be in sweet reverie, *I interrupt* gently to tell him: "By the way, I love your books." He smiles to thank me.
> Amy Tan, *The Opposite of Fate*, 227

Like all basic clauses, the intransitive itself can be doubled:

> *I know, I know.* I do not for a minute forget the dark gusts that roll dooms like tumbleweeds in the night across troubled America. But, for a few hours on a few days, at least I see the mixture. I know the paradox of this country.
> Ray Bradbury, *Any Friend of Trains Is a Friend of Mine*, 50

An intransitive can relieve longer patterns in the center. Here, three in a group are italicized:

> No other natural phenomenon on the planet–not even mountains five miles high, rivers spilling over cliffs, or redwood forests–evokes such reverence. Yet this same "all-powerful" ocean now proves as slavishly subservient to natural laws as a moth caught by candlelight or a rose seed blown into the Atlantic. *The ocean obeys. It heeds. It complies.* It has its tolerances and its stresses. When these are surpassed, the ocean falters. Fish stocks can be depleted. The nurseries of marine life can be varied. Beaches can erode away. Seawater, the most common substance on this earth and the most life-nourishing–at once liquid soil and liquid atmosphere–can be hideously corrupted. It can host substances that in the stomachs of oysters or clams are refined into poisons that paralyze porpoise and man alike.
> Wesley Marx, *The Frail Ocean*, 2-3

The intransitive can also provide a quick restatement at the end of a paragraph, leaving us suspended:

> Marvin bowed to the moustached man's superior wisdom and made himself at home in the posada. He settled himself at an outdoor table that commanded a good view of the

courtyard and of the road beyond it. He fortified himself
with a flagon of wine, and proceeded to fulfill his theoretical
function as called for by the Theory of Searches: viz., *he
waited*.
  Robert Sheckley, *Mindswap*, 132

Or, an abrupt conclusion:

He stood in the rain, unable to move, not knowing if the
lovers were real or simply creations of the lightning and
when it stopped, they stopped; unless of course he was
dreaming one of those dreams from which he would
awaken in that pain which is also sharpest pleasure, having
loved in sleep. But the cold rain was real; and so was the
sudden soft moan from the poolhouse. *He fled*.
  Gore Vidal, *Washington, D.C.*, 4

Or, it can itself constitute a paragraph of transition:

...and in utter abjection of spirit he craved forgiveness
mutely of the boyish hearts about him.

Time passed.

He sat again in the front bench of the chapel. The daylight
was already falling...
  James Joyce, *A Portrait of the Artist as a Young Man*, 126

Various patterns are allotted carefully to the next two paragraphs,
the short sentences arriving at key points to signal the essential events.
In each, transitive patterns join with intransitive at the end for a well-
planned conclusion, in the one a collapse into sleep, in the other the
activation of a simple movement:

The doctor went away into the mist. It was daylight now,
but everything was still grey and hazy—the pine trees floating in mist, their branches drooping like burdened wings
that no air can lift. Janek slipped into the brushwood and
raised the rusty iron door. He climbed down the ladder and
threw himself on the mattress. It was pitch-dark in the hide-
out. He got up and tried to light a fire; the wood was damp.
He got it going at last, lay down again, trying not to cry...
The silence in his ears was frightening; it was as if the whole
earth had turned to stone. *His eyes closed. Weariness numbed
his body, his mind... He fell asleep.*
  Romain Gary, *Nothing Important Ever Dies*, 3

He turned round to know if Randall and the children were
following, and saw like a shaft of light through a cloud a
momentarily opened vista between the rows of dark figures.
Something at the far end of that vista arrested his attention
for a second before the opening was closed again by the
movement of people towards the gate. Two women he had
seen like bats clinging together, in their glasses glinting
under the black canopy, two women facing him in grotesque
stillness down the rainswept vista. One of them was Emma.
Hugh stopped. The vision had gone, but as if to confirm its
reality he caught sight of the intent averted face of his son,
and his son's hand descending after a gesture of greeting.
Hugh stood still for another moment. Then he set his feet in motion.
   Iris Murdoch, *An Unofficial Rose*, 13

Below, an opening transitive stands as a topic sentence, and a final
intransitive tersely summarizes. The author summons these short basic
sentences in an urgent effort to define deeply-felt issues that threaten
the future of the world:

> *The myth of war creates a new, artificial reality.* Moral pre-
> cepts—ones we have spent a lifetime honoring—are jetti-
> soned. We accept, if not condone, the maiming and killing
> of others as the regrettable cost of war. *We operate under a*
> *new moral code.*
>   Chris Hedges, *War is a Force that Gives Us Meaning*, 35

Here, in italics, are a two-word intransitive, along with a four-word
transitive that has both direct and indirect objects. They provide syntactic relief from the longer structures around them and isolate the
speaker's actions:

> The phone rang continuously—so continuously that my sec-
> retary went home in annoyance, leaving me to answer it
> myself. Some of the calls were from the very great like Ed
> Murrow, who wanted me to extend my remarks for an even
> larger audience. *I declined.* A few wanted to know if I was
> likely to say anything that would affect the market in the
> near future. *I promised them silence.* The rest wished to
> denounce me for destroying their dream.
>   John Kenneth Galbraith, *The Great Crash, 1929*, xv

In a poignant paragraph, the second sentence, a transitive pattern, serves as a forceful topic sentence, augmented by several additional short sentences in various patterns, concluding with a series in both English and the language of the author's Chicana-mexicana-tejana traditions:

> At a very early age I had a strong sense of who I was and
> what I was about and what was fair. *I had a stubborn will.*
> I tried constantly to mobilize my soul under my own regime,
> to live life on my own terms no matter how unsuitable to
> others they were. *Terca.* Even as a child I would not obey.
> I was "lazy." Instead of ironing my younger brothers' shirts
> or cleaning the cupboards, I would pass many hours study-
> ing, reading, painting, writing. Every bit of self-faith I'd
> painstakingly gathered took a beating daily. Nothing in
> my culture approved of me. *Había agarrado malos pasos.*
> *Something was "wrong" with me. Estaba más allá de la tradición.*
> Gloria Anzaldúa, *Borderlands/La Frontera,* 38

Again in a personal memoir, several short sentences – transitive, intransitive, equative – combine with longer sentences to dramatize the author's responses to stories she has read:

> *I loved the idea of sleeping on pine needles.* I've got to say one
> of my deep regrets is that pine oils became known as such
> wonderful cleaners that the scent of pine no longer brings
> the woods to mind but rather the bus stations and nursing
> homes where sickness and adversity prevail instead of the
> freedom of open spaces. *I cried for The Little Match Girl. I hate*
> *the people who tried to make that a cute story. She was poor. Her*
> *family was poor.* She froze to death because of the indiffer-
> ence of the people inside with a fireplace and food and
> drink. *And that was that. This is not a musical. This is not fun.*
> Nikki Giovanni, *Quilting the Black-eyed Pea,* 106

Two scholars open a paragraph with an eleven-word transitive topic sentence that suggests a definition will follow. The definition unfolds in a sixty-two-word sentence:

> *Success involves more than a heart-pounding race to the finish line.*
> Our research uncovered four irreducible components of
> enduring success: happiness (feelings of pleasure or content-

ment about your life); achievement (accomplishments that compare favorably against similar goals others have strived for); significance (the sense that you've made a positive impact on people you care about); and legacy (a way to establish your values or accomplishments so as to help others find future success).

Laura Nash, Howard Stevenson, "Success That Lasts," 104

Very short sentences can drive home emphatically the key point in argumentative or expository prose. Below, a sentence of four words and one of three words succinctly re-enforce the argument:

What's true for graphics is true for aesthetics in general. Expanded supply creates expanded demand, which in turn feeds even more supply. *Over time, people learn.* They discover more about what's aesthetically possible and more about what they like. *Exposure changes tastes.*

Virginia Postrel, *The Substance of Style,* 55

In all these examples, the effect derives far more from the unmistakable relation of a short sentence to longer sentences than from any differing characteristics of the sentence types. It is, simply, the effect of a deliberately short sentence, thoughtfully positioned. Besides the sentence types mentioned thus far, the passive, for instance, or a negative, can work the same way, if it is short:

The editor of this anthology, who took part and was wounded in the last war to end war, hates war and hates all the politicians whose mismanagement, gullibility, cupidity, selfishness and ambition brought on this present war and made it inevitable. But once we have a war there is only one thing to do. *It must be won.* For defeat brings worse things than any that can ever happen in a war.

Ernest Hemingway, *Men at War,* XI-XII

Long sentences formed with a short sentence as nucleus

Related to the effects of the isolated short sentences we have been considering are short sentences that combine with free modifiers in the formation of long sentences. These can help to create a distinctive impact and texture. Below, a two-word intransitive serves as nucleus for the free modifiers that precede and follow it. The effect is emphasized by the separate three-word transitive sentence that comes along immediately afterward:

> One afternoon, in an early summer of this century, when
> Laura Rowan was just eighteen, *she sat*, embroidering a
> handkerchief, on the steps leading down from the terrace
> of her father's house to the gardens communally owned
> by the residents in Radnage Square. *She liked embroidery.*
> Rebecca West, *The Birds Fall Down*, opening paragraph

A short basic sentence in isolation, whether as a separate structure or as part of a long sentence, can bring a sentence or paragraph into gentle focus, as above, or into a firmer perspective, as in the examples that follow. Here is another intransitive placed in the middle of a long sentence:

> At the medicine-cabinet mirror, eyes still closed, *I stood*,
> hoping as always that when I opened them something
> would have happened overnight, I'd see a change.
> Jack Finney, *The Woodrow Wilson Dime*, 7

The sentence above has a base clause, with both left-branching and right-branching free modifiers. The example below opens with a short sentence as base clause, interrupted skillfully by a mid-branch. In addition, the sentence has right branches, free modifiers that *follow* the base clause:

> *The Russians*, coming from streets around the cemetery,
> *were hurrying*, singly or in groups, in the spring snow in
> the direction of the caves in the ravine, some running in
> the middle of the slushy cobblestone streets.
> Bernard Malamud, *The Fixer*, 9

Below, two right-branching sentences begin with an independent statement as the base clause. The first is a *be*-pattern. A similar brief statement, this one an intransitive, opens, and serves as the nucleus in the final sentence of the passage:

> *He is the puritan*, holding to the tradition of Socrates' cheer-
> ful indifference to bodily pleasures, but disposed to mistake
> this indifference for a rather grim and graceless asceticism.
> He can see no distinction between trust in providence and

submission to fate. *He marches*, in the filthy rags of right-
eousness, with face set towards a peak of infallible wisdom
and virtue, which even the small company of the elect have
little or no hope to climb.

F. M. Cornford, *Before and After Socrates*, 108

Here are some transitive patterns with right-branching expansions:

I examined her face, the eyes so heavily mascaraed, but large
and grey, the lines extending from her lips that the makeup
failed to hide, the creases in her forehead.

Hollis Alpert, *The Claimant*, 293

He entered the pro-cathedral, an echoing vastness of beauty
and silence, pillared in marble, rich in oak and bronze,
a temple of towering and intricate design, in which his
mission chapel would have stood unnoticed, forgotten, in
a corner of the transept.

A. J. Cronin, *The Keys of the Kingdom*, 333

Alternation of short and long segments sets an inviting pace, hinting at the action itself in the new restaurant at the concert hall designed
by Frank Gehry:

The feeling of the restaurant has undergone a sea change too.
Instead of obviously well-heeled patrons dining at a gour-
met landmark with hushed solemnity, people seem to be
having more fun ... *[The] crowd now cuts a wide swath* – young
and old, tourists and Angelenos, haute and hipster, dressed
up and dressed down. And when the hour of 10 rolls around,
another, even more diverse wave floods in, energized by the
concert or play they've just attended, talking music, talking
art, hungry and feeling like celebrating.

S. Irene Virbila, "Still ahead of the curve," FI, F3

A transitive pattern serves as base clause at the *end* of the coming
sentence, with free modifiers preceding it, that is, branching off to its left:

In the sound of the wood pigeons calling in the trees
behind them, and the sound of running water at their feet,
they unpacked their tea.

Nevil Shute, *Pastoral*, 240

Linking-verb kernels, too, may be held intact, as in the opening clause of the following right-branching sentence:

> *She looked mad*, absolutely round the bend, standing in a filthy bare hall on ragged linoleum under the dismal light of one feeble, fly-brown, naked bulb, casually dispensing thousands of pounds.
>   Angus Wilson, *No Laughing Matter*, 401

In contrast to the free-modifying sentences in the preceding examples, here is a sentence loaded with bound modifiers:

> Neglect of this rich mine of information is due in part to *the difficulty one faces in attempting to establish a suitable model in this area for modern quantification techniques that have contributed immeasurably to the formulation of historical generalizations in such areas as economic history and voting patterns.*
>   Earl W. Hayter, *The Troubled Farmer*, 3

This sentence suffers through 11 prepositional phrases, most of them in the ponderous 37-word noun phrase (italicized). Prepositional glut occurs if no attempt is made to set up short independent base clauses. The worst offenders in this overloading of patterns are the long noun phrase and nested prepositional phrases, often collaborating in clumsiness and verbal deadweight.

Creating a succinct base clause–a short sentence around which a long one is built–is a technique every writer needs to know. It is touched on only briefly here because the materials of free-modification, which allow the kernel or near-kernel to be felt as a separate entity, are taken up in other chapters.

Short sentences, in their many varieties, can help to bring clarity, impact, texture, to any kind of writing. But they must be well constructed, of course, and amicably situated with longer companions.

There never was an is without a where.
Lawrence Buell

Only a house, quiet as snow, a space for myself to go, clean as paper before the poem.
Sandra Cisneros

In 1946 a quarter meant popcorn, candy, a movie, a cartoon, and a serial, plus a trip to the projection booth to visit Snooky, who read Mickey Spillane books. And after the movie he could go next door to the Trolley Car Diner, where Jimmy, their boarder, would fry him a burger if he was not too busy.
Fannie Flagg

CHAPTER TWO

Noun Phrases

> Simplicity is not a given. It is an achievement, a human
> invention, a discovery, a beloved belief.
> William H. Gass, *Finding a Form*, 305

Except for three short words, *is not* and *is*, the two sentences above are composed entirely of noun phrases, seven of them: *Simplicity* is a noun; *a given* is a verb turned into a nominal; *It* is a pronoun. The remaining four are all nouns with modifiers. As this pair of sentences demonstrates, noun phrases do not always consist of nouns. Noun phrases are structures most often headed by a noun, but they may be headed by a pronoun, or by any other word or structure that stands in for a noun. Thus an entire clause may function as a noun phrase.

Because there are more nouns than any other part of speech in the English vocabulary, noun phrases offer a tremendous stock of meaning. Important for their content and variety, they also perform a great array of functions. In the basic sentence pattern, the noun phrase is the first component:

Sentence = Noun Phrase + Verb Phrase

Not only does the noun phrase occupy the important subject position; additional noun phrases usually appear as part of the verb phrase that fills the predicate position. Noun phrases take their places in half a dozen slots in the basic sentence patterns and are common in at least another half dozen slots in enlarged sentence patterns. This chapter will begin with a few examples of the *varieties* of noun phrases and then examples of the *slots* in which noun phrases function.

Varieties of noun phrases

In basic sentences, the components of noun phrases most frequently seen are noun alone, or with determiner (often *a, an,* or *the*), or with additional modifiers; pronoun alone or with modifiers; verbals, especially infinitives and gerunds; clauses; nominalized adjectives or other parts of speech. The most prevalent noun phrase is, of course, simply a noun or a noun with modifiers:

> *The refrigerator* hums. *A bee* thumps heavily, insistently,
> against *a windowpane.*
>> Michael Cunningham, *The Hours,* 45

> UNICEF looks after *children* in *need.*
>> Linda Fasulo, *An Insider's Guide to the UN,* 185

> *The Universal Declaration of Human Rights* is *the product* of *the UN's Commission on Human Rights,* founded in *1946,* which was then led by *former First Lady Eleanor Roosevelt,* who had *an international reputation* as *a crusader* for *human rights.*
>> Fasulo, 15

In the example above, along with nouns as headwords of noun phrases, two pronouns, *which* and *who,* function as noun phrases.

Below, four gerund phrases (*–ing* verbs) serve as appositive noun phrases, each set off by parentheses, each gerund phrase a definition of a preceding noun phrase naming a psychological condition. The entire series is object of the preposition *like.* The book's subtitle is also a gerund phrase, *cultivating vulnerability,* with a gerund that has its own object:

> Even in the 1980s, people had never heard of terms like generalized anxiety disorder (*being worried*), social anxiety disorder (*being shy*), social phobia (*being really shy*), or free-floating anxiety (*not knowing what you are worried about*).
>> Frank Furedi, *Therapy Culture,* 2

Again, three gerunds serve as noun phrases, all in object positions:

> When I heard about my brother's illness and his *dying,*
> I knew, instinctively, that to understand it, or to make an
> attempt at *understanding* his *dying,* and not to die with him,
> I would write about it.
>> Jamaica Kincaid, *My Brother,* 196

Infinitives as noun phrases are a frequent and versatile resource; here one serves as subject:

> *To leave academia* was a terrifying idea.
> Amy Tan, *The Opposite of Fate*, 54

Clauses, complete with subject, predicate, and modifiers, are widely used as noun phrases. Below, in each instance, an entire clause is a noun phrase functioning as direct object:

> And what of the circumstances themselves: Do we believe *they are simply a matter of fate?*
> Tan, 209

> We cannot always tell *how our actions or our words may affect others*.
> Jane Goodall and Marc Bekoff, *The Ten Trusts*, 145

Any part of speech may be turned into a noun phrase. Adjectives are among the most usual:

> That seemed to satisfy her, and she smiled as the crowd of *the contrite* rolled on like a piece of the sea, both of us but waves blending perfectly with its flow…
> Charles Johnson, *Dreamer*, 236

A writer can nominalize anything at all:

> There never was *an is* without *a where*. Both the bad things and the good things that happen to human beings and other life-forms self-evidently occur when their bodies are physically located somewhere, in particular locations.
> Lawrence Buell, *Writing for an Endangered World*, 55

Positions and functions of noun phrases

Slots for noun phrases in the basic sentences include subject, predicate nominative, direct object, indirect object, object of preposition, and objective complement. In expanded sentences, functions include the noun as modifier of another noun, the adverbial noun, the noun as fragment, the noun as appositive, the noun in the nominative absolute, and the noun series or catalog.

As subject in the first two examples that follow, the opening noun phrase is typical—a determiner, an adjectival modifier, and a noun. One can hardly help observing also in the first example the striking use of noun phrases as objects in the three parallel prepositional phrases, also as a direct object, and as a predicate nominative:

> *Two little girls* arrived at the big school on the same day, at the same hour, took each other's measure, and became best friends.
> Doris Lessing, *The Grandmothers*, 10

> *The night sky* is as beautiful as ever, to astronomers as well as to poets.
> Steven Weinberg, *Facing Up: Science and Its Cultural Adversaries*, 71

Instead of writing "the sky at night," Weinberg turns the noun "night" into an adjectival modifier in a noun phrase that becomes a cohesive unit and enhances rhythm.

In the sentence below, the predicate nominative in a *be*-pattern of definition is clear and efficient even though fairly long. It is easy, however, to overload relative clauses bound to the noun, as are those in this sentence:

> A rocket is a *jet-propelled missile which carries the source of its propulsion energy along with it and whose functioning is independent of the presence of an atmosphere.*
> *The Way Things Work*, 578

Below, a sentence with parallelism best suited to a speech is composed of six kernel clauses, each with a noun phrase in the direct object slot. In five of the clauses, the parallelism and the repetition of the key concept *they conserve* emphasize the treasures being conserved in those direct objects:

> These farmers produce *valuable goods*, of course; but they also conserve *soil*, they conserve *water*, they conserve *wildlife*, they conserve *open space*, they conserve *scenery*.
> Wendell Berry, *Citizenship Papers*, 170

Professional writers seldom elaborate much on a noun phrase as indirect object. Here, it is a single word:

> And she can get *me* a job on a ranch in August.
> *Windblown World: The Journals of Jack Kerouac*, 88

In an equative clause, the noun has a place in the fashioning of metaphor:

> The dictionary for me is *my Scheherazade*. Plus it can spell Scheherazade.
> Amy Tan, *The Opposite of Fate*, 222

The role of the noun phrase in similes is illustrated here, with noun phrases as the objects of the preposition *like*:

> High on the slopes of the building, burning like *flares*, sheets of flaming newspaper soared skyward, suddenly cooled, powdered, and fell like *a rain of ash*.
> Wright Morris, *The Field of Vision*, 235

> The road lay like *a length of black tape* across the desert.
> Nathaniel Benchley, *Welcome to Xanadu*, opening line

> The engine looked like *a surly, crouching animal*...
> Benchley, 6

A noun phrase functions as an objective complement in the following sentence:

> They called my aeroplanes *darts*.
> Jerry Mander, George Dippel, and Howard Gossage, *The Great International Paper Airplane Book*, 13

Nouns can modify other nouns, as has been seen earlier. Here the noun *rights* has its own adjectival modifier, and the phrase modifies *debate*:

> It is not possible to leave this topic without some consideration for the *reproductive rights* debate.
> Gayatri Spivak, "French Feminism Revisited," 63

Below, in three sentences, nouns work in pairs as modifiers of nouns:

> To get straight to the worst, what I'm about to offer isn't
> really a short story at all but a sort of *prose home* movie, and
> those who have seen the footage have strongly advised me
> against nurturing any elaborate *distribution* plans for it.
>   J. D. Salinger, *Franny and Zooey*, 47

> The task in this book was to present a theory of syntax from
> the *communication-and-cognition* perspective.
>   Robert D. Van Valin, Jr. and Randy J. LaPolla, *Syntax*, 640

> Something of literally *life and death* importance had hap-
> pened in mortal history...
>   J. B. Phillips, *Ring of Truth*, 36

Noun modifiers of nouns sometimes accompany adjectives or
serve in a noun-adjective compound:

> Leaves long dead and brittle as old *butterfly* wings, an aqua
> *candy* wrapper, flecks and dust and *seed-sized* snips of *gutter*
> chaff all hurried in a rustling revolution under our eyes...
>   John Updike, *The Centaur*, 130

> *Pursuit* planes were traded for additional *cargo* ships or
> retained for *emergency invoice* duty and *small-parcel* service;
> trucks and tanks were procured from the *ground* forces
> and used for *short-distance road* hauling.
>   Joseph Heller, *Catch-22*, 259

> She bought the green *glove silk* slip and the *tea-colored* lace.
>   Katherine Anne Porter, *Flowering Judas and Other Stories*, 200

Noun modifiers can also be used as adjectivals in more unusual
arrangements, here as a kind of appositional substitute for "moonless":

> It was a dark night, *no moon*, but the stars diffused a very
> faint luminescence over everything, a light like softest
> sound, touch of fur on ebony.
>   John Fowles, *The Magus*, 275

Science writers often deposit noun collocations and noun compounds as modifiers of other nouns, in an attempt toward economy and accuracy:

> Brodinsky *et al* further show that *activity-related* changes in
> *neurotransmitter* expression also occur in isolated neurons
> *in vitro*, hinting that a *cell-autonomous* mechanism—a mechanism that depends solely on the neuron in question, and
> not on external factors—regulates *neurotransmitter* output.
> Martyn Goulding, *A Matter of Balance*, 517

Noun modifiers can stand in adverbial slots as well:

> They heard the whistles of tugboats, *all day and all night long.*
> James Baldwin, *Another Country*, 51

> It goes *a long way back, some twenty years.*
> Ralph Ellison, *Invisible Man*, 19

> He added nothing to the terror of the dark, the terror generalized and mindless that had to be endured *nightlong and
> night after night.*
> William Golding, *Free Fall*, 161

The noun as fragment

A few years ago a staff member at a large university, cleaning out an old cabinet in the English department's offices, came across a neat black box. Inside were long-unused rubber stamps, twenty or more, apparently in the distant past employed to mark student papers. It is easy to visualize an overburdened writing teacher efficiently, firmly, perhaps even angrily, stamping with red ink the margins in stacks of student compositions: AWK. AGR. NOT CLR. CHOP. JARG. TRNS NDED. SPLT INF. COMM SPLS. RUN-ON. And what was probably regarded as the greatest of all student sins, FRAG. I remember a teacher long ago who announced that any student paper containing a fragment automatically received an F, unless the student had labeled the fragment "intentional."

Nowadays writing teachers are more likely to recognize that many professional writers use sentence fragments repeatedly and artfully, often several at a time, in criticism, journalism, fiction, biography, history, essays. Often the fragments are linked semantically or syntactically to words in the preceding and following sentences. Some are like appositives in their relation to words that precede or follow. Fragments are still usually avoided, however, in legal, medical, scientific, and engineering documents, treatises, articles, and even correspondence.

But use of fragments is not limited to personal writing. Below, in a journalistic tribute to a distinguished writer, the first paragraph is composed of three fragmentary sentences, each one a noun phrase elaborated by a clause that begins with *who*. The three are gathered together in the pronoun *those* at the beginning of the next sentence:

> A highly accomplished journalist who brought his acute powers of observation to subjects ranging from world wars to the Irish American experience. A successful screenwriter who immersed himself in Hollywood's bizarre and cantankerous creative process. A dyed-in-the-wool New Englander who wrote perceptively and noncondescendingly about the social and cultural rituals of the West Coast.

> Those were among the reminiscences offered Wednesday by close friends and colleagues of John Gregory Dunne...
> Reed Johnson and Renee Tawa, "An Appreciation," E4

Although a series of fragments can create a lyrical quality, they can become tiresome. But here in a vivid memoir, ten fragmentary sentences, each an elaborated noun phrase, form four paragraphs of metaphorical, poetic expression of relationships and experiences:

> Lights reflected. Lights of white-hot friction, of gases burning, of the incredible burning of ice. Lights that strike, then vanish in a flash.

> Lights that strike and go on even after flashing, having set fires. Lights that blot out, lights that dwindle. Lights that cycle predictably, and lights whose cycles you cannot foretell.

> Lights glowing warm on wicks, inside glass chimneys. Beckoning the snowshoe-er from the windows of a cabin collared by snow.

> Lights long lost–squelched throughout a long journey, like the light of a comet–then igniting finally in the soul. Soul igniting as the blue lights reflect its image back to it, saying, The light of nature, born of the universe, is in you.
> Trudy Dittmar, *Fauna and Flora, Earth and Sky*, 216

This sentence unites the fragmentary concepts, and its run-on punctuation continues the fragmentary momentum:

> I'm still enthralled by light, that's a fact, and you can't grab it.
> Dittmar, 216

Here are fragments of varying length which manage to retain a somewhat lyrical or poetic quality along with their directness and brevity:

> So much, then, for these things.
> Robert Graves, *Count Belisarius*, 415

> Stopping, he looked for daylight. Yes, it was there. The light was there. *The grace of life still there. Or, if not grace, air.*
> Saul Bellow, *Mosby's Memoirs and Other Stories*, 184

Here are three fragments of deliberately increasing length:

> Sleep, and the approach of sleep. The pouring texture, beginningless and endless, that fulfills a dream. The dream-song at the end of little Jean's famous poem, "The Playlanders," which she had written, all magnificently, at Inglesse, when she was five—that masterpiece of alliterative spellings, with its wonderful, and somehow so world's-end, mountain, Juhoohooa.
> Conrad Aiken, *Ushant*, 364

Fragments are used here in an appealing juxtaposition of eleven in a row, each consisting of or containing one or more noun phrases. All are in apposition to the page's title, *A House of My Own*, naming what the house is not and is:

> Not a flat. Not an apartment in back. Not a man's house. Not a daddy's. A house all my own. With my porch and my pillow, my pretty purple petunias. My books and my stories. My two shoes waiting beside the bed. Nobody to shake a stick at. Nobody's garbage to pick up after.

> Only a house quiet as snow, a space for myself to go, clean as paper before the poem.
> Sandra Cisneros, *The House on Mango Street*, 108

Noun phrases as appositives and nominative absolutes

Noun phrases of the sort occasionally punctuated as fragments often function as appositives, separated from their surroundings by a dash or a comma. Below, a noun phrase appositive comes at the climax of the sentence, as is often the case:

> Despite its great variety of natural wonders, California is best known to many outsiders for just one thing–
> *earthquakes.*
> Robert Iacopi, *Earthquake Country*, 4

Here a climactic appositive comes after a long, long wait:

> To audiences who had been forced to sit through plays in which love was the motive of the intrigue, but who had an instinctive feeling that love, though all very well in its way, was not really quite so important as the dramatists pretended, for after all there were politics, golf, getting on with one's job and all sorts of other things, it was a welcome relief to come upon a dramatist for whom love was a tiresome, secondary business, *a quick gratification of a momentary impulse whose consequences were generally awkward.*
> W. Somerset Maugham, *The Summing Up*, 88

The paragraph below consists of one sentence. Except for the six words in the main clause, it is all one long noun phrase appositive, seventy-one words:

> He taught Russian at Waindell College, *a somewhat provincial institution characterized by an artificial lake in the middle of a landscaped campus, by ivied galleries connecting the various halls, by passing on the torch of knowledge from Aristotle, Shakespeare, and Pasteur to a lot of monstrously built farm boys and farm girls, and by a huge, active, buoyantly thriving German Department which its Head, Dr. Hagen, smugly called (pronouncing every syllable very distinctly) "a university within a university."*
> Vladimir Nabokov, *Pnin*, 9

The nominative absolute is almost a clause. It consists of a noun phrase with a partial predicate:

> He smoked briefly, *his eyes following a pattern of concrete blocks in the school building.*
> J. D. Salinger, *Franny and Zooey*, 153

Since the nominative absolute functions as a sentence modifier, not tied directly to any one referent in the main clause, it is easy to use. It is easy to form as well: one simply drops the verb out of a clause or changes it to a participle, and what remains is a major noun phrase with whatever is left of the predicate:

> They faced each other on the floral rug, *feet apart* and *elbows crooked in uncertain attitudes*, as if about to begin some ritual of which neither had learnt the cues. "I'll show you," Bertrand chimed, and jabbed at Dixon's face.
> Kingsley Amis, *Lucky Jim*, 213

Noun phrases as subjects of verbals and as items in a series

Nouns act as subjects of participles, in arrangements that are not really absolute constructions, not fully independent, not sentence modifiers. Here, a noun twice heads a participial phrase, all used to fill a subject slot:

> *Lowell, resting in the wing on the floor of the stage, Lowell recuperating from the crack he had given his head,* was a dreamy figure of peace in the corner of the proscenium, a reclining shepherd contemplating his flute ...
> Norman Mailer, *The Armies of the Night*, 42

The preceding example also serves to introduce the next important use of noun phrases to be demonstrated here, the noun series. It usually consists of three or more noun phrases, sometimes even split up, as in the first example:

> *His origins* are obscure, *his parentage, even his name.*
> Arthur Knight, *The Liveliest Art*, 40

These noun catalogs often occur at the end of a sentence, swelling out a prepositional phrase with multiple objects:

> Prose fiction, that form which "takes the minutest impressions," is linked with *epic, chronicle, memoir, fable, essay, case history, biography, report, prose romance, and what have you, letter, rogue's tale, anecdote.*
> Richard Stern, *Honey and Wax*, x

The preceding series was effectively broken up toward the end. Here are two more catalogs as objects of a preposition, each one rounded off by a final item longer than the rest. The first is summed up by a noun phrase as appositive. In the second, the final item in the series is a nominative absolute:

> They mar themselves with *cacophonies, jagged rhythms, ugly words and ugly thoughts, colloquialisms, clichés, sterile technical terms, headwork and argument, self contradictions, cleverness, irony, realism—all things which call us back to the world of prose and imperfection.*
> Robert Penn Warren, *Selected Essays*, 4-5

> Any list of the great British works of epic fantasy must begin *with* Paradise Lost, *with its dark lord, cursed tree, invented cosmology and ringing battle scenes, its armored angelic cavalries shattered by demonic engines of war.*
> Michael Chabon, *Dust and Demons*, 25

Below, noun catalogs are inserted at three key points, twice as complements in a pattern of equative clauses, once in the direct object slot, finally cut off with an impatient *etc., etc.*

> I am *a novelist, painter, sculptor, philosopher, draughtsman, critic, politician, journalist, essayist, pamphleteer*, all rolled into one, like one of those portmanteau-men of the Italian Renaissance.

> I am a portmanteau-man (like 'portmanteau-word'). I have been *a soldier, a yachtsman, a baby, a massier, a hospital patient, a traveler, a total abstainer, a lecturer, an alcoholic, an editor, and a lot more.* So I have met other *editors, alcoholics, lecturers, patients, soldiers, etc., etc.*
> Wyndham Lewis, *Blasting and Bombardiering*, 3

Avoiding the long noun phrase with bound modifiers

With nouns making up the largest share of our general vocabulary, any edicts against nominal style—and many have been advanced—become hard to obey. The best advice, in general, does not worry so much over the length or number of noun phrases as about the way they are made long and the way they are distributed—with a strong preference for commas and nonrestrictive modifiers (also called *loose* or *free modifiers*) like those in the series above, rather than bound modifiers.

Here is a trio of bound modifiers, with lumpy noun phrases as subject, postponed subject, object of a preposition, and noun complement:

> *The control of these fundamental protective systems and the*
> *channeling of them into team play and individual effort that*
> *possess logic and reason acceptable to the individual's culture*
> represent the mental hygiene of athletic endeavor.
>   Joseph P. Dolan and Lloyd J. Holloway, *The Treatment*
>   *and Prevention of Athletic Injuries*, 1

> It is encouraging to note *the progress made by beekeeping to*
> *meet the challenging times, particularly in connection with the*
> *difficult problem of pesticides as they relate to the keeping of bees*
> *in the highly cultivated areas where bees are needed for pollination.*
>   John E. Eckert and Frank R. Shaw, *Beekeeping*, 458

> At that time I surveyed a major portion of the work written
> on gene structure and I was struck by *the numerous instances*
> *of independent discovery, periods of obscurity, and spurious philo-*
> *sophic attitudes that subsisted underneath the apparently smooth*
> *transition of ideas and experimental progress that reviews and*
> *texts alike tend to produce.*
>   Elof Axel Carson, *The Gene*, v

The examples above are riddled with prepositions, one locked inside another, and heavy, too, with embedded relative and subordinate clauses. They are bad mostly because of what goes into them, not because of how much of it there is. Free modifiers, well-planned, are one solution, and perhaps the most useful forms—in addition to the appositive and the nominative absolute, briefly seen here—await us in later chapters.

Pronouns

Pronouns are important to style in both fiction and nonfiction. Although few, they are among the most frequently used words in the language because they relieve the writer of having to use the same nouns over and over. Pronouns themselves are often repeated and varied to help establish a posture in relation to the readers, frequently creating an impression of informality, or of authority, and at times a speaking voice. They serve also in maintaining cohesion, whether in narrative or formal writing.

Some vital roles of pronouns in storytelling are illustrated in the quotation below, contributing to the author's relaxed conversational voice, all the while advancing item by item the path of the description. Echoing the idiom of ten-year-old Bobby himself in a small town in the 1940s as well as the idiom of the period, the author employs twenty pronouns in this paragraph:

> *He* had a mother, a father, and a grandmother and had never known *anyone who* had died. *He* had seen only photographs in store windows of the boys *who* had been killed in the war. *He* and *his* best friend, Monroe, were now official blood brothers, an act so solemn that *neither one* spoke on the way home. *His* big sister, Anna Lee, a pretty blue-eyed blond girl, was quite popular with *all* the older boys, *who* would sometimes hang around the house and play catch or throw the football with *him*. Sometimes *he* was able to make a quarter off the guys just to leave *them* alone on the front porch with Anna Lee. In 1946 a quarter meant popcorn, candy, a movie, a cartoon, and a serial, plus a trip to the projection booth to visit Snooky, *who* read Mickey Spillane books. And after the movie *he* could go next door to the Trolley Car Diner, where Jimmy, *their* boarder, would fry *him* a burger if *he* was not too busy.
> Fannie Flagg, *Standing in the Rainbow*, 9

In recent years, several widespread changes have come about that have affected the ways professional writers use pronouns in nonfiction as well as fiction. One change is the increasing popularity of colloquial genres—bylined essays by columnists in newspapers and other periodicals, short and long autobiographies and memoirs, books of collected essays and speeches, and contributions to websites. The use of email for both business and personal correspondence also finds many of us writing in a more casual way.

Conversational tones appear in discussions of technical subjects, especially computers, software, and the vast environment of which they are a part. Some writers of technical manuals have switched from the third person to the second person: instead of "the user should be aware that," they write "you should be aware that…, then you do this and next you do that." With a dozen instances of the pronoun "you" in a paragraph or two, however, it is easy to sound preachy or invasive.

Despite these trends, some articles and documents in technical, academic, and professional fields—law, some sciences, medicine, engineering, literature, history—continue to avoid first person pronouns and use other pronouns sparingly. The style sheet of *Renaissance Quarterly*, for example, revised in 2002, specifies: "Please avoid the use of 'I,' 'me,' and 'my' in the text of articles. Throughout, avoid gender-specific language and chronologically vague terms like 'early modern'." Such a dictum is perhaps intended to maintain a boundary between the personal and the academic, to encourage precision, and to end generic use of masculine pronouns.

Indeed, widespread changes have come about because editors, writers, teachers, and the public no longer tolerate the generic use of masculine pronouns, a usage that for centuries was regarded as standard and was made compulsory by style sheets. Most of today's good writers, without awkwardness, write in ways that are gender-neutral. It is much easier if, from the start, one writes without using masculine pronouns generically. Once they have been written, they are like weeds, hard to dig out.

First-person pronouns can be very effective in autobiographical writing. Below, they join with other pronouns to help the author share her deep feeling and experience as she describes her work just after the events of September 11, 2001:

> Compiling this book quickly in the strange awful time *that* dawned on *us* last September became for *me* a way of surviving *that* time, and in the process *I* reopened in *my* own veins the intimate connection between the will to survive and the need to feel useful to *something* or *someone* beyond *myself*... Writing, which was both painful and palliative for *me*, turned out to be *my* own way of giving blood in a crisis.
> Barbara Kingsolver, *Small Wonder*, xv

Again, first person pronouns are central to expressing the crisis of an author who, returning from a funeral ceremony for her father, finds that her home, possessions, and book manuscript have been destroyed by fire:

> *I* then found for *myself*, and laid eyes on and touched, the ashes of *my* Book of Peace. The unroofed sun shone extra brightly on a book-shaped pile of white ash in the middle of

the alcove. *I* had been working at the table with the hand-stenciled flowers; the pages had been to the right of the computer. The ashes of *my* Book of Peace were purely white paper and words gone entirely white. The temperature here in the middle of the room had not been hotter than by the wall. *I* held in *my* hands the edges of pages, like silvery vanes of feathers, like white eyelashes. Each one fanned out into infinitely tinier vanes. Paper had returned to woodgrain. *I* touched the lines, and they smeared into powder. *I* placed *my* palm on this ghost of *my* book and *my* hand sank through it. Feathers floated into the air, became air, airy *nothing*.

    Maxine Hong Kingston, *The Fifth Book of Peace*, 34

In nonfiction dealing with less personal subjects, pronouns are on occasion used to display friendliness with the reader. Here *you* and *we* along with several other pronouns work effectively for a computer specialist addressing a general audience, conveying a tone of friendly urgency:

Mirror Worlds are devices for showing *you* the big picture, the whole. Every Mirror World has the same goal, in the end: to show *you* the whole thing at once, the whole *whatever* this Mirror World is tracking. Yes, *you* can plunge in and explore the details.

    David Gelernter, *Mirror Worlds*, 50

In the next passage, the style is carried forward by pronouns, assertive clauses, rhetorical questions, and metaphor:

The big picture is a cipher. The whole is simply too complicated to comprehend. Can *we* afford to go on this way? *Who* will accept responsibility? Is ant-mindedness *our* fate? *What* are *we* going to do about *it*?

    Gelernter, 33

Personal pronouns often help to convey a sense of the author's personal speaking voice. The first person pronoun creates a sense that the author is speaking, sometimes as if in conversation, sometimes as if seated at a seminar table, or standing at a lectern. Below, in the first four sentences of the book, Atwood uses *I* and about a dozen other pronouns:

> When *I* was a student of English literature, in the early 1960s, *we all* had to read an important critical text called *Seven Types of Ambiguity* (1930). *This* erudite book, *it* is astonishing to note, was written by William Empson when *he* was only twenty-three. *It* is also astonishing to note that when *he* was in the full throes of composition *he* was expelled from the University of Cambridge for being found with contraceptives in *his* room.
>
> *This* is a fitting commentary on how *we* are all stuck in time, less like flies in amber – nothing so hard and clear – but like mice in molasses; because surely nowadays *he* would be expelled for being found *without* contraceptives in *his* room.
> Margaret Atwood, *Negotiating with the Dead*, xv

In essays, memoirs, or advice-books, authors often shift from *I* to *we* as in the following passage, thus including other persons like the speaker, here other writers:

> *We* could go on to make explicit what has been implicit. *We* could talk about inspiration, or about trances and dream visions, or about charms and invocations – all of them linked with poetic traditions of long standing; then *we* could go one step further and talk – as *many* have – about the shamanistic role of the writer.
> Atwood, 179

Authors referring to themselves as *I* or *we* on occasion address the readers directly as *you*. Sometimes, in fact, the *we* or *you* includes both writer and reader:

> All writers learn from the dead. As long as *you* continue to write, *you* continue to explore the work of writers who have preceded *you*; *you* also feel judged and held to account by them. But *you* don't learn only from writers – *you* can learn from ancestors in all their forms.
> Atwood, 178

Below, in the introduction to a book, a teacher of writing uses 26 pronouns on the first half-page. As she begins, she speaks as part of an authorial *we* that also includes the readers and other people; her *you* includes herself and the reader. Her *I* and other pronouns help create a voice that is personal and informal, now and then breezy, but in the next instant thoughtful or pedagogical:

> Life is not orderly. No matter how *we* try to make life so, right in the middle of *it we* die, lose a leg, fall in love, drop a jar of applesauce. In summer, *we* work hard to make a tidy garden, bordered by pansies with rows or clumps of columbine, petunias, bleeding hearts. Then *we* find *ourselves* longing for the forest, where *everything* has the appearance of disorder; yet *we* feel peaceful there.
>
> *What* writing practice, like Zen practice, does is bring *you* back to the natural state of mind, the wilderness of *your* mind where there are no refined rows of gladiolas. The mind is raw, full of energy, alive and hungry. *It* does not think in the way *we* were brought up to think—well-mannered, congenial.
>
> When *I* finished *Writing Down the Bones* and people in *my* workshops read *it*, *I* thought *I* would not have to say *anything else*. *I* felt embarrassed to say, "Steve, *you* ought to be more specific there." *I* thought *he* would retort, "*We* know. *You* already told *us* in chapter eight."
> Natalie Goldberg, *Wild Mind*, xiii

Personal pronouns are indispensable also in creating the distinctive voices of newspaper columnists, especially humorists:

> *I* ignored *them* at the bank. *I* snubbed *them* at the shopping mall. *I* banished *them* from the bedside table, the bathroom, the kitchen. Just when *I* thought *I* was rid of *them, they* burst like unleashed pathogens from new hosts: restaurant walls, church signposts, showroom catalogues. Something has to be done about *them*, *I* tell *you*, or *I* may sicken unto death.
>
> *I* refer, of course, to Motivational Quotes. Those 10-cent soupçons of wisdom from the great and the not-so, exhorting *us* to throw off the weights of lethargy, strike out on the road to self-improvement, and become the Olympians *we*'re destined to be.
> Louis Bayard, "I'm Maxed Out on Maxims," B04

In the next passage another humorist opens his column by adeptly using pronouns and other devices to create the effect of *two* speaking voices in a make-believe dialog:

> *I* suppose *you*'ve heard by now that *I* had the gout. *Everybody* seems to know. No, *I* don't want to hear about *your* grandfather's gout. With the possible exception of *your* grandmother, *nobody* is less interested in hearing about *your* grandfather than *I* am. No, the gout does not make people ill tempered. *I* have nothing against *your* grandfather – although *I* must admit that even before the onset of *my* own affliction, stories concerning the inflammation of *his* joints would not have been high on *my* list of compelling narratives.
> Calvin Trillin, *With All Disrespect*, 30

In contrast to columnists writing for a broad popular audience, scientists and journalists in a number of specialized publications customarily write in a more formal style, making little if any use of the first person *I*. But they often use the first person plurals, *we, us,* and *our,* to refer to the human race in general:

> The universe around *us* exhibits structure on all scales. Stars are not scattered uniformly through space; they are grouped into galaxies. *Our* sun is one of several hundred billion stars in the Milky Way galaxy, a highly flattened disk 100,000 light-years across. The Milky Way, in turn, is one of tens of billions of galaxies in the observable universe. *Our* nearest large galactic neighbor is about two million light-years away. But galaxies are not randomly sprinkled like raisins in a muffin. Between 5 and 10 percent are grouped into clusters containing up to 1,000 galaxies in a volume a few million light-years across.
> Michael A. Strauss, "Reading the Blueprints of Creation," 54

On the same page, the writer intersperses two uses of the second-person *you*, perhaps simply for variety or possibly to establish a more individual connection to the reader:

> When *you* point a telescope at the night sky, the eyepiece reveals stars, planets and galaxies. But without further information, *you* will not know which objects are small and nearby or large and far away. Fortunately, the telescope can

provide that information. For galaxies, the key is that *we* live in an expanding universe. Galaxies are receding from one another, and the more distant a galaxy is, the faster it is moving away from *us*.
    Strauss, 54

In the following example, a neurobiologist uses *our, us,* and *we* in a similar way to refer to all human beings:

Attention is an important feature of consciousness. Events that do not command *our* attention hardly exist for *us*, even if they influence how *we* perceive, feel or react. Attention, in the sense of concentration, sharpens the actual states of consciousness. The more *we* concentrate on one single event, the more other events will fade out of *our* consciousness.

In everyday life, *our* brains perceive and process a great deal of information that never reaches *our* consciousness.
    Gerard Roth, "The Quest to Find Consciousness," 34

Roth also makes effective use of the pronoun *one* and *one's*. The possessive appears four times in the following extract, from the same page as the preceding quotation:

The characteristic stream of consciousness consists of two forms: background and actual. Background consciousness encompasses long-lasting sensory experiences, such as a sense of personal identity, awareness of *one's* physical body, control of that body and intellect, and *one's* location in space and time. Other elements include the level of reality of *one's* experiences and the difference between that reality and fantasy. Background consciousness provides the foundation for the second type: actual consciousness. The concrete, sometimes rapidly alternating states of actual consciousness include awareness of processes in *one's* own body and the surrounding environment; intellectual activities, such as thinking, imagining and remembering; emotions, feelings and needs (such as hunger); and wishes, intentions and acts of will.
    Roth, 34

Gender-neutral pronouns

Plurals are usually gender-neutral. Occasionally, writers use *he or she* (not *he/she*), but do not write it repeatedly because of the awkwardness it creates. A few authors alternate use of the masculine and feminine pronouns. The writers of a book on "software-enabled technology" try this tactic:

> …users–especially beginners–are simultaneously very intelligent and very busy. *They* need some instruction, but not very much, and the process has to be rapid and targeted. If a ski instructor begins lecturing on meteorology and alpine ecology, *he* will lose his students regardless of *their* aptitude for skiing. Just because a user needs to learn how to operate a program doesn't mean that *he* needs or wants to learn how *it* works inside.
> Alan Cooper and Robert Reimann, *About Face 2.0*, 34-35

Elsewhere in the text, to balance out the uses of the masculine *he* as a generic, the same writers use the generic *she*. Here is an example:

> When a small child encounters an angry dog, *she* instinctively knows that bared fangs signal great danger even without any previous learning.
> Cooper and Reimann, 249

Rather than alternating masculine and feminine pronouns, which are often pages apart, one might consider using plurals and some changes in syntax:

> If a ski instructor begins lecturing on meteorology and alpine ecology, students may lose interest regardless of their aptitude for skiing. Just because users need to learn how to operate a program doesn't mean that they need or want to learn how it works inside.

> A small child encountering an angry dog instinctively knows, even without any previous learning, that bared fangs signal great danger.

These sentences leave no doubt that skiers, computer users, and small children facing angry dogs may be of either sex.

The use of masculine pronouns as generics was encouraged in many grammars and style sheets until the late twentieth century. These thoughtful writers, however, in 1910, ignored the prescriptions:

> The actual necessity for food is governed by three fundamental laws: first, age; second, activity or work, and third, the temperature of atmosphere or environment. If some study is devoted to experimentation, the student will soon become familiar with *his or her* requirements, measured or determined by age, occupation, temperature, the amount of fresh air breathed every day, the mental condition, whether disturbed or tranquil, and feeding *themselves* will become one of the most fascinating studies and duties within the scope of *their* daily employment.
> Eugene Christian and Mollie Griswold Christian, *250 Meatless Menus and Recipes*, 67

Judicious use of personal pronouns through many pages of a recent book marks the language of a concert pianist and music critic writing amiable reminiscences about pianists as well as his ideas about the piano itself. Here *his or her* is used once only, and it does not call attention to itself:

> There are different kinds of tonal beauty in piano sound, and each pianist can develop a personal sonority that makes *his or her* work recognizable...
> Charles Rosen, *Piano Note: The World of the Pianist*, 24

His or her becomes cumbersome, however, if used repeatedly. The author chose instead in the following paragraph to revert to use of generics:

> ...the pianist who looks soulfully at the ceiling to indicate the more spiritual moments of lyricism is a comic figure, and so is the performer who throws *his* hands into the air to indicate a daredevil recklessness. Both are outdone in unintentional comedy by the pianist who gestures wildly only with *his* right hand, while *his* left remains securely planted on the ivories as if *he* were afraid that *he* will not easily find its place again.
> Rosen, 10

Here is one way to remove the masculine pronouns:

> ...the pianist who looks soulfully at the ceiling to indicate
> the more spiritual moments of lyricism is a comic figure,
> and so is the performer who throws both hands into the air
> to indicate a daredevil recklessness. These two are outdone
> in unintentional comedy by the pianist who gestures wildly
> only with the right hand, while the left remains securely
> planted on the ivories as if in fear that it will not easily find
> its place again.

One common device to avoid masculine generic pronouns is to use the plural "their" to refer to a singular antecedent. The two examples that follow are from a book published in 2003:

> No one expects *the speaker* to bring chips or to take off *their*
> shoes, but the speaker seeks, and is praised for, as much
> warmth and familiarity as possible despite the formal nature
> of the occasion.
> John McWhorter, *Doing Our Own Thing*, 47

> Typically, *the student or even professor* standing at the
> microphone has a three-by-five index card in *their* hand
> with a few general points to hit.
> McWhorter, 48

In the first example, another choice might be to use plurals. In the second sentence, one could simply omit *their*.

Gender-free nouns

Gendered nouns are usually thought of as a matter of word choice, that is, of diction rather than syntax, but getting rid of them brings surprising bonuses to style in general, and these changes often involve syntax. Rosalie Maggio, author of *The Nonsexist Word Finder*, makes this important observation:

> By replacing fuzzy, over-generalized, cliché-ridden words
> with explicit, active words and by giving concrete examples
> and anecdotes instead of one-word-fits-all descriptions, you
> can express yourself more dynamically, convincingly, and
> memorably...

Writers who talk about brotherhood or spinsters or right-handed men miss a chance to spark their writing with fresh descriptions; they leave their readers as uninspired as they are. Thoughtless writing is also less informative. Why use, for example, the unrevealing *adman* when we could choose instead a precise, descriptive, nonsexist word like *advertising executive, copywriter, account executive, ad writer,* or *media buyer.*

The syllable "man" as in "adman," has been abandoned in many job titles. Writers find alternatives that do not include the suffixes *–woman, –man,* and *–person.* Among them: *police officer, mail carrier, council member, member of Congress, chair, moderator, delivery driver, housekeeper, government official* (not *statesman*), *newspaper writer, sports lover, third-base player, con artist, emcee, service member, vegetable seller, weather reporter, caretaker, federal agent.* Maggio lists some gender-free words: *workers, immigrants, people, voters, civilians.*

Good authors avoid also a multitude of compounds and phrases that include the noun "man." With a little ingenuity, writers find substitutes for: *man and wife, man in the moon, manhandle, manhole, manned space flight, manmade, man on the street,* and many others. Even when converted to a verb, the word *man* sometimes runs into trouble:

> A majority of the panelists also rejects the verb *man* when used to refer to an activity performed by women. Fifty-six percent of the panel (61 percent of the women and 54 percent of the men) disapprove of the sentence *Members of the League of Women Voters will be manning the registration desk.*
> *The American Heritage Dictionary of the English Language,* 1061

One could simply substitute "staffing," without any change of syntax, but that does not tell what is happening here. Better to improve meaning, syntax, and style:

> Citizens who wish to register to vote may do so at a desk staffed by volunteers from the League of Women Voters.

A number of gendered nouns involve female suffixes, among them *–ette, –enne, –trix,* and *–ess.* Professional writers nowadays avoid such dated terms, reminiscent of the days when Amelia Earhart was referred to as an "aviatrix." The suffix "–ette" as in *usherette* and *majorette* is both diminutive and female; "–enne" as in *comedienne* and *equestrienne,* and "–ess" as in *stewardess* and *sculptress,* indicate femaleness. Most writers now use *usher* and *major, comedian* and *equestrian,* and *flight attendant* and *sculptor* for both sexes. When referring to an adult, good writers use "man," not "boy," and "woman," not "girl," unless there is a specialized context calling for the juvenile term.

Today's writers are fortunate in having at hand the vast resources of English vocabulary and syntax to assure that what they write is gender-neutral and fair. Noun phrases, including pronouns, figure strongly in their choices.

We went to Italy, we went to Ireland, we went to Williamsburg, we went to Montreal, we went to St. Martin, and Mark drove and I navigated and Julie suggested wrong turns and Arthur fell asleep.
Nora Ephron

Many times during the night I woke to listen, listen, but there is no sound at all. The silence is as thick and soft as wool. Will the snow never stop falling?
May Sarton

It is men tormenting and killing a bull; it is a bull being tormented and killed.
Max Eastman

CHAPTER THREE

Verb Phrases

About adjectives: all fine prose is based on the verbs
carrying the sentences. They make sentences move.
Probably the finest technical poem in English is Keats's
Eve of Saint Agnes. A line like:

> *The hare limped trembling through the frozen grass,*

is so alive that you race through it, scarcely noticing it,
yet it has colored the whole poem with its movement—
the limping, trembling, and freezing is going on before
your own eyes.

> F. Scott Fitzgerald in a letter to his daughter,
> Frances Scott Fitzgerald, *The Crack-Up*, 303

MOST VERBS are action words. A few assert a state of being
rather than an action. The very essence of a sentence, something *said*
about a subject, often depends on verbs: it is the verb phrase that does
much of the *saying*.

These generalizations apply not only to the main predicate verb
but to verb phrases of other kinds as well—participles, gerunds, infinitives—which are labeled *verbals* because they remain verb-like even
while behaving like other parts of speech. F. Scott Fitzgerald, advising
his daughter "about adjectives," directs her attention to verbs. In his
example from Keats, "limped" is the *finite verb*, the verb that carries
tense and fills the predicate position. As a verb, it does indeed make the
sentence "move," to use Fitzgerald's word, but it also describes, as
might an adjective. And the two *nonfinite verb* forms, "trembling" and

"frozen," (a present participle and a past participle) also impart a feeling of movement in the manner of verbs and at the same time describe in the manner of adjectives.

The skilled writer can install verb phrases almost anywhere, as F. Scott Fitzgerald's own prose demonstrates. Once he jotted in his notebook a sentence composed entirely of verbs:

> Forgotten is forgiven.

Here he has converted two verbs—past participle forms—into nouns, a subject and a predicate nominative, thereby activating a normally static structure, the equative clause.

One important secret of success in writing is proficiency in using both the finite and nonfinite forms of verbs. Writers can create strong or subtle predicates, can introduce participles, gerunds, and infinitives into different positions within the kernel, can bring verbals into numerous locations alongside the basic kernel positions. Wherever verbs and verbals are placed, they enrich what is *said* by bringing with them their normal constituents—their attached subjects, complements, and modifiers.

Verbs can help to animate other structures, their energy level becoming almost contagious. Their intensities and rhythms invigorate other parts of speech and syntactic arrangements to create sustained patterns and levels of activity. In the extraordinary prose below, *racing …leaping…tumbling* and other verbs transmit their rushing rhythms and motion to the prepositions and nouns that follow:

> After Inniscarra the hills gather closely, and the river laughs out loud. It dances, it prances, it rushes, it slides, calm for a moment then onward again, stream racing stream, leaping and tumbling, wild Bacchanalian, wine from the mountains, froth from the ecstasy blown through the reeds. Mile after mile, past larch woods and beech woods and fern-covered hillsides, castles, and 'standing stones' cresting high ground. In comes the torrent from wild Knockabrocka, bringing turf waters from Aghabullogue; down comes the water from Carriganish.
>
> Robert Gibbings, *Lovely is the Lee*, 190

Some predicates with actions in series

Finite verbs, skillfully chosen, save a writer from added clauses and assorted modifiers. Actions can be set forth singly or one after the other, their juxtaposition or sequence itself meaningful. Thomas Jefferson's verbs, by their very sequence, illustrate the increasing violence:

> He has plundered our Seas, ravaged our Coasts, burnt our towns, and destroyed the Lives of our People.
> *Declaration of Independence*

Here are some contemporary sentences that also rely strongly on the particular sequence of the predicate verbs; although these verbs fall naturally, some are placed in a carefully devised order. The first example comes from a novel that has as its title a one-syllable active verb, *Thinks*. Active predicate verbs, mostly one-syllable, chronicle a series of routine actions that signal the end of a played-out affair:

> She *slept* badly and *woke* before daybreak. Instead of waiting for her alarm to ring, she *got up, showered, dressed, drank* a cup of coffee, and *loaded* her car.
> David Lodge, *Thinks*, 339

Next, a sequence of parallel predicates in a memoir unfolds a series of sense experiences:

> Suddenly I *could see* the sun glinting off the water of Stockholm harbor and I *could smell* the fresh clean air. I *could feel* the velvet seats of the opulent movie theatre where I saw a six hour version of *Fanny and Alexander*. I *could hear* the hiss of the samovars and the sound of Russian being spoken.
> Emily Prager, "Swedish Food," 48

A parallel syntactic trio of verb phrases increases precision and implies an order of activity at the end of the following sentence:

> Writing is much more premeditated than speaking: we are allowed to mull over our words for an awfully long time before setting them down, and once they are down, on the page or screen, we can *look at them, puzzle over them, revise them*.
> Ben Yagoda, *The Sound on the Page*, xxxi

Below, predicate verbs form a series of enthusiastic imperatives:

> One of the few things I know about writing is this: *spend it*
> *all, shoot it, play it, lose it,* right away, every time. *Do not hoard*
> what seems good for a later place in the book or for another
> book; *give it, give it all, give it now.*
> Annie Dillard, *The Writing Life,* 78

Repetitive actions, even beyond those named, are implied in nine
short independent clauses that form the compound sentence below.
Five terse abutting clauses using the verb *went* with the same subject
(*we*) list the actions performed as a group; these are followed by four
short clauses connected by *and,* each with a different subject and different verb to identify actions of the individuals in the group, one by
one:

> We went to Italy, we went to Ireland, we went to Williamsburg,
> we went to Montreal, we went to St. Martin, and Mark drove
> and I navigated and Julie suggested wrong turns and Arthur
> fell asleep.
> Nora Ephron, *Heartburn,* 101

A string of sentences, each consisting of a pair of contrastive
clauses, is marked by assertive predicates:

> He was a staunch churchman, but he laughed at priests.
> He was an able public servant and a courtier, but his views
> on sexual morality were extremely lax. He sympathized
> with poverty, but did nothing to improve the lot of the poor.
> It is safe to say that not a single law has been framed or one
> stone set upon another because of anything that Chaucer
> said or wrote; and yet, as we read him, we are of course
> absorbing morality at every pore.
> Virginia Woolf, *The Common Reader,* 17

Again, in this and the next series of short independent clauses, the
active predicates are strongly assertive. Below, the rhythm and emphasis help to direct attention to the trio of nouns—*craft, nuance, or*
beauty—as well as to the verb phrase at the end of the second sentence:

> Writers and intellectuals *can name,* we *can describe,* we *can*
> *depict,* we *can witness*—without sacrificing craft, nuance, or
> beauty. Above all, and at our best, we may sometimes help
> question the questions.
> Adrienne Rich, *Arts of the Possible,* 167

In fiction as well as discursive prose, predicate verbs can be given an added insistence by using a series, or more than one, that simply repeats the verb itself. From the closing page of a novel:

> So the coffin was enclosed and the soil did not come directly upon it. But then, how did one get out? One *didn't, didn't, didn't!* You *stayed*, you *stayed!*
>   Saul Bellow, *Humboldt's Gift*, 471

The –ing *verb or verbal*

The present participle in the conjugation carries the strongest sense of immediacy, of ongoing existence or activity, and sometimes of force, no matter where it is placed. Helped by an auxiliary, an object, and prepositional phrases, it serves as a predicate in "we are of course absorbing morality at every pore" in the example above from Virginia Woolf. When an –*ing* verb appears outside the predicate as an adjectival modifier, it is simply referred to as the present participle. When it functions as a noun, it is called a gerund. The –*ing* forms and the infinitive are often drawn into service together, several at a time, a generous accumulation in a sentence, paragraph, or series of paragraphs. Before such typical groupings are illustrated, however, here are a few examples of each one more or less alone, for a sense of the way each works.

The –ing *form as predicate*

> The deadline for the second edition *was fast approaching*.
>   Katharine Graham, *Personal History*, 449

> The sunlight then *was edging over the treetops*, and after I'd caught three more nice fish, it was level with my left shoulder, full and warm.
>   Fred Chappell, *I Am One of You Forever*, 34

> Harry's heart *was pumping frantically* now that he knew they were on the right track.
>   J. K. Rowling, *Harry Potter and the Order of the Phoenix*, 776

The –ing form as present participle-adjectival

It was a *searing* Valley afternoon.
Sandra Tsing Loh, *Depth Takes a Holiday*, 91

"James," she said, urgent, *appealing*, afraid.
Doris Lessing, *The Grandmothers*, 303

A lovely *soaring* summer day this; winter sent *howling* home
to his arctic.
Virginia Woolf, *A Writer's Diary*, ed. Leonard Woolf, 124

The –*ing* words and fragmentary nature of the diary entry above appropriately convey a sense that the action is happening now, this very day. No examples appear here, but use of such fragments and –*ing* words often attempts a stronger sense of immediacy and urgency in advertising and headlines, as well as in news broadcasts.

The –ing form as gerund (nominal)

Often suggesting a continuing process, gerunds occupy noun positions such as subjects, objects of verbs, and objects of prepositions:

Comparing the New Woman with the female aesthetes
can also help us refine our sense of both groups' politics.
Talia Schaffer, *The Forgotten Female Aesthetes*, 15

I remember *seeing him a good many times* before I first spoke
to him.
C. P. Snow, "Rutherford," 4

It also isolated Adams: ...he was cut off from the advice and
contacts that in Washington were his for the *asking*.
Olivier Bernier, *The World in 1800*, 151

A prolific writer uses five –*ing* verbs as gerunds, objects of prepositions, to describe the continuing process of revising his novels. Linking the verbals by a repeated use of *and*, he sets a rhythm that suggests the actions themselves:

I have never written a novel yet (except *Thank you, Jeeves*)
without *doing* 40,000 words or more and *finding* they were
all wrong and *going* back and *starting* again, and this after

filling 400 pages with notes, mostly delirious, before *getting* into anything in the nature of a coherent scenario.
　　P. G. Wodehouse, *P. G. Wodehouse: In His Own Words*, 149

The infinitive

Infinitives often impart as much vigor as finite verbs:

To trust is *to let go*.
　　Margaret Atwood, *Surfacing*, 224

I learned *to bind books*. Then *to throw pots*.
　　Danny Gregory, *Everyday Matters*, 12

Mrs. Kelley reflected that, besides flying, one thing she had neglected and would like now *to have done* was *to learn to swim*.
　　John Hersey, *Here to Stay*, 18

The past participle

Past participles tend to perform a descriptive function:

What a thrill, what a shock, to be alive on a morning in June, prosperous, almost scandalously *privileged*, with a simple errand to run.
　　Michael Cunningham, *The Hours*, 10

…the Darwin of our times is changing. Traditionally, he is a bluff, warm, helpful fellow, *racked* with illness yet *prepared* to push on nevertheless.
　　Michael Ruse, "The Darwin Industry: A Guide," 222

Mixed examples

Most of the time, writers don't confine themselves to a single form of the verb or verbal but use several forms in combination. The examples that follow show a mixed collection of verbs and verbals. In general, the first group consists mostly of *–ing* participles and gerunds, the second group, infinitives, and the third group, past participles. One should notice the predicate materials – adverbials and direct objects – that fill out the verb phrases. With free modifiers, set off by commas, the syntax allows a complex series of actions to be easily comprehended.

Verb phrases headed by present participles can also serve as *bound* (restrictive) modifiers, as in the first example below. The second and third excerpts contain present participles as bound modifiers followed by more present participles, set off from them by commas, as a long free-modifying series:

> The little girls sat *watching the streets grow duller and dingier and narrower...*
> Katherine Anne Porter, *Pale Horse, Pale Rider*, 40

> They came *ambling and stumbling, tumbling and capering, kilting their gowns for leap frog, holding one another back, shaken with deep fast laughter, smacking one another behind and laughing at their rude malice, calling to one another by familiar nicknames, protesting with sudden dignity at some rough usage, whispering two and two behind their hands.*
> James Joyce, *A Portrait of the Artist as a Young Man*, 192

> He hinted at himself *striding recognized down exotic streets, walking in sandals through dust, moving slowly behind an ox-cart or a rickshaw, or a dog-sled, kicking aside the encumbrance of a cashmere robe, a furred cloak, shading his eyes from the sun, sheltering his head from the snow, regarding unmoved typhoon and flood, seeing with familiarity such scenes as the quiet eye could not envisage, laughing and looking easily and speaking intimately in strange tongues*; yes, he agreed, he was a stranger.
> Shirley Jackson, *The Sundial*, 95-96

More often, the entire participial verb phrase is a free or nonrestrictive modifier, easy to hook on or insert and making important contributions without new whole clauses:

> *Driving a small car on the motorway at 70 mph, with another car alongside him*, he is impelled to imagine himself in a dodgem, *wanting to bounce cheerfully off this other vehicle.*
> Frank Kermode, *Pieces of My Mind*, 389

An author engages in word-play with an opening present participle, followed by a predicate with the same verb's past tense:

> *Concluding these reflections*, he concluded these reflections...
> John Barth, *Lost in the Funhouse*, 126

A predicate verb (*awaken*) and a verb transformed to a noun (*tremble*) combine with three present participles to describe a vivid sequence of remembered experiences:

> For example, after a year in jail, I'd awaken in a tremble,
> *reliving* all the terror, *seeing* it all again with ten-fold intensity,
> *remembering* for days afterward.
> Neil Cassady, *Collected Letters, 1944-1967*, 95

When there is more than one participial phrase, there may be no clear idea of sequence across them. They may appear simultaneous both with one another and with the main clause, especially when some of the actions described are mental. On the other hand, a sequence may be implied, strengthened too by adverbs, across space or time:

> At a distance he can see the tall line of a dozen or more
> aqueduct arches, *commencing suddenly, suddenly ending;*
> *coming now from nowhere, now going nowhere.*
> James Gould Cozzens, *Morning Noon and Night*, last page

—*Ing* verbs that hold down nominal slots, the very useful gerunds, retain also some of their action-giving, verb-like qualities. In the next excerpt are four such verb forms where one might expect to meet nouns, giving effective variety and life:

> *Turning* from professional details and daily *winning* to con-
> sideration of these more fundamental problems requires not
> only the means of *acquiring knowledge* but also an opportu-
> nity and a stimulus for *examining its broader significance.*
> George Gaylord Simpson, *The Meaning of Evolution*, 3

A gerund phrase also works as a subject in this reminiscence:

> *Stealing watermelons on dark and rainy nights was* a pious duty
> when I was a boy.
> Donald Day, *Uncle Sam's Uncle Josh*, 5

In a more intricate formation, the gerund is tied to its noun to serve as subject of the sentence. *Shape-shifting* becomes a seductive opening to a sentence that names it as one of the *wonders* soon to be identified in a series of clauses with unusually graphic finite verbs. Commas instead of semicolons or periods to separate the clauses enhance the rapid movement imparted by the verbs:

> *Shape-shifting* is one of fairy tale's dominant and characteristic wonders: hands are cut off, and reattached, babies' throats are slit, but they are later restored to life, a rusty lamp turns into an all-powerful talisman, a humble pestle and mortar becomes the winged vehicle of the fairy enchantress Baba Yoga, the beggar changes into the powerful enchantress and the slattern in the filthy donkeyskin into a golden-haired princess.
>   Marina Warner, *From Beast to the Blonde*, xix

Often, as in the preceding example, the gerund's own verbal activity is closer to the described experience than a noun alone would be, if substituted. Gerunds are impressively flexible as to effect and position. Below, three gerunds serve as objects in a trio of parallel prepositional phrases:

> They were grateful to me for *believing* in them, for *educating* them, for the practice of freedom, for *urging* them to become critical thinkers able to make responsible choices.
>   bell hooks, *Teaching Community*, 19

In a book on how war seduces and corrupts entire societies, the author expresses a sad truth in a prepositional phrase with a gerund as object:

> The cause, sanctified by the dead, cannot be questioned without *dishonoring* those who gave up their lives.
>   Chris Hedges, *War is a Force that Gives Us Meaning*, 145

Two gerunds, objects of prepositions, lead into an ironic commentary in a novel:

> He moved to Gloucester fairly recently from Cambridge, and has that high-table trick of *being able* to make urbane conversation about any topic whatsoever *without saying* anything memorable or profound.
>   David Lodge, *Thinks*, 23

In the next two sentences, a social critic responds to her own challenge to *make work visible,* by using thirteen *–ing* words, gerunds, to name a long list of domestic chores and several contrasting pursuits:

> However we resolve the issues in our individual homes,
> the moral challenge is, put simply, to make work visible
> again: not only the *scrubbing* and *vacuuming,* but all the
> *hoeing, stacking, hammering, drilling, bending,* and *lifting* that
> goes into *creating* and *maintaining* a livable habitat. In an
> ever more economically unequal world, where so many of
> our affluent devote their lives to ghostly pursuits like *stock*
> *trading, image making,* and *opinion polling,* real work, in the
> old-fashioned sense of labor that engages hand as well as
> eye, that tires the body and directly alters the physical world,
> tends to vanish from sight.
> Barbara Ehrenreich, *Maid to Order,* 103

Although they function as nouns, the verb-like qualities of gerunds, below, describe potent actions—*forcing, filing,* and *hiring:*

> Among NOW's first actions were *forcing* newspapers to elimi-
> nate sex-segregated help-wanted ads and *filing* a formal com-
> plaint against NASA that charged discrimination in the *hiring*
> not only of astronauts but also for top-level posts in its
> administration.
> Martha Ackmann, *The Mercury 13,* 176

Next, in an autobiography, a gerund series stands in apposition to a direct object:

> We also devised ordeals, which we suffered, as tests of
> courage, *walking bare-legged through stinging nettles, climbing*
> *high and difficult trees, signing our names in blood and so forth.*
> Evelyn Waugh, *A Little Learning,* 59

Writers rely frequently on the infinitive phrase. In perhaps its most common form as a way of expanding finite verbs, the dependent infinitive or a chain of such infinitives, can open up a main verb phrase for important expansions, often widening into the major stretch of the sentence:

> I was not quite conscious of it at first, but then it came again
> a bit stronger, until I was sure I heard it, and then as I was
> reading I began *to wait for it, and to make spaces in sentences for*

it, to enjoy it, and finally to play with the words and with the
audience, to swoop and glide and describe arabesques with all
the nutty abandon of Donald Duck on ice skates.
Shana Alexander, *Life Magazine*, 30B

Infinitive phrases occupy nominal slots in all kinds of writing, sometimes as subject and complement in a *be*-pattern but also in many other
arrangements of varying complexity:

To enjoy good houses and good books in self-respect and decent
comfort, seems to me *to be the pleasurable end toward which*
all societies of human beings ought now to struggle.
William Morris, *The Ideal Book*, I

To picture himself passing the limit would be *to admit into his imag-*
ination the reality of death; and this even now he could not do.
Iris Murdoch, *An Unofficial Rose*, 6

The infinitive of purpose has a unique dynamics. Here in the first
example, four such infinitives help to define a book's purpose. Also
effective as definitions are two gerund phrases in the second sentence:

We envision information in order *to reason about, communi-*
cate, document, and preserve that knowledge—activities nearly
always carried out on two-dimensional paper and computer
screens. *Escaping this flatland* and *enriching the density of data*
displays are the essential tasks of information design.
Edward Tufte, *Envisioning Information*, 33

The infinitive of purpose often begins simply with *to* rather than *in*
order to. In many kinds of prose it serves as a forceful introductory
device, sometimes as sentence modifier:

To find deeper meaning, one must become able to transcend
the narrow confines of a self-centered existence and believe
that one will make a significant contribution to life—if not
right now, then at some future time.
Bruno Bettelheim, *The Uses of Enchantment*, 4

In the next example, repetition of the infinitive's verb creates a
pause emphasizing the silence being described:

Many times during the night I woke to *listen, listen,* but there
is no sound at all. The silence is as thick and soft as wool.
Will the snow never stop falling?
　May Sarton, *From May Sarton's Well,* 15

Among verb phrases, infinitive structures are probably given the least
attention in discussions of style; they don't deserve this slighting.
Essential for any writer who wants to cultivate ease and economy of
style, they are natural, normal, efficient, and all the types converge
effortlessly in many different sorts of prose. Here, in the ordinary
course of things, four infinitive phrases help to develop three sentences:

There will always be the Christmas rush, the Summer
Vacation in Europe and there will always be many more
people who prefer *to fly during the daytime rather than at night.*
These people are willing *to pay more for these privileges. To fill
their flights* the airlines have been forced *to give a good break to
others who will use their services at less popular times.*
　Jim Woodman, *Air Travel Bargains,* 9

In past years many manuals of style sternly warned writers against
using "split" infinitives, that is, infinitives with a word or words inserted
between the "to" and the verb. Such uses can be awkward, but most
often they are fine, a fact acknowledged in 1993 by *The Chicago
Manual of Style* when they dropped the usage from their list of "errors
and infelicities."

…in order to understand a medical condition, physicians
need *to not only examine the patients but listen to them…*
　Deborah Tannen, *Gender and Discourse,* 6

When such institutions run off the rails, the challenge is *to
honestly analyze the failure and correct the flaw* so that the institution can regain legitimacy and trust.
　Orville Schell, "Gray Lady and a Greek Tragedy," R12

Below, the split infinitive in the second sentence perhaps may create more appropriate emphasis than would the conventional arrangement. The reference is to a World Family Tree on the internet:

So far it has tied together seventy-five thousand family trees,
a total of 50 million names. The goal, once unthinkable, is *to
eventually document and link every named human who ever lived.*
　Stewart Brand, *The Clock of the Long Now,* 91

In his classic *A Grammar of the English Language*, George O. Curme defended the split infinitive in nine pages mostly devoted to "a large number of characteristic examples taken from the author's much larger collection." Included is Willa Cather's line:

> How satisfactory it would be to really know…
> *The Song of the Lark*, 421

Past participles often join infinitives and gerunds in basic functions and as modification before, during, or after a main clause. Like present participles, they are usually nonrestrictive modifiers. Here a sentence opens with four past participles and ends with a present participial:

> *Repudiated, embraced, attributed, claimed*, it turns up everywhere, changing shape with the times.
> Patricia Meyer Spacks, *Boredom*, xi

Opening participles, like the four italicized above and the one below, can serve as a cohesive device by making clear the relationship of an idea or action completed earlier to one that is about to be named:

> Leonardo da Vinci was praised for a spectacle he devised in 1493 that featured seven gyrating planets. *Entitled* Il Paradiso, it was one of the first court entertainments totally enclosed in a specially created and permanent environment where an aristocratic audience was presented with calculated visual and aural delights.
> Carol Lee, *Ballet in Western Culture*, 56

Here in a sentence introduced by a past participial modifier, a biographer describes Nikita Krushchev's responses to books given to him by his son:

> *Emboldened* by his father's reaction to *Zhivago*, Sergei produced Solzhenitsyn's *First Circle* and *Cancer Ward* and George Orwell's *1984*. At these, however, Krushchev's responses drew the line; "He didn't like them," Sergei said.
> William Taubman, *Krushchev*, 628

Some past participles, like the above, are reduced passive assertions, economical in the making of sentences because they eliminate the need for a separate passive clause. In the following deft sentence, the opening verbal appears to be a playful faked passive, or an abbreviated active *having overslept*:

> *Overslept*, he awoke with a bang and was splashing cold water on his face when the landlady knocked.
> Bernard Malamud, *A New Life*, 364

Taken from a passive statement, the material that accompanies the past participle is often a prepositional phrase, sometimes of agent or of instrument:

> *Tossed from side to side by the sharp turns, jerked forward by the sudden stops, his ear assailed by shrieking brakes and surly horns,* he goes on talking or reading his paper, and reaches his destination heedless of the miracle that has brought him there.
> William K. Zinsser, *The City-Dwellers*, 78

In the left-branch above, the third phrase (*his ear assailed*) shows the function of the verb phrase within the larger structure known as the nominative absolute, a form exemplified in the preceding chapter and to appear again later. The two participial phrases that precede it make another point about the past participial phrase: its pastness may not come across strongly. The essence of the past participle is rather its passivity, and it may be used to represent, as it does here, an action performed upon the subject of the main clause at the same time that the action of the main clause is going on. But this is not always so. The front-shifted position, especially, can be used for an economical summary or prior action, as in the next example, after which the main clause arrives; out of it, the action grows:

> *"Morally" weakened by fifteen years of service on the Editorial Committee, and physically disturbed by the approach of my sixty-third year*, I agreed to abandon my normal habits of life and become (for a season) a statistical debauchee.
> Don Cameron Allen, *The Ph.D. in English and American Literature*, VII

And here is a past participle in a nominative absolute, accompanying two opening adjectives:

> Insoluble, unsolvable, the chord *suspended* – was it never to
> find resolution?
>   Conrad Aiken, *Ushant*, 60

The passive verb

Otters eat clams. The verb is in the active voice: the subject performs the action. *Clams are eaten by otters.* The verb is in the passive voice: the subject receives the action. Which form you choose depends on whether you have previously been writing about otters or clams. One of the uses of the passive is to shift the topic or the emphasis. Another use is to move the noun phrase that was the subject of discussion to a new location in the sentence, usually toward the end, where you can easily add as many modifiers as you like:

> *Clams are eaten by otters, those charming, popular furry sea crea-*
> *tures, clever in that they use tools – the otter uses a stone to crack*
> *the clam shell – and so great is their need for food that they daily*
> *consume 25 per cent or more of their body weight (some weigh*
> *more than 90 pounds), thereby reducing the shellfish population,*
> *according to the Alaska Department of Fish and Game.*

For good or ill, the passive can be used to leave out the agent. You can relieve the otters of blame:

> *Clams are being eaten at such a rate that the shellfish population*
> *is disappearing.*

The passive can thus be used if the performer of the action is unknown or if the writer does not wish to place responsibility.

There are, as with other inversions, many reasons for turning to the passive, including the need for special emphasis or rhythm, for strategic rearrangements of different kinds to aid modification or to increase cohesion, for adjustments in a parallel series, and for certain more thematic effects, often providing contrast with the active verbs.

The most basic result of the passive is the change made in what is emphasized. It is the nature of brief English utterance, such as short kernel patterns, to send the primary stress toward the end of the sentence. It is therefore the nature of the passive to direct this emphasis at the phrase of agent or of instrument, or at both, or, when neither is there, at whatever happens to appear last (unless it is a pronoun):

> I was tormented by strange hallucinations.
> Vladimir Nabokov, *Nabokov's Congeries*, 91

> We are made kind by being kind.
> Eric Hoffer, *The Passionate State of Mind*, 77

> His round sunburned face was marked by a certain watchful innocence.
> Carson McCullers, *Reflections in a Golden Eye*, 2

> Every apartment I ever stayed in was loaded with them.
> Andy Warhol, *The Philosophy of Andy Warhol*, 23, writing about cockroaches

Changing the sentence below from passive into active demonstrates how much more effective and understandable the passive can be, as composed by the author. First, a rewritten active version:

> *The Buddhist version of interior arrangement, where one strives to create a particular atmosphere with aesthetic minimalism, with an eye for simplicity, affirms in my own imagination this process of thinking and writing.*

> In my own imagination, this process of thinking and writing is affirmed by the Buddhist vision of interior arrangement, where one strives to create a particular atmosphere with aesthetic minimalism, with an eye for simplicity.
> bell hooks, *Remembered Rapture*, 40

Below, the author has placed two passive verbs in parallel clauses that open two successive sentences. The verbs themselves draw emphasis as descriptions emerge of the ways distinctive facial characteristics relate to personal characteristics:

> The thinness of his lips *was emphasized by* a narrow line of dark moustache; it seemed a hard, almost cruel mouth until he smiled, and then an expression of unexpected kindliness would irradiate his whole face. The general gauntness of his looks *was accentuated by* the deep sockets from which his eyes looked out, always rather sadly.
> George Woodcock, *The Crystal Spirit*, 3

Next, the clipped assertion that follows the charge of loud active verbs uses the passive to stress the quiet, italicized simplicity of the past participle *said*:

> Do not worry about making your characters shout, intone, exclaim, remark, shriek, reason, holler, or any such thing, unless they are doing it for a reason. All remarks can be *said*.
> Shirley Jackson, "Notes for a Young Writer," 239

Again, the passive form has allowed a writer to save until the end, for emphasis, the appropriate last word:

> Her body, if concealed at all, is concealed *by a water lily, a frond, a fern, a bit of moss, or by a sarong—which is a simple garment carrying the implicit promise that it will not long stay in place.*
> E. B. White, *The Second Tree from the Corner*, 108

> Hemingway's short stories and novels are concerned *with the fundamentals of life, such as death.*
> Richard Armour, *American Lit Relit*, 152

The particular effects that the passive can impart on the phrase of agency are illustrated in the examples that follow. Here the passive moves the agent to the beginning of the sentence for a change in emphasis:

> *By its multitude of memories* memory will be driven to distraction.
> James Gould Cozzens, *Morning Noon and Night*, 17

> *By the husbands of his wife's friends*, Graham was considered lucky.
> Eric Ambler, *Intrigue*, 5

Below, the phrase of agency is compounded:

> The order was carried out on the twenty-ninth of November, *not by the public executioner, but by a gravedigger…*
> Roland H. Bainton, *Here I Stand*, 123

Sometimes the agent is dropped altogether, when it is unknown, well known, or unimportant—or the writer chooses for other reasons to omit it. The passive form makes this economy possible.

> A warning should be posted, at this point, as to chronology.
> John Hersey, *The Algiers Motel Incident*, 264

> From the window all that could be seen was a receding area of grey.
> Anita Brookner, *Hotel du Lac*, 7

> The town was occupied, the defender defeated, and the war finished.
> John Steinbeck, *The Moon Is Down*, 11

> The creation of the entirely artificial environment that is now the Sacramento Valley was not achieved at one stroke, nor is it complete to this day.
> Joan Didion, *Where I Was From*, 22

When present, the agent can also be accompanied by a phrase of instrument, as it is in this double structure:

> He was then received into the convent *by* the brethren *with the kiss of peace* and again admonished *by* the prior *with the words*…
> Roland H. Bainton, *Here I Stand*, 27

More often, though, the phrase of instrument occurs when the agent is not directly mentioned:

> The plays are stuffed like badly made beanbags *with false feeling, false knowledge, false humanity*.
> Jack Kroll, "Theater of Crisis," 23

A secondary result of the passive is the creation of past participles for use in various adjectival slots, many of which have been seen earlier in this chapter. Not all adjectives ending in *–ed*, however, are past participles generated in this way. Three below are *stained, blistered, and exiled*:

> In that kindly light the *stained* and *blistered* paint of the bungalow and the plot of weeds between the veranda and the dry waterhole lost their extreme shabbiness,

and the two Englishmen, each in his rocking chair, each
with his whisky and soda and his *outdated* magazine, the
counterparts of numberless fellow-countrymen *exiled*
in the barbarous regions of the world, shared in the
brief illusory rehabilitation.
　　Evelyn Waugh, *The Loved One*, 7-8

Here we come to a third area of the passive's use as a syntactic jug-
gler. In addition to its ability to shuffle words for emphasis or for ease
of modification, it can also adjust structures for smoother or clearer
transition. The passive thus becomes a device for cohesion. Often the
passive makes for a quick transition from the sentence in which it
occurs to the opener of the sentence that follows. Here two passives
placed back to back bring together for emphasis and coherence the
agent and the passive core of the next sentence:

And whether it be genuine disgust, joy, grief, pity, shame
or desire – it is accompanied *by a vague sense of gratification.*
We are gratified by the discovery that we are not all shame
and show, that there are elements in our inner make-up as
organically our own as the color of our eyes and the shape
of our nose.
　　Eric Hoffer, *The Passionate State of Mind*, 115

The shape of the passive itself frequently helps to shape larger passages. We meet it amid other sentences, and its own syntactic order
directs us through the larger order of words, helping to unify it. Related
to this cohesive function is the use of the passive to make possible a
consecutive development of the same subject:

You see, *books* had been happening to me. Now *the books*
were cast off back there somewhere in the churn of spray
and night behind the propeller.
　　The Langston Hughes Reader, 317

The subject is able to get our attention at the beginning of each sentence only because the passive is used for the second.
　　Below, a versatile grammar joins active forms and two passives,
making possible successive views of the same subject from different
angles. This parallelism of first person openers is just right for the
stages of an elaborate self-identification:

I am an invisible man. No, *I* am not a spook like those who haunted Edgar Allan Poe; nor am *I* one of your Hollywood-movie ectoplasms. *I* am a man of substance, of flesh and bone, fiber and liquids – and *I might even be said* to possess a mind. *I* am invisible, understand, simply because people refuse to see me. Like the bodiless heads you see sometimes in circus sideshows, it is as though *I have been surrounded* by mirrors of hard, distorting glass.

Ralph Ellison, *Invisible Man*, opening lines

The adept use of almost alternating passive and active verbs in the opening of a book review tends to mirror the pattern of history being described: women *are often overlooked*, they *appear*, they *have been written about*, they *made a mark*, and so on.

Women are often overlooked in the writing of history, and they appear only seldom in the great sagas that have been written about the conquest and settlement of the West. Most women on the frontier were confined to home and farm, and companionship was limited to husbands, children and other women. But at least a few made a mark in their own lifetimes, only to disappear from the historical record.

Jonathan Kirsch, "Maverick minds, kindred spirits," R2

Again, below, alternation and passive verbs make for effective emphasis and cohesion:

We heard Killdeers last evening. Small Crested Flycatchers, Summer Yellow-birds, Maryland Yellow-throats, and House Wrens are seen as we pass along our route; while the Spotted Sandpiper accompanies us all along the river. Sparrow Hawks, Turkey Buzzards, Arctic Towhee Buntings, Cat-birds, Mallards, Coots, Gadwalls, King-birds, Yellow-breasted Chats, Red Thrushes, all are noted as we pass.

Jorie Graham, *Materialism*, 89

Why did author-scientist Isaac Asimov arraign his fellow scientists for their frequent use of the passive? Asimov accuses them of

interlarding every statement with a semiwithdrawal in the shape of a qualifying phrase, and then translating the whole into a grammatical construction peculiar to the scientific paper – the Impersonal Passive.

Isaac Asimov, *From Earth to Heaven*, VI

Asimov explains further in a note on the same page:

> As an example of this inspiring form of writing I give you
> the solemn phrase, "It was earlier demonstrated by the
> investigator that–" Very few scientists are brave enough to
> dare to write, "I once showed that–"
> Asimov, vi

Not all scientists write this way, of course. But it does happen:

> It *may possibly be thought strange* that more *has not been said*
> in this book about the modern, very powerful techniques–
> various forms of chromatography and spectrometry, for
> example–now *being increasingly applied*, together with useful
> methods of statistical analysis, by a growing number of
> investigators to the study of olfaction. The value of all these
> procedures *should certainly not be underestimated.*
> William McCartney, *Olfaction and Odours*, 190

Nor is it only scientists who write in the manner Asimov attacks.
Besides its use by writers in many fields, it is found in committee
prose–not addressed by one writer to prospective readers, but by a
staff, some official body, an institution, corporation, government
agency, or the like, to readers in whom it displays no personal interest.
The impersonality, however chilling, is thus an accurate reflection of
authorship, impersonal because collective–making a consensus prose
for which responsibility would be as hard to fix actually as it is grammatically. There is indeed something mysterious and unnerving about
the next icy official pronouncements:

> It is hereby stipulated that coverage under this policy does
> not include damage caused in any manner by windstorm
> to paint or waterproofing material applied to the exterior
> of the building(s) or structure(s) covered hereunder. The
> value of paint or waterproofing material, being excluded
> from the coverage as above stated, shall not be considered in
> the determination of actual cash value when applying the
> Co-Insurance Clause applicable to loss from windstorm.
> "Windstorm Exterior Paint and Waterproofing
> Exclusion Clause," an insurance company policy

> A bachelor's degree in a broad program of general educa-
> tion, granted by a college or university of recognized stand-
> ing, is normally requisite for admission, but is not sufficient

in itself. An examination of an applicant's academic record is made to determine whether he has established a strong affirmative case in regard to the character of his general education, and his fitness for graduate work in his proposed subject of study. Letters of recommendation from persons who are in a position to analyze the candidate's abilities and to estimate his promise are given very serious consideration. The results of the Graduate Record Examination are used as a supplementary objective check on the candidate's aptitudes and knowledge. In the consideration of applicants, regard is given to character and promise as well as to scholastic attainment. A personal interview is not required. If a candidate wishes to present himself for an interview or if he wishes to learn further about the program of study, he is welcomed...

A Graduate School Announcement

TO ALL REGISTRANTS:
When you report pursuant to this order you will be forwarded to an Armed Forces Examining Station where it will be determined whether you are qualified for military service under current standards. Upon completion of your examination, you will be returned to the place of reporting designated above. It is possible that you may be retained at the Examining Station for more than 1 day for the purpose of further testing or for medical consultation. You will be furnished transportation, and meals and lodging when necessary, from the place of reporting designated above to the Examining Station and return.

"Order to Report for Armed Forces Physical Examination," U. S. Selective Service System Form 223

There can be no doubt about these excerpts being officialese, and we can at least respond to them on these grounds–even though we hardly enjoy reading them. Yet we may still wish to object in the case of the middle one, the announcement from a university, and wonder if its composers might have avoided inflicting interested students with such a sense of anonymous cold authority. It would have been easy enough to substitute an inexact but warming "we" for the unspoken agent of all that momentous paperwork, serious consideration, and decision-making. And matters are not helped by eight uses of the old-fashioned generic pronouns.

In the account below, however, the impersonality of tone seems appropriate. With the exception of the opening impersonal passive "It will be remembered," the commentator presents us with a series of rapid actions, of orders and imprisonments and inquisitions assailing the defenseless Essex, and later Hayward and Wolfe, and recorded aptly by the passive grammar, with its submerged, threatening agency. The heavy passives give the actions the weight of history, conveying not just the threatening swift action of events but their gravity, lasting importance, and the power of almost invisible agents:

> *It will be remembered* that when Essex made his tempestuous return from Ireland, against the queen's orders, in September of 1599, *he was suspected and remitted* to custody. On November 29, *censure was pronounced* on him in Star Chamber. In March *he was allowed* to return to his own house in charge of Sir Richard Berkeley. In June of 1600 *he was tried before special commissioners, censured, and ordered* to remain a prisoner in his house and not to execute any of his offices. Great *stress was laid* on Hayward's book during these proceedings as evidence of Essex's ambitions and intentions, and in July *Hayward was summoned to court and examined.* The printer Wolfe *was also questioned* and revealed that three weeks after the first printing of Hayward's book, the Archbishop of Canterbury had ordered the dedicatory epistle to Essex *cut out.* All later editions *were burnt* in the Bishop of London's house – to the financial grief of the printer, he complained. Hayward *was again examined.*
>   Lily B. Campbell, *Shakespeare's Histories*, 187

Syntax works in a thematic way also in these biographical notes about poet Ezra Pound, the passive receiver of the actions in a chain of events:

> On May 3, 1945, Pound *was captured by Italian partisans and taken* to Genoa for interrogation by FBI agents; on May 24 *he was confined* in a military stockade, where *he was held* for nearly five months. *Flown* to Washington on November 18 and *reindicted for treason*... A jury found him to be of unsound mind and *he was committed* to St. Elizabeth's hospital...
>   *American Poetry: The Twentieth Century*, v. 1, 918

Below, this time in a novel, a matter-of-fact reportorial style, cryptic and objective, uses passives to suggest the impersonal workings of public justice:

> In the early summer of 1902 John Barrington Ashley of
> Coaltown, a small mining center in southern Illinois,
> *was tried* for the murder of Breckenridge Lansing, also
> of Coaltown. He *was found guilty and sentenced* to death.
> Thorton Wilder, *The Eighth Day*, 3

With these last examples we have returned from complaints against the passive to a discussion of what might be called making thematic capital of the implications carried by the passive voice. The results are remarkably varied, and a small further sampling will conclude this chapter. In the following passage, a superstitious heritage assumes some sort of divine command coming down through the ages as the agent behind rules and taboos:

> There are the rules and the laws; *they are well made. It is
> forbidden* to cross the great river and look upon the place
> that was the place of the Gods—*this is most strictly forbidden...*
> *These things are forbidden—they have been forbidden* since the
> beginning of time.
> Stephen Vincent Benét, "By the Waters of Babylon," 3

The agent of this passive is unexpressed, simply because it is unknown:

> *Passport kontrol!* Somewhere down the train the words
> were barked.
> Catherine Drinker Bowen, *Adventures of a Biographer*, 6

Aside from these matters of agency or its absence, there is another way in which the passive becomes thematic, having to do with the nature of passivity itself. In the next sentence, at the end of a long coordinate chain, the active verbs of motion culminate in a single passive form, emphasized by the following adverb and appropriate to a shift from active to passive conveyance:

> They sailed and trailed and flew and raced and crawled and
> walked and *were carried*, finally, home.
> John Knowles, *Indian Summer*, 4

The next paired clauses seem almost a study in transformation, analyzing the two sides of the same verbal coin—the contrast between active and passive predication and, in a given case, its moral implications:

> It is men tormenting and killing a bull; it is a bull being tormented and killed.
> Max Eastman, *Art and the Life of Action*, 90

Two near-kernels are now paired in another contrast, this time the humorous juxtaposition of two kinds of death, one active and the other passive:

> In New York, I should die of stimulus. In Boston, I should be soothed to death.
> Van Wyck Brooks, *A Chilmark Miscellany*, 9

Another paired contrast between active and passive involves what the author refers to as "the dynamic of reading and writing." Here it is an active infinitive in contrast to a passive infinitive:

> The writer by implicit contract with readers promises *to interest them*; they in turn tacitly agree to allow themselves *to be interested*.
> Patricia Meyer Spacks, *Boredom*, xi

A contrast between passive and active responses to the paranoia sometimes faced by aspiring writers is expressed by a teacher of writing by using passive verbs in the first clause and then using mainly active verbs in the advice that follows:

> You can be defeated and disoriented by all these feelings, I tell them, or you can see the paranoia, for instance, as wonderful material. You can use it as the raw clay that you pull out of the river: surely one of your characters is riddled with it, and so in giving that person this particular quality, you get to use it, shape it into something true and funny or frightening.
> Anne Lamott, *Bird by Bird*, 11

A similar contrast, again a passive contrasted to an active, marks the sentence below:

> It was the deep and enduring belief that people *be permitted to define* themselves, not just by gender but by ability, inclination, and character.
>   Anna Quindlen, *Loud and Clear*, 208

Death happens to be the subject of the next example, the description of a corpse. The passive structure renders a sense of action locked into the rigidity of death:

> The body lay on the back, the head toward the door.
> A candlestick *was yet clutched* in the right hand.
>   Robert Penn Warren, *Wilderness*, 228

One brief selection displays almost every kind of verb and verbal discussed in this chapter and illustrates the vitality of verbs in good prose. The vigorous active verbs, a dozen or more describing a player's on-stage physical actions, find a contrast in the closing lines that include passives (*a book made of* and *being read*) to portray the comparative quiet of reading and mental awareness. Carol Muske-Dukes, poet, novelist, critic, writes about actor David Dukes, her late husband.

> He would play Hamlet, the Duke of Albany, Timon. He was Aubrey Beardsley, Teddy Roosevelt, Henry Carr. He leapt from a balcony in Dracula's cape, he fenced his way downstage, shouting, as Hotspur–he pedaled a bike onstage, walked on his hands, peeled an orange, sang a rhyming soliloquy, quoted Dada. He was a physical actor who had to observe carefully how the body moved; he was a cerebral actor who feared overthinking his parts. I think about his experience as an actor and believe in some eerie, proactive way it recreated the experience of reading, of being inside a book made of intense audience regard, being "read" as he acted–and conscious of that reading.
>   Carol Muske-Dukes, *Married to the Icepick Killer*, 173-174

Hot soup on a cold day, cold soup on a hot day, and the smell of soup simmering in the kitchen are fundamental, undoubtedly even atavistic, pleasures and solaces that give a special kind of satisfaction.
                    Julia Child and Simone Beck

Profound was Gary's relief the next morning as he bumped and glided, like a storm-battered yacht, into the safe harbor of his work week.
                    Jonathan Franzen

The cool globes of dew or rain broke in showers of iridescent spray about his nose; the earth, here hard, here soft, here hot, here cold, stung, traced, and tickled the soft pads of his feet.
                    Virginia Woolf

The limping earnestness of his speech disappeared; he talked as he drank, abundantly.
                    Desmond Hall

CHAPTER FOUR

Adjectives and Adverbs

> Your coloring words, particularly adjectives and
> adverbs, must be used where they will do the most
> good. Not every action needs a qualifying adverb,
> not every object needs a qualifying adjective. Your
> reader probably has a perfectly serviceable mental
> picture of a lion; when a lion comes into your story
> you need not burden him with adjectives unless
> it is necessary, for instance, to point out that he is
> a green lion, something of which your reader might
> not have a very vivid mental picture.
>
> Shirley Jackson, *Come Along with Me*, 239-240

> After a while, I find myself starting to feel hungry
> for an adverb...
>
> Christopher Ricks, *Dylan's Visions of Sin*, 467

ADJECTIVES AND ADVERBS are "coloring words," but this is not to deny their importance or to suggest that their roles are somehow inferior to those of nouns and verbs. Often the noun and the verb simply state the known or given information, and it is the adjective or adverb that carries the news of the sentence.

Adjectives and adverbs offer to writers extraordinary resources and subtleties. Along with nouns and verbs, they are *content words*, the four word classes forming the great bulk of the vocabulary whose main job is to carry content or meaning. Although the inflected forms and the placements of content words give help in depicting the syntactic structure of sentences, that task is left mainly to the much smaller group labeled *structure words* or *function words*–prepositions, conjunctions, determiners and the like, auxiliaries, some pronouns–only a few hundred all told but the most frequently used words in the language, words such as *a, an, the, this, that, my, and, to, on, but, for, can, has*, for example. The remarkable richness of English word classes, including adjectives and adverbs, and the ways they work ingeniously together in sentences invite creative variety, as seen in the examples that follow.

Adjectives and adverbs in short sentences

Sometimes in the *be* and linking verb equative patterns, the adjective is doubled or even further expanded, offering a significant enlargement of meaning:

> The relationship is *disgraceful, disgusting.*
> Janet Frame, *Scented Gardens for the Blind*, 194

> The noise had been *so loud, so sharp.*
> William Golding, *The Pyramid*, 4

> My career at Fontlands was *short and inglorious.*
> Havelock Ellis, *My Life*, 125

> He sounded *weary, hurt.*
> Bernard Malamud, *The Assistant*, 88

> He felt *porous and pregnable.*
> Vladimir Nabokov, *Pnin*, 20

> The lawn is *green* and *clean* and *quiet.*
> Julia Alvarez, *How the Garcia Girls Lost Their Accent*, 85

What is clear is the tendency of the third slot, especially after *be* and linking verbs, to carry the *new* information of the sentence. When the adjective appears in front of nouns as part of other patterns, it is still often responsible for much of the new descriptive material. Here, in front of a noun complement in a *be* pattern, it is the adjective that carries the news and draws the stress:

> But his life energy was *cheerful* stuff.
> Iris Murdoch, *Bruno's Dream*, 19

You're a *patient* person.
Ann Beattie, "The Rabbit Hole as Likely Explanation," 70

Below in a sentence with a direct object, the modifier *another* draws emphasis equal to or exceeding that on the noun it precedes:

They started *another* war.
Rebecca Wells, *Little Altars Everywhere*, 169

Adjectives to make contrasts

In some of the preceding examples with adjectives used in pairs, at times the two adjectives are almost synonymous: *disgraceful, disgusting; loud, sharp; porous, pregnable*. Pairs of adjectives are also often used in various kinds of syntactic arrangements to establish contrasts:

Value judgments may be *informed or uninformed, responsible or irresponsible*.
Walter Kaufmann, *The Faith of a Heretic*, 335

An art critic makes subtle choices of descriptive adjectives, here including two differentiating pairs:

The visual system has a drive to perceive objects and so a built-in good will towards the pictorial enterprise, allowing liberties. The marks can be *selective or tendentious, coherent or fantastic* in the visual behaviour they demand and the experience the behaviour brings.
Michael Baxandall, *Words for Pictures*, 158

Below, after a neat braiding of a contrastive pair of adjectives and a pair of nouns, the authors also take advantage of a pair of adjectives similar to each other in meaning:

Hot soup on a *cold day, cold soup* on a *hot day*, and the smell of soup simmering in the kitchen are *fundamental*, undoubtedly even *atavistic*, pleasures and solaces that give a special kind of satisfaction.
Julia Child and Simone Beck, *Mastering the Art of French Cooking*, volume 2, 3

The mobility of adverbs

Adverbs have a place, an optional niche, at the end of any kernel. But they become the most mobile of all speech parts and are able to work in positions almost anywhere in the sentence. Beginning with adverbial openers, here are examples of some of the many positions:

> *Gently* he stopped the machine.
> Romain Gary, *Nothing Important Ever Dies*, 108

> *Slowly* I tapped along the way. *Obediently*, I turned.
> John Wain, *Death of the Hind Legs*, 73

> *Slowly*, the sky blew up.
> Philip Wylie, *The Answer*, 15

> *Outside*, the darkness was total.
> Brian Moore, *The Emperor of Ice-Cream*, 102

> *Next* I moved the slate.
> Rose Tremain, *The Way I Found Her*, 276

> He was *always* two men.
> Alan Paton, *Too Late the Phalarope*, 3

> We come, *then*, to the question of art.
> Ralph Ellison, *Shadow and Act*, 82

> All that life *soon* faded.
> John Hersey, *Here to Stay*, 167

> The two *finally* went on their way.... He moved *slowly*.
> Rupa Bajwa, *The Sari Shop*, 3

Examples are everywhere. Also we often see adverbs as modifiers of adjectives, one of the adverb's most useful functions:

> The man's face grew *visibly* paler.
> Romain Gary, *Nothing Important Ever Dies*, 110

> It was *very* hot and bright and the houses looked *sharply* white.
> Ernest Hemingway, *The Sun Also Rises*, last page

The service was *fatiguingly* long.
John Updike, *Olinger Stories*, 160

Sometimes adverbs appear in pairs. Here each adverb is preceded by the intensifier "so," also an adverb:

She laughed so easily, so often.
Chimamanda Ngozi Adichie, *Purple Hibiscus*, 85

Given the high mobility and flexibility of the adverb, how does a writer decide exactly where in the sentence it works best? Consider the placement of the adverb *unfortunately* in the following descriptions of linguists' attention to children's language learning:

The acquisition of complex sentences *unfortunately* has not received nearly as much attention as the acquisition of syntactic phenomena in simple sentences.

The acquisition of complex sentences has *unfortunately* not received...

The acquisition of complex sentences has not received, *unfortunately*, nearly as much...

The acquisition of complex sentences has not received nearly as much attention, *unfortunately*, ...

Unfortunately the acquisition of complex sentences has not received...

One need not find fault with any of the choices above. The decision would probably depend on what *sounds* best and fits best in relation to the sentences that precede and follow. The writers actually chose none of the above but wrote:

The acquisition of complex sentences has not received nearly as much attention as the acquisition of syntactic phenomena in simple sentences, *unfortunately*.
Robert D. Van Valin, Jr., and Randy J. LaPolla, *Syntax*, 646

The writers may have wanted to emphasize the adverb, or to link the idea to the sentence that followed. Adverbs are among the most useful devices for establishing cohesion.

The adverb in longer patterns

Like the single adverb, longer adverbial patterns are often extremely mobile. Next, adverbial phrases and subordinate clauses occupy various positions:

> *On the edge of the silted and sanded up Old Harbor, right where the Hawley dock had been,* the stone foundation is *still there.*
> John Steinbeck, *The Winter of Our Discontent,* 50

Often single adverbs—or adverbial phrases or clauses—serve admirably as sentence openers. It may be that as many as one-fourth of the sentences in English and American fiction begin with adverbial modifiers. At times opening adverbials join with others to create effective links from one sentence to another and establish a thematic unity as in this fictional passage about the boredom of a news writer:

> *When he was thirteen and a baseball zealot,* his sister had ridiculed his interest in baseball games by saying, "They're all the same except for the score." *At the time,* the remark had seemed to him symbolic of her deep, feminine ignorance of what was truly important in life, but he *later* decided she had aptly described not only baseball games but also political campaigns. He found international affairs even more repetitious. *Whenever he floated into the Foreign Affairs section,* he *always* seemed to be writing a story he had written *two or three times before,* usually about Cyprus. *For a while,* he considered the possibility that the Greeks and Turks on Cyprus had some way of knowing *when* he was going to be assigned to Foreign Affairs. *All over the island* people would say, "He's there! He's there!" in Greek or Turkish, a signal for everyone to haul out the bombs and Bren guns for *yet* another chapter of the dreary conflict—absolutely indistinguishable from the chapter he had dealt with *a year before.*
> Calvin Trillin, *Floater,* 25

Adjectives and adverbs in isolated positions

As adjectives and adverbs take up their positions, as they are arranged, developed, or expanded, they answer such questions as "Which one?" "What kind?" "How?" "When?" "Where?" and many more. The information they bring, ready to arrive at almost any point in a sentence, often makes its appearance marked by commas. Both adjectives and adverbs may be isolated this way in free positions for particular emphasis, set off by punctuation. Adjectives thus deployed are often what are called appositional adjectives, discussed in chapter 10. However they are classified, their impact in a given sentence may be considerable. Here, for instance, what remains most forcibly with us is the highlighted adjective at the end:

> I care about that moment which was true and inspiring. I saw it only a few seconds, but it will remain with me, *imperishable.*
> Henry Miller, *Henry Miller on Writing*, 123

And the terse *dead* abruptly closes this sentence with appropriate finality:

> A few minutes later he slumped from his chair, *dead.*
> Jerry Allen, *The Thunder and the Sunshine*, 238

In this isolated use, as elsewhere, past and present participles are often found working as adjectives, and with adjectives. Below, the sentence itself appears fixed by the last past participle:

> Onlookers young and old line the curb, *transfixed.*
> Sidney Petrie, *What Modern Hypnotism Can Do for You*, 11

Here the present participial phrase interrupts the sentence just as the building it modifies interrupts the described view:

> Our living room looked out across a small back yard to a rough stone wall to an apartment building which, *towering above,* caught every passing thoroughfare sound and rifled it straight down to me.
> Ralph Ellison, *Shadow and Act*, 187

Participles and pure adjectives are used in similar ways:

> The lamp had been standing cobwebbed in a corner,
> *unplugged.*
> John Updike, *Of the Farm,* 27

> He thought of crawling under his bed and hanging onto
> one of the legs but the three boys only stood there, *speckled*
> *and silent, waiting,* and after a second he followed them
> a little distance out on the porch and around the corner
> of the house... He stopped a few feet from the pen and
> waited, *pale but dogged.*
> Flannery O'Connor, "The River," 35

> Early in the afternoon on Christmas, after a good meal
> with Paul Smith, pastor of St. Monica's, Great Plains,
> Father Urban got on the train for Duesterhaus, *tired.*
> J. F. Powers, *Morte d'Urban,* 90

> The moon had passed behind a cloud and the water looked
> dark and malevolent, *terribly deep.*
> Norman Mailer, *The Naked and the Dead,* 13

> Troops of grimed and burly laborers, a few women among
> them, ran hither and thither, *toiling, cursing.*
> John Barth, *Giles Goat-Boy,* 177

Here is a long participial sentence opener that might be labeled "dangling modifier" if it appeared in a student paper. In such a sentence the participial phrase needs to have handy the noun that it modifies, and that is not the case here:

> *Having rarely, so far as is known, given a penny to a cause for a*
> *charity, indifferent to the improvement of others while preoccupied*
> *with the improvement of himself,* it never came into Holmes's
> head to contribute to the usefulness of an institution.
> Edmund Wilson, *Patriotic Gore,* 796

To get rid of the dangler, the last part of the sentence, after *himself,* might be rewritten: *Holmes never thought about contributing to the usefulness of an institution.*

Now here are isolated adverb modifiers:

> From mind the impetus came and through mind my course
> was set, and therefore nothing on earth could really surprise
> me, *utterly*.
>   Saul Bellow, *Henderson the Rain King*, 156

> We have a variety of answers, most of them probably right
> for some god, *somewhere*.
>   Mary Barnard, *The Mythmakers*, 90

> Every once in a while, and *faintly*, the wind moves the
> airplane on its landing gear struts.
>   Richard Bach, *Stranger to the Ground*, 34

> She held the paper bag containing two bottles close to her
> side, *a little furtively*.
>   William Van O'Connor, *Campus on the River*, 54

> This is not how Dostoevsky meant, *intellectually*, for the
> history of Myshkin to come out, but it is how, *imaginatively*,
> it had to come out.
>   R. P. Blackmur, *"The Idiot:* A Rage of Goodness," 142

> Perhaps they reminded me, *distantly*, of myself, *long ago*.
> Perhaps they reminded me, *dimly*, of something we
> had lost.
>   James Baldwin, *Tell Me How Long the Train's Been Gone*, 480

Adjectives and adverbs in inverted position

The process of inversion can also bring about the front-shifted emphasis of isolated adjectival and adverbial phrases. Adjectival phrases open
the first two examples, below; an adverbial phrase opens the last one:

> *Profound* was Gary's relief the next morning as he bumped
> and glided, like a storm-battered yacht, into the safe harbor
> of his work week.
>   Jonathan Franzen, *The Corrections*, 201

Looming, ubiquitous are the dangers of prodigality,
of valuing change just for its own sake, of destroying
the basic elements that give significance to living.
　　Richard G. Lillard, *Eden in Jeopardy*, VI

Outside the lounge could now be heard the rhythmic crunch
of steel-tipped boots and the bellow of the commands.
　　David Walder, *The Gift Bearers*, 69

Catalogs of modifiers

A catalog of adjectives opens the next sentence:

Diligent, well-meaning, oppressed, loyal, affectionate, and
patriotic, this princess is not yet corrupted by her question-
able powers.
　　Michael Dobson and Nicola J. Watson, *England's
　　Elizabeth*, 172

Here is another list of adjectives—marked off by dashes—in the
middle of a sentence:

He was my sister Mimi's crazy husband, a mystical child of
darkness—*blatantly ambitious, lovable, impossible, charming,
obnoxious, tirelessly active*—a bright, talented, sheepish, tricky,
curly-haired man-child of darkness.
　　Joan Baez, "Foreword," VII

An opposite technique to the careful placement and demarcation
of isolated adjectives is the deliberate piling up of a number of modifiers immediately in front of a headword as in the first example or as
predicates after *he* in the second:

Whereas the truth was, as he alone knew, that the heavens
were a *glorious blazing golden limitless* cathedral of unending
and eternal light...
　　John Knowles, *Indian Summer*, 27

Everything he writes is written as an *angry, passionate, generous, fumbling, rebellious, bewildered and bewildering* man.
　　Sean O'Faolain, *The Vanishing Hero*, 108

In the following excerpt, the biographer uses a catalog of adjectives at the end of the sentence to contrast with adjectivals used earlier in the sentence:

> It is one of the peculiarities of her posthumous reputation that the full, immense extent of her life's work has only revealed itself gradually, changing the twentieth-century perception of her from the delicate lady authoress of a few experimental novels and sketches, some essays and a "writer's" diary, to one of the most *professional, perfectionist, energetic, courageous,* and *committed* writers in the language.
> Hermione Lee, *Virginia Woolf,* 4

In a short conversation, an author who consistently makes effective use of adjectives relies on fourteen adjectival and participial forms:

> "That Sengupta, I swear," Sorava went on. "What a *skinny, scrawny, sniveling, driveling, mingy, stingy, measly, weaselly* clerk! As far as I'm concerned he's *finished with, done for, gone for good."*
>
> *"Khattam-shud,"* Haroun said quietly.
>
> "That's *right,"* his mother answered. "I promise. Mr. Sengupta is *khattam-shud."*
> Salman Rushdie, *Haroun and the Sea of Stories,* 210

The result of such insistent modification, such an emphatic welter of description, is often highly charged and emotive. A similar result may come from groups of hyphenated modifiers mixing noun and adjective forms:

> Analyzing the comedian's problem in this new business, it seemed to me that the *bizarre-garbed, joke-telling* funster was ogling extinction.
> Fred Allen, *Treadmill to Oblivion,* 5

> He loved *hitherto-unthought-of, thereafter-unthinkable* combinations of instruments.
> Randall Jarrell, *Pictures from an Institution,* 136

In an unusual arrangement, a catalog of mostly adjective modifiers is punctuated as a sentence fragment and artfully inserted between two short sentences. Syntactically, it might be attached to the preceding sentence but, punctuated as it is, its meaning looks both backward and forward:

> My daughter arrived. *Smart, sensitive, cheerful, at school*
> *most of the day, but quick with tea and sympathy on her return.*
> My characters adored her.
> Alice Walker, *In Search of Our Mothers' Gardens*, 359

The importance of a discerning and versatile handling of adjectives and adverbs is apparent. When properly chosen and located, these parts of speech are able to clarify, qualify, or intensify an idea. But they cannot save a bad idea. Unnecessary modification can even disable some words that look vigorous standing on their own.

Adjectival color and clarity

The following sentences demonstrate successful paragraphs that are heavily adjectival, highly colored. They are attractive and colorful but selective, because their adjectives have all been chosen, assigned, and fastened together with attention to rhythm, clarity, impact, and focus.

> Father Urban, *fifty-four, tall and handsome but a trifle loose in*
> *the jowls and red of eye*, smiled and put out his hand.
> J. F. Powers, *Morte d'Urban*, 17

> In the *somber* background, a *single, stark, leafless* tree spreads
> *gnarled* branches atop a *dark, volcano-shaped* hill. The image
> is *emblematic* of Petrina's reading, her re-presentation, of
> Milton's epic. Of all Milton's *visual* interpreters, Petrina
> is the artist for whom Paradise is most decisively and
> tragically *lost*.
> Wendy Furman and Virginia Tufte, "Metaphysical Tears:
> Carlotta Petrina's Re-Presentation of Paradise Lost,
> Book IX," 86

They were standing in a *large, circular* room. Everything in here was *black* including the floor and ceiling—*identical, unmarked, handle-less black* doors were set at intervals all around the *black* walls, interspersed with branches of candles whose flames turned *blue*, their *cool shimmering* light reflected in the *shining* marble floor so that it looked as though there was *dark* water underfoot.

J. K. Rowling, *Harry Potter and the Order of the Phoenix*, 770

He lifted his *heavy* eyes and saw leaning over him a *huge* willow-tree, *old* and *hoary*. *Enormous* it looked, its *sprawling* branches going up like *reaching* arms with many *long-fingered* hands, its *knotted* and *twisted* trunk *gaping* in wide fissures that creaked faintly as the boughs moved.

J. R. R. Tolkien, *The Fellowship of the Ring*, 127

He had a *momentary, scared* glimpse of their faces, *thin and unnaturally long*, with *long, drooping* noses and *drooping* mouths of *half-spherical, half-idiotic* solemnity.

C. S. Lewis, *Out of the Silent Planet*, 44

Adjectives in the next example are perfectly selected to help give a human view of sensory perceptions attributed to Elizabeth Barrett Browning's cocker spaniel:

The *cool* globes of dew or rain broke in showers of *iridescent* spray about his nose; the earth, here *hard*, here *soft*, here *hot*, here *cold*, stung, traced, and tickled the *soft* pads of his feet.

Virginia Woolf, *Flush: A Biography*, 12

And here, an author brilliantly combines usual and unusual adjectives, precisely applicable, with past participles, nouns and metaphors:

Dr. Harvey greeted me at the door in a red-and-white plaid shirt and a thin, solid-blue Pendleton tie that still bore a mildewy $10 price tag from some earlier decade. His face was blowsy and peckled, runneled with lines, though he didn't quite seem his eighty-four years. He had an eagle nose, alert eyes, and stubbed yellow teeth. His white hair was as fine as corn silk and shifted with the November wind over the bald patches on his head.

Michael Paterniti, *Driving Mr. Albert*, x

Next a series of three forceful adjectives is emphatically deployed after a participial phrase; there follows a sequence of participial phrases that add detail to scene and characterization, helped by a pair of bound appositive adjectives:

> There she was, walking down the street along the win-
> dowsill, step by step, *stout, safe, confident,* buried in her
> errands, clutching her handbag, stepping aside from the
> common women *blind* and *heavy* under a week's provisions,
> prying into the looking-glasses at the doors of furniture
> shops.
> Dylan Thomas, *Adventures in the Skin Trade,* 5

In the sentences below, a well-chosen adjective in front of almost every noun helps to create the emphatic rhythms, vigor, and persuasiveness of the author's tribute to Martin Luther:

> Luther's *audacious* declaration initiated a *religious* movement
> and *intellectual* current of which we are a part 463 years later.
> His *penetrating theological* critique of the *existing* order and
> his *persistent* resistance against the *prevailing religious* hierar-
> chy exposed a *decadent* Christianity and *corrupt* church.
> Cornel West, *Prophetic Fragments,* 258

From the same paragraph, another sentence further demonstrates this insistent adjectival style:

> Never before or after has a *biblical* professor in a university
> performed such *prophetic* gestures of *gargantuan* propor-
> tions, nor has a *traditional* intellectual engaged in *organic*
> activity with such *astounding* results.
> West, 258

Below, adjectives combine with adjectivals including present and past participles and nouns. Adverbial intensifiers— *less, downright, won-derfully*—add to the lively assortment:

> The *first hundred* pages of the book constitute a *dense* but
> *sparkling* digest of *key* ideas on soul, flesh, mind, death and
> the afterlife—a *jet* flight through *Western* philosophy from
> Plato to Locke that takes in the *familiar* (*Platonic* forms), the

less *familiar* (the *Hippocratic* theory of humors) and the downright *esoteric* (the iatrochemistry of Joannes Baptista van Helmont). Happily, Porter was a wonderfully *gifted* explicator of all that is *abstruse* and *difficult*. Even so, this is not a section to read while *sleep-deprived* or *suffering* from a *crashing* hangover.
    Andrew Miller, "Losing Their Religion," 11

On the same page, Miller makes apt choices of adjectives in the objective complement *thinkable* and the modifier *robust*:

Sapere aude ("Dare to be wise"), the Enlightenment battle cry, made, little by little, everything thinkable. "Should free inquiry lead to the destruction of Christianity itself," the dissenting minister Joseph Priestley declared in the robust style of the times, "it ought not, on that account, to be discontinued."
    Miller, 11

Here is a rather elevated though frequent adjectival formation, the adjective plus dependent prepositional phrase:

They come to him *murmurous with imaginative overtones, heavy with evocative memories* ...
    Lord David Cecil, *The Fine Art of Reading*, 282

It can be used less formally:

Sometimes his face swelled *purple with anger*, and he pounded on the door till he was sobbing with exertion.
    Doris Lessing, *In Pursuit of the English*, 173

Dan was *restless with suppressed belligerence*.
    Lessing, 184

A mood is articulated in a pattern that uses the same adjective five times:

It was a *good* peace, that spread. Those were *good* leaves up there, with a *good*, bright sky beyond them. This was a *good* earth beneath my back, soft as a bed, and in all its unexamined depths was a *good* darkness.
    William Golding, *The Pyramid*, 56

Adjectival styles often succeed in nonfiction descriptions of first-hand experience. A cellist calls on adjectives (and adverbs as well) to answer the question, "How do the members of a string quartet play together and tour together year in and year out, without killing each other?" Below, the adjectives are italicized, but it is worth noting also the acuteness of the adverbs, among them *destructively, harshly, personally, ferociously*:

> Conversely, there is a danger that *individual* criticisms can become destructively *hurtful* and *bitter*. If they are voiced too harshly and personally, no one ends up in a *fit* state to play. After all, the *deep* feelings conjured up when we play *great* music already make us feel *vulnerable*. In addition, nearly all playing requires *maximum* self-confidence and *complete physical* ease and relaxation, even (or especially) in music of *great* intensity and ardour, or that is *rapturous* or *celebratory*. So suggestions or criticisms ferociously barked at a colleague with an anger bordering on hatred, or with *withering* contempt, are likely to be *counterproductive*, and are bound to be avoided—something that is not always easy.
> David Waterman, "Four's a Crowd," cı

Adverbial energy and rhythm

Adverbs are often used to modify the adjectives, and they become an important part of the rhythm of adjectival styles. There are also what might be called adverbial styles, sentences in which much of the content, much of the interest, or perhaps the real punch, ends up with the adverbs:

> It was *lightly*, yes. But it was *not briskly*, it was *not very fast*.
> Mark Van Doren, "The Watchman," 75

> If he said he had written a fairy-story with a political purpose, we cannot *lightly* suppose he spoke *lightly*.
> C. M. Woodhouse, "Introduction," ıx

> He drank *eagerly, copiously*... The limping earnestness of his speech disappeared; he talked as he drank, *abundantly*.
> Desmond Hall, *I Give You Oscar Wilde*, 139

So one day he *silently* and *suddenly* killed her.
D. H. Lawrence, *Etruscan Places*, 198

Lightning spit *all around him*; rain cut *in at his face*; thunder crashed *against his eardrums*. Another bolt of lightning, *closer*. Then another, *closer still*.

Clay looked *up, straight, right up into the sky.*
William Goldman, *Soldier in the Rain*, 308

It was *always* going to be like this, *always, always.*
John Wain, *A Travelling Woman*, 47

Here, from the same book, a paragraph moves into adverbial fragments:

He stopped *in amazement*. She was laughing. *Not mockingly, or with the effect of covering up other emotions she might otherwise betray. Simply laughing, unaffectedly, from sheer amusement.*
Wain, 47

Intensifiers and qualifiers

All the adverbs just gathered live up to the nickname they share with adjectives as "coloring words." But there is a particular case against a particular kind of adverb. Listen to the objections expressed by a poet and essayist. She names some of the worst offenders:

With regard to unwarinesses that defeat precision, excess is the common substitute for energy. We have it in our semi-academic, too conscious adverbs—awfully, terribly, frightfully, infinitely, tremendously...
Marianne Moore, *Predilections*, 9

Below energy has succumbed to excess:

It is obvious that people dwelling upon a treeless and *often absolutely* vegetationless coast would turn to the sea for their food and for other necessities.
Ivan T. Sanderson, *Follow the Whale*, 33

An excess of adverbs, especially if they end in *–ly*, can at times set up an unintended rhythm, as in the following sentence. One can easily remove them:

> The essays pioneered an *entirely* new model of communication (one that *apparently* defies traditional rhetoric) that we have not *culturally* assimilated and that makes Emerson so *intellectually* refreshing and so worth reading still.
> Robert Atwan, *The Best American Essays*, XI

In this classic scene from *Lucky Jim*, shifts in modifiers parody the style and indicate the futility of a student paper:

> It was a perfect title, in that it crystallized the article's niggling mindlessness, its funereal parade of yawn-enforcing facts, the pseudo-light it threw upon non-problems. Dixon had read, or begun to read, dozens like it, but his own seemed worse than most in its air of being convinced of its own usefulness and significance. "In considering this strangely neglected topic," it began. This what neglected topic? This strangely what topic? This strangely neglected what? His thinking all this without having defiled and set fire to the typescript only made him appear to himself as more of a hypocrite and fool. "Let's see," he echoed Welch in a pretended effort of memory: "Oh, yes; *The economic influence of the developments in shipbuilding techniques, 1450 to 1485.*"
> Kingsley Amis, *Lucky Jim*, 16

Adverbs as cohesive devices

The mobility of the adverb can help hold sentences together. An adverb at the beginning of a sentence can tie it to the preceeding sentence:

> He recognized the feeling. *After that*, he recognized the man.
> Wright Morris, *The Field of Vision*, 16

> There! Out it boomed. *First* a warning, musical; *then* the hour, irrevocable.
> Virginia Woolf, *Mrs. Dalloway*, 5

> *There* fear stiffened into hatred. *Here* hatred curdled from despair.
> Phillip Toynbee, *Prothalamium*, 67

Adjectives in adverb roles

Adjectives sometimes encroach on adverb territory for particular effect. A brief selection will show the informal, sometimes colloquial, sometimes intensified, results of a functional shift that puts adjectives where adverbs would be expected:

> The trunk and the branches and the twigs were *terrible* black.
> William Golding, *Pincher Martin*, 177

> They stayed indoors till the colliers were all gone home, till it was *thick* dark, and the street would be deserted.
> D. H. Lawrence, *Sons and Lovers*, 76

> It was *full* dark now, but still early...
> James Agee, *A Death in the Family*, 19

These last examples remind writers that our language is richly flexible, responsive to innovative molding by skilled hands. Adjectives and adverbs are prime materials for experimenting.

*Austen does more without words than most writers do
with them.*
                    Patricia T. O'Conner

*Immense piles of gold flared out in the southeast, heaped in
soft, glowing yellow right up the sky.*
                    D. H. Lawrence

The door swung open on darkness.
                    Penelope Mortimer

*All the way home in the taxi and in the lift up to her flat on
the seventh floor Mrs. Liebig kept on talking.*
                    Angus Wilson

CHAPTER FIVE

Prepositions

> It must here be observed that most, if not all,
> prepositions seem Originally formed to denote the
> *Relations of Place*. The reason is, this is that grand
> *Relation*, which *Bodies or Natural Substances* maintain
> at all times one to another, whether they are con-
> tiguous or remote, whether in motion, or at rest...

> But though the original use of Prepositions was to
> denote the Relations of Place, they could not be
> confined to this Office only. They by degrees
> extended themselves to Subjects *incorporeal*, and
> came to denote Relations, as well *intellectual* as *local*.
>
> James Harris, *Hermes or A Philosophical Inquiry*
> *Concerning Universal Grammar*, (1751), 266-9

ALTHOUGH most prepositions are small words, often thought of
as relatively empty of meaning, they are vital to all kinds of prose,
partly because many of them do indeed "denote the relations of place"
to people. Ten prepositional phrases express this reciprocity in the sentence below from a novel. A character speaks about her grandfather:

> He had grown up in the Middle West, in a house dug out
> of the ground, with windows just at earth level and just at
> eye level, so that from without, the house was a mere
> mound, no more a human stronghold than a grave, and
> from within, the perfect horizontality of the world in that
> place foreshortened the view so severely that the horizon
> seemed to circumscribe the sod house and nothing more.
>
> Marilynne Robinson, *Housekeeping*, 3

The paired phrases *from without* and *from within* organize the reader's perceptions, and astute choices of the phrases and several multi-sylla-ble words, along with thoughtful positioning, help this phrase-laden sentence to flow rather well.

From a short story, fourteen prepositional phrases make up all except eight words of the 53-word sentence below, among them a series of locational phrases beginning with *in*, setting the scenes as in a play. The repetition and the careful positioning help to avoid the lumpiness that sometimes comes with heavy use of such phrases:

> Naturally for the rest of my life I longed to see her, not only in doorways, in a great number of places – in the dining room with my aunts, at the window looking up and down the block, in the country garden among zinnias and marigolds, in the living room with my father.
> Grace Paley, *The Collected Stories*, 326

Twelve prepositional phrases make up the bulk of the two sen-tences in the opening of a book review, below. In the first sentence, after the words *is set*, six locational phrases are patterned, lined up in a row – *in, at, of* and then *in, at, of* – forming two parallel sequences that succeed well in descriptive content and moderately well in rhythm. The second sentence is helped by parallelism of two phrases begin-ning with *for*:

> *Don't Look Back*, the first of Karin Fossum's police procedurals to be published in the United States, is set *in* a picturesque Norwegian village *at* the foot *of* a mountain, *in* a valley *at* the edge *of* the sea. But there's no mistaking this psychologi-cally astute, subtly horrifying crime study *for* a cozy village mystery, or its soulful detective *for* one of those brainy European sleuths who make a parlor game of homicide.
> Marilyn Stasio, "Crime," 14

The versatility of prepositions, the variety of relationships they can show, and their relevance to place, quiescence, motion, and metaphor have received little attention by writers on style, whose main concern has been to quote John Dryden's rule to avoid ending a sen-tence with one. There is a story that when an editor revised one of Winston Churchill's sentences because it ended with a preposition, the author wrote in the margin: "This is the sort of nonsense up with which I will not put." Professional writers can and do end good sentences with prepositions, or with words that function as either prepositions or adverbs. Some examples:

> Down below, our carpenters worked at the new leak,
> and presently called to Tulp to rig the pumps and free her,
> so that they might know what the new leak amounted *to*.
>   John Masefield, *Live and Kicking Ned*, 113

> "English," we think today, is something more than the
> teaching or the reading of words as words but something
> less also, less surely, than the teaching of the private life
> the words came *out of*.
>   Archibald MacLeish, "What Is English?," *A Continuing
>   Journey*, 257

Like adverbs and adjectives, the prepositional phrase can occupy various positions in a sentence, although one must take care that the phrase is tied to the intended word and not to an unintended one. The *Los Angeles Times* columnist who wrote the sentence below took delight in exploring possible locations of the first two prepositional phrases:

> A man chasing a cat with a broom in his underwear is
> ambience by any definition.
>   Jack Smith, *How to Win a Pullet Surprise*, 1

There are times when a prepositional phrase may fit at several points. In the sentence that follows, the phrase can be attached at the beginning as it is here, or at the end, or at three other places: *At a steady pace, the barefoot competitor gradually passed all the other runners.*

A preposition can itself have different kinds of objects. A noun or pronoun generally stands as the object of a preposition, as in *at the store, with him*; or a possessive noun or pronoun, *at Tiffany's, of his*. A preposition may take as its object a gerund, *by looking*, or an adverb, *until now*, or a clause, *under whatever it was*.

But the object of the preposition is not the only facet of the basic definition open to great variety. Harold Whitehall's division of prepositions into five groups distinguishes several possible relations: location, direction, association, agency, and time.[1]

---

[1] *Structural Essentials of English* (New York: Harcourt Brace, 1951).

Location

Examples of the emphasis prepositions can give to "place" have been seen at the opening of this chapter. Location can be more than just place; it can provide atmosphere:

> Two wooden beds stood *in the midst of* a clutter of squarish wooden chairs, their upholstery worn.
> John Espey, *The Anniversaries*, 207

> Rats stir *in* the weeds, *among* the graves.
> William Styron, *Lie Down in Darkness*, 327-328

> Lifetimes ago, *under* a banyan tree *in* the village of Hasnapur, an astrologer cupped his ears—his satellite dish *to* the stars—and foretold my widowhood and exile. I was only seven then, scabrous-armed from leaves and thorns.
> Bharati Mukherjee, *Jasmine*, 3

Direction

Prepositions indicating direction may be literal, as in the first example, or metaphorical as in the two phrases that end the second example:

> We continued *across* the foyer *to* a dreamlike bank of windows, turned left *up* a pale flight of marble steps, left again, *through* two doorways, and *into* the Assembly Room.
> John Knowles, *A Separate Peace*, 157

> Beauvoir revisits the house of childhood in her *Memoirs of a Dutiful Daughter*, in order to unmask and analyze its illusions, and to recount the long journey *out of* it, *away from* it.
> Emily R. Grosholz, *The Legacy of Simone de Beauvoir*, 188

Association

Prepositions may also perform the general function of "association," generally meaning "associated with," or "in relation to":

> They are rich, of course, obscenely rich *by the world's standards*; but not *rich rich*, not New York City rich.
> Michael Cunningham, *The Hours*, 91

Brandy and port make a wonderful difference *to* meat and game soups, just as a little dry white wine makes all the difference *to* several of the fish soups.
Jane Gregson, "Soup," 341

Agency

Prepositions of "agency" mean something like "done by" or "for the purpose of":

Perhaps it is natural for a man who has destroyed something to try to restore a balance *by* creating something.
John Steinbeck, *The Winter of Our Discontent*, 131

Maybe it zooms in *for* a closeup, or maybe it zooms out *for* the big picture. Maybe a sentence tells us the result of something that happened in another.
Patricia T. O'Conner, *Words Fail Me*, 98

Austen does more *without* words than most writers do *with* them.
O'Conner, 196

Time

Almost any preposition can introduce a reference to time:

It was a good sign if they wanted to see a house again *in* what you might call the middle *of* the night.
Jane Smiley, *Good Faith*, 3

Word had gone round *during* the day that old Major, the prize Widdle White boar, had had a strange dream *on* the previous night and wished to communicate it to the other animals.
George Orwell, *Animal Farm*, 15

Prepositions with multiple objects

One small word of only two to five letters—*at, to, in, by, on, of, with, over, above*, and others—can bring into play not just one object but a sequence of nouns, or words that stand in for nouns, and can position them to become the very heart of the sentence. Various configurations help toward different effects and open up the objects, especially the final one, for extensive elaboration. In this example, the preposition *about* has four objects, the last one enlarged into a detailed description, itself using four additional prepositional phrases:

> A relentless work, with decadence in every detail, it is a novel *about decay, the death of morality, the corruption of the spirit, the transformation of Paris into a city of greed and heartless development driven by a few desperate men whose only goal is profit.*
> Susan Salter Reynolds, "Discoveries," RII

In the same review, the final item in a series of five objects of the preposition *with* consists of a quotation from the book being discussed. The variety of the materials that can be included and the ease of creating a construction of this kind make such a phrase a versatile, useful item in a writer's repertoire:

> The novel is crammed *with exotic, expensive things—clothing, furniture, jewelry, even "strange plants whose foliage derived an odd vitality from the splendor of poisonous blossoms both light and dark."*
> Reynolds, RII

In the next example, from a memoir, the mode of connecting multiple objects of a preposition exhibits them individually and together:

> I love being in Germany among my friends; it is a return *to a place and a language and a cultural tradition* that my parents never ceased to mourn.
> Thomas Laquer, "Prelude," 100

Intellectual and poetic relationships

Skilled hands on occasion enlist prepositions to help establish relationships that are "incorporeal" or "intellectual," to repeat the words of James Harris quoted at the beginning of the chapter, and such uses at times become eloquent, even poetic. The brilliant syntax of Abraham Lincoln's sentences of 1863, memorable both for what they say and the way they say it, includes a path of 26 prepositions moving from the locational to the intellectual, from the field at Gettysburg to the "unfinished work" needed in a democracy so that

> government of the people, by the people, for the people,
> shall not perish from the earth.

The parallelism in Lincoln's conclusion adds to its eloquence as is often the case in public speeches. In our own time as well, writers continue to find ways, often quite simple, to make prepositions function with remarkable expressiveness. The ones that follow are from fiction:

I lived *to* sounds...
John Hersey, *A Single Pebble*, 18

Immense piles of gold flared out in the southeast, heaped in soft, glowing yellow right *up* the sky.
D. H. Lawrence, *Sons and Lovers*, 285

The winter wore away, and in the parks the trees burst *into* bud and *into* leaf.
W. Somerset Maugham, *Of Human Bondage*, 685

And laughing again for joy, he went out of the chapter houses to where the sun piled *into* the open square of the cloister.
William Golding, *The Spire*, 3

The door swung open *on* darkness.
Penelope Mortimer, *The Bright Prison*, 125

The houses were dark *against* the night, and a little lingering warmth remained in the houses *against* the morning.
John Steinbeck, *The Moon Is Down*, 147

Prepositions as verbs or adverbs

Still another transference results in some of the most striking of the preposition's stylistic effects. The English preposition has long carried a latent verbal force, as in William Shakespeare's *The Tempest*, "I shall no more *to* sea!" In many of the preposition's modern appearances in otherwise verbless clauses, it seems to have been simply left behind after the omission of *be* or some other verb of being. Used repeatedly in questions, as in the first example, the construction can carry a heightened emotional force that might feel overdrawn and old-fashioned in some contexts:

> And *for* what? *For* what this agony of concentration? *For*
> what this hell of effort? *For* what this intense withdrawal
> from the poverty and squalor of dirty brick and rusty
> fire escapes, from the raucous cries and violence and
> never-changing noise? *For* what?
> Thomas Wolfe, *You Can't Go Home Again*, 508

> Tie-dye scarves *for* the ladies, *for* the men a home-brewed
> lemon and licorice and aspirin syrup…
> Truman Capote, *Breakfast at Tiffany's*, 173

Some prepositional fragments only locate, without implied movement:

> Again shelves *to* the ceiling, filled neatly with gleaming
> canned and glassed foods, a library for the stomach.
> *On one side*–counter, cash register, bags, string, and that
> glory in stainless steel and white enamel, the cold cabinet,
> in which the compressor whispered to itself.
> John Steinbeck, *The Winter of Our Discontent*, 14

In other cases, the preposition clearly imparts a verbal force, a *motion*:

> Right *down* the road *to* their own station wagon, where the
> lights were on.
> Wright Morris, *The Field of Vision*, 250

> Back *to* his plan.
> Garson Kanin, *Remembering Mr. Maugham*, 47

A great train, bound for Manchester, drew up. Two doors opened, and *from* one of them, William.
D. H. Lawrence, *Sons and Lovers*, 81

Out of bed on the carpet with no shoes.
William Golding, *Pincher Martin*, 178

Past a block of big homes, fortresses of cement and brick inset with doorways of stained and beveled glass and windows of potted plants, and then halfway *up* another block, which holds a development built all at once in the Thirties.
John Updike, *Rabbit, Run*, 10

On with the story. *On with* the story.
John Barth, *Lost in the Funhouse*, x

Multiple prepositions: virtuosity and excess

Many sentences, if the rhythm suits what is being said, can be successful, although preposition-heavy. Here is a calculated excess, a deliberate pileup of prepositional phrases:

> While Mrs. Kelley slept, hundreds *of* millions *of* gallons *of* rain, part *of* the fantastic load *of* water that had been shipped by the hurricane designated as Diane during its voyage up the Atlantic Ocean, were being bailed out on certain hills *of* northern Connecticut and were washing down them toward Winsted.
> John Hersey, *Here to Stay*, 7

In the next example, with directional prepositions rather than *of*, the sheer number of prepositional phrases again appears for a special purpose; movement, progression are unmistakable:

> The procession of men and women *from* the street *into* the station and *down* the escalators *towards* the trains becomes a movement *from* a world above *to* an underworld of death.
> Ralph Freedman, *The Lyrical Novel*, 258

All the way home *in* the taxi and *in* the lift *up to* her flat *on* the seventh floor Mrs. Liebig kept on talking.
Angus Wilson, *A Bit off the Map and Other Stories*, 107

Heavy concentrations of prepositional phrases below are controlled to suggest an almost biblical tone:

> …this was the miracle *of* the age, and *of* the succeeding age, and *of* all ages to come… But there were giants *in* the earth *in* those days, and they spoke *in* the name *of* the nation, and people followed them.
>> Forrest McDonald, *E Pluribus Unum*, last paragraph

Below, these extreme examples of embedded prepositional phrases create awkward unintended rhythms:

> There remain cases *in* which the inadequacies *of*
> a conventional orthographic record cannot be put
> *to* rights *by* assumptions drawn *from* generalizations
> *about* the language and dialect *in* which the poem
> is composed or *from* hypotheses *about* the meaning
> or the meter *of* the poem.
>> Rulon Wells, *Essays on the Language of Literature*, 129

> My purpose in presenting this paper is twofold: First, I want
> to unburden myself *of* something *of* a crisis *in* my thinking
> *about* the uses *of* experimental psychology *in* the study *of*
> cognition, and second, I want to talk *about* my current interests *in* research.
>> James Deese, "Behavior and Fact," 515

It is easy to identify the problem but hard to solve it. One could try using verbs where possible, instead of nouns and prepositions, and also one could reduce the frequency of the word *of*. The preposition *of* contributes to the unevenness of many forewords and prefaces, including this two-paragraph example, its flow impaired by 26 *of*'s.

> The plan *of* this anthology has emerged from two decades *of*
> experimentation with that indispensable course which is
> designed to introduce students to the greatness and variety
> *of* English literature. A number *of* the editors began with the
> scattergum survey, which represented almost every notable
> writer in relatively brief selections; later, like so many *of* our
> contemporaries, we turned to the intensive teaching *of*
> selected major writers, considered outside *of* their historical
> and literary contexts. The broad survey achieved inclusiveness by dispersion, at the expense *of* proper emphases and *of*

study in depth. The close study *of* relatively few writers, on the other hand, was arbitrarily selective, and gave the student few points *of* historical and literary reference; it left him with embarrassing gaps in literary knowledge, very little sense *of* chronology, and almost no experience *of* the way that the works *of* even the most original writers are rooted in tradition and share the characteristic qualities and preoccupations *of* their age.

The [book] is designed to provide the texts and materials for a course which will combine the values *of* emphasis and range by presenting major authors in the context *of* the major literary traditions *of* their times. It includes the best and most characteristic writings *of* the great writers–not *of* some, but *of* all great writers (other than novelists), and in sufficient quantity to allow the instructor considerable latitude *of* choice while still achieving a study in depth. It also supplies the literary settings *of* the major authors by including copious examples *of* other writers and writing, excellent in themselves and also representative, in each age, *of* the reigning literary forms and the chief movements *of* convention and revolt, tradition and innovation.

Preface to a literary anthology

Because of its many possible uses–in such diverse phrases as in spite *of*, a kind *of*, at the expense *of*, the necessity *of*, the idiomatic *of* course, and the indispensable genitive, *of* plus an object to show possession–the preposition *of* is difficult to avoid even when it makes the text lead-footed. On the other hand, at the end of the following example, *of the wrath of God* could easily have been edited to *of God's wrath*:

Gin alone, however, she has just pointed out, is often enough quieting in the fullest sense, and the poetic connection between death and intoxication gives a vague rich memory of the blood of the sacrament and the apocalyptic wine of the wrath of God.

William Empson, *Some Versions of Pastoral*, 237

The change would have altered the intended emphasis and actually rendered the sentence less balanced, less poetic. This example only points to the advisability of paying close attention to the preposition *of* in the editing process, even if it may finally be allowed to remain.

Careless use can bring problems, but prepositional phrases are indispensable for all kinds of prose and are available for striking metaphorical and poetic effect. Here, achieving a pleasant rhythm, are seven ordinary prepositional phrases – time, direction, location, association – concluding with a metaphor:

> We talked. He agreed to meet. *On a weekday just after
> Thanksgiving*, I drove south *from Maine through dead leaves
> and chimney smoke, past trees* that appeared *in a chill
> autumn mist like candelabra.*
> Michael Paterniti, *Driving Mr. Albert*, 237

The variety of descriptive effects that prepositional phrases can bring is well displayed in the illustrations that follow:

> The brown-domed gentleman took off his glasses and,
> unbending himself, looked *up, up, up at tall, tall, tall Victor,
> at his blue eyes and reddish-brown hair.*
> Vladimir Nabokov, *Pnin*, 103-104

> Garden delights aren't limited *to the sense of sight.* Fragrances
> mingle *with the splash of a fountain, the buzz of a bee*, the
> warmth *of the sun, the cooling touch of a breeze.* Finally, gar-
> dens provide the general kinesthetic pleasures *of moving in
> and through a space.*
> Stephanie Ross, *What Gardens Mean*, 3

Words that alternate as adverbs or prepositions join vividly with other action structures to enliven a short story written during his college years by a future president:

> Up again, up-up – the wind catches the high curved prow
> and swings it over, the low stern slides into a trough. Over
> you heal – over until you must hang far out over the upper
> gun'nle, all your weight on the paddle. Slowly at first then
> with a swift pivot the canoe heads into the wind again.
> Desperately you paddle now, dip-pull, dip-pull – your
> shoulders ache   your throat swells   it seems as though
> your very heart must be torn out.
> Ronald Reagan, Pre-Presidential Papers

He made the Emperor laugh and the horse couldn't better him,
so he stayed. And I stayed. And we became friends.
Jeanette Winterson

They snipped the ribbon in 1915, they popped the cork,
Miami Beach was born.
Norman Mailer

The raisins and almonds and figs and apples and oranges and
chocolates and sweets were now passed about the table and
Aunt Julia invited all the guests to have either port or sherry.
James Joyce

The room was very full and who were they all?
Gertrude Stein

CHAPTER SIX

Conjunctions and Coordination

> Beside that there are conjunctions, and a conjunction
> is not varied but it has a force that need not make
> any one feel that they are dull. Conjunctions have made
> themselves live by their work.
> Gertrude Stein, *Lectures in America*, 213

T HE COMMON CONJUNCTIONS – *and, but, for, or, nor, yet,* and *so* – are structural words that *conjoin* the elements of a coordinate structure. Their work is to connect similar units – words, phrases, clauses, or even sentences. Professional writers often use a conjunction as a sentence opener, a position where it helps with cohesion, just as it does when it links two main or base clauses into a compound sentence.

Conjunctions also make helpful contributions to style, especially to set or simulate a rhythm or pace suited to the content:

> When we choose to be the gardener, we make a deal with
> nature: we will abide by certain rules in growing plants, *and
> the plants will accede to our shaping them somewhat to our needs
> and pleasures.* We will supply water, loamy soil, a modicum
> of nutrients, and moderate temperature, *and the impatiens
> will bloom brightly from May to October.*
> Jerry Minich, *A Small Garden*, 14

For a contrasting rhythm, the next example displays *and* repeatedly in a compound sentence connecting one clause after another. This sort of movement is best suited to a free-flowing narrative style and usually inappropriate to suggest the precise logical relationships and qualifications required in formal writing:

> There was a crowd of kids watching the car, *and* the square was hot, *and* the trees were green, *and* the flags hung on their staffs, *and* it was good to get out of the sun *and* under the shade of the arcade that runs all the way around the square.
> Ernest Hemingway, *The Sun Also Rises*, 94

A combined use of *and* and *so* in the first sentence below is followed by two short sentences that begin with *And*. Conjunctions help drive the swift narrative that enlivens the opening pages of the novel:

> He made the Emperor laugh *and* the horse couldn't better him, *so* he stayed. *And* I stayed. *And* we became friends.
> Jeanette Winterson, *The Passion*, 4

Conjunctions play a role in the traditional labeling of sentence types. Conjunctions joining independent clauses characterize what have been called *compound sentences. Subordinators* and *relatives,* bringing a dependent clause to join an independent clause, characterize what have been called *complex sentences.* The label *simple sentence* refers to a sentence with one independent clause and no dependent ones. The joining of ideas in compound structures–placing them side by side, especially without connectors–is sometimes called *parataxis.* This term contrasts with *hypotaxis,* which involves arrangement of ideas in *main* and *subordinate* structures, or *independent* structures and *dependent* ones.

Omission of conjunctions

One name for refraining from conjunctions is *asyndeton.* Often whole clauses are juxtaposed in this somewhat noncommittal way. Fully independent, they are not attached to one another, they touch but are not connected. Below we see their judicious use by professional writers:

> The streets were empty, the slates shone purple.
> Sean O'Faolain, *I Remember! I Remember!*, 18

> The fog had all gone, the wind had risen.
> C. S. Lewis, *That Hideous Strength,* 175

The sun was up, the farm was alive.
   Evelyn Waugh, *The End of the Battle*, 258

We need the weather and the wind, we must wait upon
these things, we are dependent on them.
   Harry Berger, Jr., *The Allegorical Temper*, 240

Households aren't just training grounds for citizenship and
allegiance to contracts, they're small governments in themselves, and like the democratic nation, they must be founded
on the illusion of loving partnership.
   Laura Kipnis, *Against Love*, 168

She is thirteen, she will be fourteen, fifteen, sixteen.
It takes time.
   Penelope Fitzgerald, *The Blue Flower*, 136

Quite often, as is true of these, whether in groups of two or three
or more, such clauses are kernel clauses. Minimal utterance invites
minimal connection. Here three abutting clauses appear alongside separate kernels and near-kernels:

We beguile. We make apologies and protestations.
We wonder, we surmise, we conjecture. We weave a
daisy chain.
   Huntington Brown, *Prose Styles*, 81

Longer clauses may not work as well:

He is given to anger and to vengefulness, he has scorned
women only to be enthralled to Britomart, he has won the
armor of Achilles.
   Kathleen Williams, *Spenser's World of Glass*, 157

Where the paratactic clauses are appropriate, they can seem particularly so. Their connection often feels rapid, abrupt, thus imparting
a sense of urgency or speed:

She must rush, she must hurry, before it was too late.
   John Steinbeck, *The Winter of Our Discontent*, 198

Ibrahim had abandoned this place again, his eyes were on
the road, the arrival at the same airport…
   Nadine Gordimer, *The Pickup*, 267

> Then he was up again, running faster than ever, then the
> dogs were gaining on him again.
>> George Orwell, *Animal Farm*, 58

The feeling of rapidity becomes that of a quick sequence triggered almost automatically:

> They snipped the ribbon in 1915, they popped the cork,
> Miami Beach was born.
>> Norman Mailer, *Miami and the Siege of Chicago*, 11

> Then one day she went back to Australia. They exchanged
> three letters. Six months later Danby had taken up with
> Adelaide. *She was sweet, she was there.*
>> Iris Murdoch, *Bruno's Dream*, 18

> His father died, his mother died, there was no money left.
>> *Murdoch*, 19

Here syntax slides forward as easily, as automatically, as the described mechanism:

> The last screw came out, the whole lock case slid down,
> freeing the bolt.
>> David Wagoner, *The Escape Artist*, 244

Below we see the leveling effort of parataxis to convey the uneventful:

> ...but nothing ever happened. The waiters had been polite,
> the drinkers had been polite, the streets were quiet.
>> Normal Mailer, *An American Dream*, 190

A traffic light's abrupt succession of red and green is caught by the paratactic phrases of the next offering:

> It is a myth, the city, the rooms and windows, the steam-
> spitting streets; for anyone, everyone a different myth, an
> idol-head with traffic-light eyes winking *a tender green, a
> cynical red.*
>> Truman Capote, *Local Color*, 13

The parataxis that follows, both clauses and phrases, does not seem at all fast or abrupt, however. Neither is it uneventful. It is relaxed, the easy rendering of the rhythms of an easy time:

> *Everyone was beautiful, and gentle, everyone was poor, no one was*
> *smart.* One summer evening they danced in the half-light,
> and when they were tired of dancing they lay down *in the*
> *forest, on the beach, on mattresses, on the bare floor.*
> Stephen Spender, "September Journal," 397

Below, after a conventional series of noun phrases with the last connected by *and*, additional noun phrases in the series are set off by periods in one long fragment and a shorter one:

> Technically, the Badlands is chaparral. The hills are filled
> with *sage, wild mustard, fiddleheads and live oaks. Bobcats,*
> *meadowlarks, geckos, horned lizards, red tailed hawks, kestrels,*
> *coach whip snakes, king snakes, gopher snakes. Rattlesnakes*
> *and coyotes.*
> Percival Everett, "909," 122

Semicolons, dashes, and colons as connectors

Instead of using commas to separate (or connect) paratactic constructions as in some of the preceding examples, it is more conventional, especially in nonfiction, to use semicolons or dashes.

> No author can be fully trusted when describing the quality
> of his own work; I verge on dangerous ground when writing
> about this piece.
> John Kenneth Galbraith, *The Great Crash 1929*, Preface

> The last hour was quite phenomenal–2,600,000 shares
> changed hands at rapidly declining prices.
> Galbraith, 103

> By then, 16,410,030 sales had been recorded on the New York
> Stock Exchange–some certainly went unrecorded–or more
> than three times the number that was once considered a fab-
> ulously big day.
> Galbraith, 117

In both nonfiction and fiction, colons sometimes punctuate paratactic constructions, especially if the second item results from or explains what precedes:

> That's what predators do: they kill prey.
> Yann Martel, *Life of Pi*, 109

Items in series

Besides its function in the additive, compound type of sentence and its omission in certain paratactic constructions, the conjunction also operates in a more particular type of structural connection, the *series*. The common series, the juxtaposition of three or more like elements, is deceptively straightforward and is capable of a great many syntactic variations, the most frequent of which either repeat a conjunction between each pair of elements, or omit even the final written conjunction between the last two elements.

> And almost every tale she had told him was a chronicle
> of *sickness, death, and sorrow.*
> Thomas Wolfe, *You Can't Go Home Again,* 46

> *Suffering, weakness, death* are not, in themselves, tragic;
> this is common knowledge.
> Elizabeth Sewell, *The Human Metaphor,* 138

An even more common variation, in which the conjunction is repeated, results in a smoother construction, less abrupt and clipped. The elements still receive more clear-cut distinction and strong individual emphasis than in the basic single-conjunction series:

> In the kitchen they had *grits and grease and side meat and coffee*
> for breakfast.
> Carson McCullers, *The Heart Is a Lonely Hunter,* 204

> In the distance the houses were the houses in a Victorian
> print, *small and precisely drawn and quiet*; only one child
> a long way off.
> Graham Greene, *The End of the Affair,* 27

In a long sentence that opens with the conjunction *or*, the conjunction *and* appears nine times to connect a lavish and varied series that is at the end gathered together with *all of this*, used twice:

> Or the market on a Saturday morning, where the colours
> of the fruits and vegetables and the colours of the clothes
> people are wearing and the colour of the day itself, and the
> colour of the nearby sea, and the colour of the sky, which is
> just overhead and seems so close you might reach up and

touch it, and the way the people there speak English (they
break it up) and the way they might be angry with each
other and the sound they make when they laugh, all of this
is so beautiful, all of this is not real like any other real thing
that there is.
     Jamaica Kincaid, *A Small Place*, 79

Just as they are used in a series for conscious stylistic effects, conjunctions are also employed in various combinations within short
rhetorical patterns, often with a highly stylized and balanced result:

They were *neither* citadels *nor* churches, *but* frankly *and*
beautifully office-buildings.
     Sinclair Lewis, *Babbitt*, 5

Her face was worn *but* her hair was black, *and* her eyes
and lips were pretty.
     Bernard Malamud, *Idiots First*, 153

Implicit in this discussion of balance and order achieved through
the careful use of conjunctions is the need for parallelism between the
elements of the series or structure in question. Sometimes the parallelism of a seemingly balanced construction is deliberately disturbed,
and the conjunction is then used to separate words or phrases in the
attention-getting absence of the expected parallelism.

The correlatives

The conjunctions *and, but, or, nor* are often combined with and preceded by certain *precoordinators*, respectively *both, not, either, neither*, to
form the basic *correlatives* or correlative conjunctions: *both... and, not
(only)... but (also), either... or, neither... nor*. The use of correlatives to
join the parts of a coordinate structure establishes a unique relationship between the elements of the structure. As with simple coordinate
structures, a certain parallelism usually exists between the elements of
the correlative structure:

He's *either* got to send that diploma back, *or* get them
fifty goats from somewhere.
     William Faulkner, *The Hamlet*, 81

> From now onwards Animal Farm would engage in trade
> with the neighboring farms: *not*, of course, for any commer-
> cial purposes, *but* simply in order to obtain certain materials
> which were urgently necessary.
>
> George Orwell, *Animal Farm*, 66

The parallelism, obviously, need not be heavy-handed or even particularly striking, and may at times not exist at all. On the other hand,
it may be emphasized by a repetition of the correlative structure. Note
that the second *neither* is understood:

> He had *neither* companions *nor* friends, church *nor* creed.
>
> James Joyce, *Dubliners*, 109

The correlative creates an order all its own, a logical progression
or inevitability in which the idea introduced by the precoordinator is
known to be incomplete and remains in suspension until finally
resolved—that is, until the missing material is supplied as introduced by
the conjunction.

> *Not only* were the furnishings old, intrinsically unlovely,
> and clotted with memory and sentiment, *but* the room itself
> in past years had served as the arena for countless hockey
> and football (tackle as well as "touch") games, and there
> was scarcely a leg on any piece of furniture that wasn't badly
> nicked or marred.
>
> J. D. Salinger, *Franny and Zooey*, 122

Creating a sense of disorder, a paired construction, *and/or*, is hard
to read and to categorize because of the slash:

> Among readers of literary works, the most popular category
> is fiction, with 45 percent of the population reading novels
> and/or short stories. About 12 percent read poetry, while
> about 4 percent read plays.
>
> National Endowment for the Arts, *Reading at Risk*, 7

Reading "and slash or" is like bumping into a pothole. One might
prefer instead: "reading novels or short stories or both."

Conjunctive adverbs (sentence connectors)

A number of connectives can be grouped together and classified as *conjunctive adverbs,* or *sentence connectors,* so called because they share the qualities of both a coordinating conjunction and a kind of adverbial sentence modifier. Coordinating conjunctions are always found between the clauses they connect; conjunctive adverbs are more flexible both in placement and effect. The rigidity and formality of many conjunctive adverbs in stressed position at the beginning of a sentence can be softened by moving them. The following sentences display some common conjunctive adverbs in different syntactic positions:

> Invariably, *also,* the latest presents from Ramona's admirers were displayed.
> Saul Bellow, *Herzog,* 193

> Miss Brodie, *however,* had already fastened on Mary Macgregor who was nearest to her.
> Muriel Spark, *The Prime of Miss Jean Brodie,* 73

> *Indeed,* everyone who knew Matt recognized it and all our friends came to sympathize with him and with me and to see how we took our misfortune.
> Joyce Cary, *Herself Surprised,* 56

Other common conjunctive adverbs include *too, hence, consequently, nevertheless, then, otherwise, on the other hand, likewise, therefore,* and *similarly.* Their placement in the sentence, as the examples indicate, is generally a matter of the writer's discretion, but certain habits of punctuation are usually followed; the adverb is set off from the rest of the sentence by commas, and, when joining two independent clauses, is preceded by a semicolon and followed by a comma. Even the semicolon is sometimes waived, here with the effect of an informal parataxis. The following is a rather daring usage, however, even for the professional writer:

> She was willing to die for him, *therefore* could he not live for her?
> Robert Penn Warren, *World Enough and Time,* 367

Overuse is the most frequent problem with conjunctive adverbs, and the result may be clumsy, stilted, or both. Professional writers employ few of these rather weighty connectives, especially in fiction, where their use is generally limited to the shorter and more common ones.

Coordination

Coordination is the linking of structures of equal grammatical rank–single words and phrases in elementary compound groups, independent clauses in compound sentences, and even entire sentences. The coordinating conjunctions and the correlatives serve to join the grammatically equivalent elements. But it is overly simple to describe the conjunctions as coordinators without certain qualifications. Even *and* is not purely a coordinator. Whatever the units it combines, it indicates continuous and repeated action, as in: *They talked and talked and talked. We went around and around.* The words *but* and *yet* indicate contrast, opposition, or negation; *so* and *for* show several relationships, among them purpose, cause, result, or inference; *or* and *nor* indicate what might be described as alternation, choice, or opposition. Obviously, conjunctions cannot be considered as empty connecting words–as Gertrude Stein remarked, a conjunction "has a force," and each brings opportunity for considerable subtlety.

Some situations in which the process of coordination combines elements both grammatically and logically equal are at the level of single words:

> The *raisins* and *almonds* and *figs* and *apples* and *oranges* and *chocolates* and *sweets* were now passed about the table and Aunt Julia invited all the guests to have either *port* or *sherry.*
> James Joyce, *Dubliners*, 201

The calculated arrangement of this type of coordination, in the extreme, produces some striking effects by the juxtaposition of logically disparate elements:

> Once upon a time *and* a very good time it was there was a moocow coming down along the road...
> James Joyce, *A Portrait of the Artist as a Young Man*, 7

> The room was very full *and* who were they all?
> Gertrude Stein, *Selected Writings of Gertrude Stein*, 12

Linking of disparate syntactic units constitutes shorthand in which the author tosses in a phrase to perform the task that would seem to demand a clause:

> I realized then that I never had forgotten it, *and* a good
> thing too.
>   James Gould Cozzens, *Children and Others*, 104

Loose coordination also appears in a great deal of common grammatical connection. Some expert writers, unless they want special, extreme effects, contain the flow to produce a controlled coordinative statement. Examples of such middle-of-the-road coordination follow, in structures of varying complexity:

> The stains on the ceiling assumed strange shapes, *and* she
> invented stories around them, *but* after a while she would be
> sweating with terror or the force of her own imagination,
> *and* all the time Sister Alfreda sat *and* wordlessly waited
> the Hour.
>   Auberon Waugh, *The Foxglove Saga*, 252

> They plummeted a few feet *and* then little parachutes
> opened *and* drifted small packages silently *and* slowly down-
> ward toward the earth, *and* the planes raised their throttles
> *and* gained altitude, *and* then cut their throttles *and* circled
> again, *and* more of the little objects plummeted down, *and*
> then the planes turned *and* flew back in the direction from
> which they had come.
>   John Steinbeck, *The Moon Is Down*, 151

> He looked out of his clouded eyes at the faint steady light-
> ning in the east. *But* he calmed himself, *and* took out the
> heavy maize cakes *and* the tea, *and* put them upon a stone.
> *And* he gave thanks, *and* broke the cakes *and* ate them, *and*
> drank of the tea. Then he gave himself over to deep *and*
> earnest prayer, *and*, after each petition, he raised his eyes *and*
> looked to the east. *And* the east lightened *and* lightened, till
> he knew that the time was not far off. *And* when he expected
> it, he rose to his feet *and* took off his hat *and* laid it down
> on the earth *and* clasped his hands before him. *And* while he
> stood there the sun rose in the east.
>   Alan Paton, *Cry, the Beloved Country*, 277

A psychological calm or resolution results when syntax combines with vocabulary reminiscent of the King James Bible, as in the last example above. Good coordination often seems more appropriate than subordination for concluding passages, especially in narrative prose. Coordination is free from the careful weighting, ordering, and evaluating of subordination, and even when a coordinative statement is cast in a highly conscious design, the imposed structuring seems just that–imposed–resulting from poetic rather than analytic attention, implying aesthetic order or resolution rather than an authentic rendering of the ultimately irresolvable shades of logical distinction in a complex reality. More subordination in the following passages would destroy the relaxed, slackened quality of the predominant coordination:

> He turned out the light *and* went into Jem's room.
> He would be there all night, *and* he would be there
> when Jem waked up in the morning.
>> Harper Lee, *To Kill a Mockingbird*, closing lines

> She has left the quill *and* ink *and* paper in the cell. She does
> not want to write for a time. She wants to think with her
> feet on the soil *and* her fingers on the breeze, *and* her nose
> in the hair of her daughter.
>> Charmaine Craig, *The Good Men*, third paragraph from end

> He smiled *and* took her hand *and* pressed it. They got up
> *and* walked out of the gallery. They stood for a moment
> at the balustrade *and* looked at Trafalgar Square. Cabs *and*
> omnibuses hurried to *and* fro, *and* crowds passed, hastening
> in every direction, *and* the sun was shining.
>> W. Somerset Maugham, *Of Human Bondage*, closing lines

> *And* at last I step out into the morning *and* I lock the door
> behind me. I cross the road *and* drop the keys into the old
> lady's mailbox. *And* I look up the road, where a few people
> stand, men *and* women, waiting for the morning bus. They
> are very vivid beneath the awakening sky, *and* the horizon
> beyond them is beginning to flame. The morning weighs on
> my shoulders with the dreadful weight of hope *and* I take
> the blue envelope which Jacques has sent me *and* tear it
> slowly into many pieces, watching them dance in the wind,
> watching the wind carry them away. *Yet*, as I turn *and* begin
> walking toward the waiting people, the wind blows some of
> them back on me.
>> James Baldwin, *Giovanni's Room*, closing lines

This same effect can be prolonged over several terminal paragraphs:

> *And* Kino drew back his arm *and* flung the pearl with all his might. Kino *and* Juana watch it go, winking *and* glimmering under the setting sun. They saw the little splash in the distance, *and* they stood side by side watching the place for a long time.
>
> *And* the pearl settled into the lovely green water *and* dropped toward the bottom. The waving branches of the algae called to it *and* beckoned to it. The lights on its surface were green *and* lovely. It settled down to the sand bottom among the fern-like plants. Above, the surface of the water was a green mirror. *And* the pearl lay on the floor of the sea. A crab scampering over the bottom raised a little cloud of sand, *and* when it settled the pearl was gone.
>
> *And* the music of the pearl drifted to a whisper *and* disappeared.
> John Steinbeck, *The Pearl*, closing paragraphs

> *And* seeing it *and* holding it, he felt a complete bursting *and* astonishment *and* delight that he had at last caught hold of this, *and* after this surely there was nothing else to learn *and* he yielded himself because he was in fact back on Brab *and* he felt the sure sense of his horse's gallop *and* he wanted to gather him up *and* hold him together for the jump, *and* it came to him then that it was a splendid run, a magnificent run, from there to here, *and* opening his eyes wide *and* seeing them there *and* not here, with Ellen up on the Appaloosa, he could hear the excited grating sound of his own breath *and* he drew on everything he had left *and* called out in a voice that shook him, "What a run! What a run!"
>
> *And* they all lurched out of their poses for an instant *and* he wondered if he had actually spoken, *but* he wanted to laugh because it did not matter, *for* he felt old Brab gathering himself up, *and* Apple was holding level, *and* the two horses launched out in a true thrust of confident power *and* he felt the lifting start of the sailing, soaring, beautifully clean leap.
> John Espey, *The Anniversaries*, closing paragraphs

Strange thing, time. It weighs most on those who have it least.
Ian Caldwell and Dustin Thomason

*He is the one person who has to be at a Dylan concert and
the one person who can't go to a Dylan concert.*
Christopher Ricks

What, she wonders, is wrong with her?
Michael Cunningham

*Very few writers really know what they are doing until
they've done it.*
Anne Lamott

*Cats know exactly where they begin and end. When they walk
slowly out the door that you are holding open for them, and
pause, leaving their tail just an inch or two inside the door,
they know it. They know you have to keep holding the door
open. That is why their tail is there. It is a cat's way of maintaining a relationship.*
Ursula K. LeGuin

CHAPTER SEVEN

Dependent Clauses

> *When* in the Course of human Events, it becomes
> necessary for one People to dissolve the Political
> Bands *which* have connected them with another,
> and to assume among the Powers of the Earth, the
> separable and equal Station *to which* the Laws of
> Nature and of Nature's God entitle them, a decent
> Respect to the Opinions of Mankind requires *that*
> they should declare the causes *which* impel them to
> the separation.
> *Declaration of Independence*, opening sentence

A DEPENDENT clause of 50 words begins the Declaration of Independence. The 71-word sentence also includes four shorter dependent clauses. Clauses as long as the first one appear more often in documents from the past than in today's prose but, judiciously and imaginatively constructed, shorter dependent clauses continue to serve well in formal discourse, other nonfiction, and narrative.

This eloquent sentence spoken by Franklin Delano Roosevelt derives part of its strength from a dependent clause:

> The only thing we have to fear is fear itself.
> First inaugural address, 1933

Instead of the dependent clause "we have to fear," he could have used an adjective, "the only *fearful* thing is fear itself," or an infinitive alone, "the only thing *to fear* is fear itself." The dependent clause he chose, however, gives added weight, creates parallel rhythms and stresses for the three segments, a cadence: the *only* thing, we *have* to fear, is *fear* itself.

The weight and texture of the deliberations reported in a 2004 government publication are well served by syntax that makes frequent use of dependent clauses. Almost any paragraph can illustrate. Here, each dependent clause is italicized:

> The agencies cooperated, some of the time. But even such cooperation *as there was* is not the same thing as joint action. *When agencies cooperate*, one defines the problem and seeks help with it. *When they act jointly*, the problem and options for action are defined differently from the start. Individuals from different backgrounds come together in analyzing a case and planning how to manage it.
> *The 9/11 Commission Report*, Authorized Edition, 400

Dependent clauses are widely used in both nonfiction and fiction. Their predictable rhythms make them a frequent choice in ceremonial and other formal prose. Dependent clauses flourish also in the opening chapters and narrative passages of novels, where authors often want to impart details quickly. The opening fifty sentences of five recently published prize-winning novels contain from 23 to 53 such clauses, many of them quite short. The first example, italicized below, begins a novel:

> Strange thing, time. It weighs most on those *who have it least.*
> Ian Caldwell and Dustin Thomason, *The Rule of Four*, 5

> *When the trainer answered with his usual "Hey, there,"*
> Mr. Maybrick said "Dick!," and then Dick said, "Oh, Al."
> He always said it just like that, *as if he were expecting something good to happen, and Mr. Maybrick had happened instead.*
> Jane Smiley, *Horse Heaven*, 10

> There are two-toed sloths and there are three-toed sloths, the case being determined by the forepaws of the animals, *since all sloths have three claws on their hind paws.*
> Yann Martel, *Life of Pi*, 3

> Everything about him made a contrast to the older brother, *whose frame had begun to sag.*
> Richard Bausch, "Requisite Kindness," 3

Below, well into a novel, the author has shifted from the quotidian conversation of the characters into a more lyrical contextualizing of their story. Each of the two sentences employs dependent clauses, some embedded in others, with remarkable force and clarity:

> Around the beginning of this century, the Queen of Thailand was aboard a boat, floating along with her many courtiers, manservants, maids, feet-bathers, and food-tasters, *when suddenly the stern hit a wave and the queen was thrown overboard into the turquoise waters of the Nippon-Kai, where, despite her pleas for help, she drowned,* for not one person on that boat went to her aid. Mysterious to the outside world, to the Thai the explanation was immediately clear: tradition demanded, *as it does to this day,* that *no man or woman may touch the queen.*
>   Zadie Smith, *White Teeth*, 161

Dozens of labels could be gathered to describe the structures displayed here under the simple heading, *dependent clauses.* This chapter will consider two large categories loosely grouped as *relative* and *subordinate.* But the *kinds* of dependent clauses and the labels they bear don't matter as much to style as the frequency, the placement, and the combinations with other structures.

Independent clauses joined to each other form a *compound* sentence. The combination of an *independent clause* and one or more *dependent clauses* forms what is known as a *complex sentence.* And there is the *compound-complex* sentence – two or more independent clauses and at least one dependent clause. Any sentence, any independent clause that is a statement (and is not unmanageably long), may be turned into a dependent clause and tacked on, or inserted into, another sentence. In most of the kernel sentence positions occupied by nouns, adjectives, or adverbs, a dependent clause may be substituted. In addition, a dependent clause may serve in other positions as either a bound or a free modifier. Nowadays, writers who are sparing in their use of dependent clauses often prefer to reduce the potential clause to structures such as the appositive, the nominative absolute, the infinitive, or the participial phrase. Some writers mix an occasional dependent clause among these. The ability to write the whole range of syntactic structures named here is worth the trouble: variation in sentence types as well as sentence lengths is a mark of the professional.

Relative and subordinate clauses

The two italicized words below form a relative clause:

> The chapters *that follow* constitute neither an intellectual
> history of Victorian English nor an ordered survey of
> Victorian letters.
> Jerome H. Buckley, *The Victorian Temper*, VII

A subordinate clause of three words starts the following example,
which also contains three additional dependent clauses:

> *If she stumbles*, she is not aware of it because she does not
> know where her body stops, which part of her is an arm,
> or foot, or a hand.
> Toni Morrison, *Beloved*, 122-123

The two-word clause and the three-word clause italicized in the
two quotations above are lower limits, the shortest examples of these
two types of dependent clause. Any clause, of course, must contain a
subject and a predicate. A *relative clause* substitutes a relative pronoun
(*who, whom, whose, which, that,* and others) for some corresponding
structure in a hypothetical independent clause. In the above two-word
example, the relative pronoun that introduces the clause stands for the
subject, and only the verb is needed to complete the clause. A *subordinate clause* has no substitution but an addition; a subordinator (*because,
if, as, while, when, that, although,* and others) is added to a complete
clause in order to connect it to the main body of the sentence. Yet to
exemplify at once the slipperiness of even these most general definitions, sometimes the subordinator or relative is understood: Let me
know the exact time [that] *you will arrive*. In the following example,
when signifies a subordinate clause. *I don't have to read* might be thought
of as a relative clause with an understood introductory *that*:

> I am not alone, then, in feeling guilty when I read a book
> I don't have to read.
> Walter Kerr, *The Decline of Pleasure*, 46

Looking at the impact of dependent clauses on style, one soon discovers that the categories overlap, that different kinds are often used in
the same sentence and in the company of other structures, and that the

kind matters less than the number, their locations, and the way they are attached or not attached to other elements of the sentence. The loose groupings, *relative* and *subordinate*, do not lead to any insights associated with the category but serve mainly to provide convenient headings for discussing an assortment of dependent clauses.

Relative clauses

Whether in first, middle, or final position, relative clauses can vary greatly in complexity, ranging anywhere from bare kernels to intricate constructions. They are perhaps most often bound into the grammatical texture of the main clause without any punctuation:

> In the storage room *that led down to the cellar* I found
> two pewter waterpots and a copper kettle.
> Tracy Chevalier, *Girl with a Pearl Earring*, 21

> They walked up to the high gaze *that gave the island its name*,
> a knoll of spruce in the corner, all hemmed around with
> a low wall of stones.
> Annie Proulx, *The Shipping News*, 185

A long relative clause beginning with *that* suspends perhaps somewhat too long the main point of the following sentence:

> I still count the little preamble *that begins as the houselights*
> *go down and the footlights glow and goes on to accompany the*
> *slow rise of the curtain on the opening scene of Carmen* as the
> most cunningly contrived passage of descriptive music
> I have ever heard.
> Charles W. Morton, *It Has Its Charms*, 71

Here a relative clause serves as a bound modifier interrupting the compound predicate:

> She saw a red-haired man *who looked faintly familiar* and
> watched him bend under a hood and then stand back to
> appraise a customized Buick with a black lacquer chassis.
> Don DeLillo, *Underworld*, 161

In final compound positions, relative clauses figure importantly in the next example:

> I grew up around a father and mother *who read every chance*
> *they got, who took us to the library every Thursday night to load*
> *up on books for the coming week.*
> Anne Lamott, *Bird by Bird*, XI

The successful logic of the following embedded sentence is helped by the comma that sets off the second *which*-clause from the first:

> The inner door, *which led to the passage, which in turn led to the*
> *storm door,* was beside the stove.
> John Steinbeck, *The Moon Is Down*, 122

Below, a *which*-clause concludes a sentence; the verbs and nouns in the dependent clause are more descriptive than most adjectives:

> He let out a laugh and reached again to stroke the dog,
> *which reeled its head in to give him a look of subjection and fealty.*
> T. Coraghessan Boyle, *Drop City*, 217

Subordinate clauses

Subordinate clauses often serve as sentence openers, but some can be attached almost anywhere:

> *Even if they grow up in the same neighborhood, on the same block,*
> *or in the same house,* girls and boys grow up in different
> worlds of words. Others talk to them differently and expect
> and accept different ways of talking from them.
> Deborah Tannen, *You Just Don't Understand*, 43

> Now the end of a semester was at hand, and Chip still
> wasn't sure *that anyone but Melissa really got how to criticize*
> *mass culture.*
> Jonathan Franzen, *The Corrections*, 40

The subordinate clause is open to a great number of variations, some so common as to have replaced the basic word order:

> I was almost swept past the subway, *so swiftly were the people milling around on the sidewalk.*
> John D. Spooner, *The Pheasant-lined Vest of Charlie Freeman*, 23

Below, the *just...so* frame operates like a correlative structure to link the subordinate clause to the subsequent main clause:

> And *just* as the mother feels acutely the slightest criticism of her child, *so* any criticism of her book even by the most negligible nitwit gave Virginia acute pain.
> Leonard Woolf, *Downhill All the Way*, 57

Instead of the tight, correlative-like structure above, the next example looks at first almost like parataxis. More likely, it is a variant of something like "As he thought more, he raged more":

> *The more he thought*, the more he raged, aloud and privately.
> John Updike, *The Same Door*, 187

> *The more power we achieve over how our bodies look, whether through genetics, surgery, drugs, or other means*, the more we will alter our outer selves to match our inner selves.
> Virginia Postrel, *The Substance of Style*, 187

This effective right-branching arrangement is capped off by a quick subordinate clause after a series of nominative absolutes:

> They sat there, he leaning back on his elbows, his face tilted upward, eyes closed, somehow more arrogant than ever, *while she read a book.*
> Audrey Callahan Thomas, *Ten Green Bottles*, 150

Ideas in dependent clauses

These examples have showed that the term *dependent* should be taken only in the grammatical sense. There need be nothing weak or second-rate about relative or subordinate clauses in comparison to the main clauses they modify. Yet writers are often encouraged to put main ideas into main clauses and lesser ideas into subordinate clauses. It is important to remember that the distinction between main and subordinate is, in general, structural, not logical, not semantic. We see below an example of important ideas displayed in dependent clauses:

> In spite of my initial shock, I admit *that I am perversely honored to be in CliffsNotes*. Look at me: I'm sitting in the $4.95 bookstore bleachers along with Shakespeare, Conrad, and Joyce. Now I'm not saying *that I've reached their same literary status…since I'm not dead yet*, I can talk back.
> Amy Tan, *The Opposite of Fate*, 10

For another instance of the power of dependent clauses to carry vital meanings, we go to an unusual twenty-first-century book that in its entirety is a close reading of Bob Dylan's songs:

> He is the one person *who has to be at a Dylan concert* and the one person *who can't go to a Dylan concert*.
> Christopher Ricks, *Dylan's Vision of Sin*, 490

Bound and free modification

Further, the question of how and where to locate ideas, in free or in bound relationships, suggests an area of difficulty with dependent clauses. Dependent clauses as bound modifiers may result in painful relative embeddings and heavy subordinate imbalance, or in slow, even, unaccented prose without the rhythms of contrast upon which good writing depends. Skillful writers can use these constructions adeptly to add details, texture, variety, and at times a neat and appropriate turn.

Dependent clauses as nominals: Wysiwyg clauses

Dependent clauses can take the place of nouns, as subjects, predicate nominatives, or objects. One group of these nominal clauses deserves a special name. Usually terse, aphoristic, pointed, occurring singly or in pairs or larger groups, *wysiwyg* (**wiz e wig**) clauses can be serious, informational, playful, humorous. In the first example, the opening clause serves as subject of the sentence and the second clause as predicate nominative:

> *What you see* is *what you get.*

Although most of the grammatical terms used in this book are traditional, you will not find *wysiwyg* in syntactic glossaries. But such clauses have existed for a long time, usually under the label "noun clauses" or "nominal clauses," with no attention to their special character or stylistic effects. Here is a pair of *wysiwyg* dependent clauses from Shakespeare written four centuries ago, imitating a line from Plautus written twenty-two centuries ago:

> *What's mine* is yours, *and what is yours* is mine.
> *Measure for Measure*, 5.1.539; Plautus, *Trinummus*, 2.2.48

A paired example, italicized below, punctuates the argument at the end of a book, one clause serving as subject, one as predicate nominative:

> For twelve tumultuous years FDR convinced a majority of his countrymen to trust his leadership by putting into practice his policies for dealing with a devastating depression and a world war. Anyone anywhere is free to measure his achievement. *What he said* was *what he did.*
> Carol Gelderman, *All the Presidents' Words*, 179

These dependent noun clauses serve as subjects of sentences:

> *What is always needed in the appreciation of art, or life*,
> is the larger perspective.
> Alice Walker, *In Search of Our Mothers' Gardens*, 5

> *What I had discovered, of course*, was a model.
> Walker, 12

> *What the black Southern writer inherits as a natural right*
> is a sense of community.
> Walker, 17

And below, a dependent noun clause serves as subject and, in the same sentence, two such clauses as compound objects of a preposition:

> *Part of what existence means to me* is knowing the
> difference between *what I am now* and *what I was then.*
>   Walker, 125

In the following example from a novel, a variation opens with *What*, an inversion split off from the rest of the dependent clause that serves as a direct object. The framing of the clause as a question under-lies a subtlety that at times characterizes the *wysiwyg* clause: it often implies (or even sets forth) a question as in the first example below:

> *What*, she wonders, *is wrong with her?*
>   Michael Cunningham, *The Hours*, 4

> *What went unsaid, but clearly implied,* was *that they had a right but not a reason to be proud of me.*
>   Percival Everett, *Erasure*, 3

The implicit question, above, in the example from a memoir-like novel, is "What went unsaid, but clearly implied?" and the implicit answer appears in the second clause.

A novella, written in the manner of memoir, intimates the drama to come, using as the direct object one of these terse nominal clauses, five crisp monosyllables:

> And at that moment I believed I knew *what would come to be.*
> When I returned the hat, I would exchange it for the man
> who wore it.
>   Lan Samantha Chang, *Hunger*, 14

Such clauses abound in book reviews, in use by good and varied company. Reviewers are usually practiced writers—novelists, poets, lit-erary editors, writing teachers, journalists, biographers, academic crit-ics, and specialists in various fields. Below, in the first sentence of a review of a novel, the reviewer expands a *wysiwyg* clause beyond the usual length to carry a good deal of essential information:

> It's easy to explain *how Lorraine Adams knows so much about*
> *the illegal Algerian community in America, about credit card*
> *fraud, about terrorism and FBI investigations. Harbor,* her metic-
> ulously constructed first novel, is based on her reporting for
> *The Washington Post.*
>
> Neil Gordon, "Under Surveillance," 7

This reviewer's second paragraph opens with a pair of *wysiwyg* clauses
as subject and predicate nominative:

> *What's harder to explain* is *how Adams is able to draw us so*
> *convincingly into the lived reality of her ensemble cast, a skill*
> *that derives less from the craft of journalism than from the art*
> *of fiction.*
>
> Gordon, 7

Like other syntactic structures, *wysiwygs* are often handy in positions where they open out for additional expansion. Here, in another
review, three of these nominal clauses serve as direct objects and set a
pattern for additional details:

> He described *what he ate, what he saw* and *what he heard,* con-
> juring the delicate fragrance of a mango grove, the slap of
> pitchy tar on the cedar planks of a hull and a peculiar black
> and-white striped wild ass – the first English description of
> a zebra.
>
> Sara Wheeler, "The Highbrow Hijacker," 19

Novelists make adroit use of *wysiwyg* patterns in writing dialogue.
Below, the first and third dependent clauses serve as objects; the second is a postponed subject after *It's* as a sentence opener:

> "I just don't understand *what the hold is.* It's clear *why she*
> *holds on to you,* but I just can't see *why you holding on to her.*"
>
> Toni Morrison, *Beloved,* 67

Here, again in a work of fiction, a character is speaking; the *wysiwyg*
clause is a direct object:

> Then I learned *just how much of an aerodynamic wonder the*
> *batten sail is* – it makes a sort of flat curve.
>
> Annie Proulx, *The Shipping News,* 113

Whether as object or predicate nominative, these clauses often function as informative or witty sentence concluders:

> The sorry fact seemed to be *that life without Alfred in the house was better for everyone but Alfred.*
> Jonathan Franzen, *The Corrections*, 564

In any syntactic position, an aphoristic quality can be conveyed by a *wysiwyg* clause. Below, it is a subject:

> *What could not be changed* must be borne. And since nothing could be changed, everything had to be borne. This principle ruled her life. It was mantra, fettle, and challenge.
> Monica Ali, *Brick Lane*, 4

Two terse nominal clauses are used here, one as object of a verb and one as object of a preposition:

> "You love *who you love*," I say. "You're blessed with *whatever you're blessed with.*"
> Alice Randall, *The Wind Done Gone*, 200

In autobiographical and biographical accounts and memoirs of various sorts, *wysiwyg* clauses at times provide the structure for witty observations or quips. Here an author describes her own and other writers' experience; the dependent clauses function as objects, the first as object of a verb, the second as object of a preposition:

> Very few writers really know *what they are doing* until *they've done it.*
> Anne Lamott, *Bird by Bird*, 22

Recounting what she has heard about another writer, the same author uses a dependent nominal clause as the object of an infinitive:

> Now, Muriel Spark is said to have felt *that she was taking dictation from God every morning—sitting there, one supposes, plugged into a Dictaphone, typing away, humming.*
> Lamott, 22

Again, these clauses appear as objects, this time in an ingenious series of sentences, imparting some wry and humorous observations. In the next to last sentence below, the *wysiwyg* clause is a predicate nominative:

> Dogs don't notice *when they put their paws in the quiche*. Dogs don't know *where they begin and end*.
>
> Cats know exactly *where they begin and end*. When they walk slowly out the door that you are holding open for them, and pause, leaving their tail just an inch or two inside the door, they know it. They know *you have to keep holding the door open*. That is *why their tail is there*. It is a cat's way of maintaining a relationship.
> Ursula K. LeGuin, *The Wave in the Mind*, 163

Another author uses dependent clauses as objects, as she reflects on her mother's reaction to the daughter's childhood refusal to practice the piano:

> I heard her mutter *that from now on I could do whatever I wanted*. She would no longer tell me what to do.
> Amy Tan, *The Opposite of Fate*, 18

These nominal clauses are at home in many kinds of nonfiction, including criticism of literature, art, and culture. Serving as predicate nominative, this *wysiwyg* clause opens with *how*:

> The mystery is always *how the two activities, seeing and painting, can become so inextricably one*.
> Joseph J. Rishel, "Paul Cezanne," 121

Sometimes writers resort to *wysiwyg* clauses when other attempts at description are not quite adequate. Below, an author setting out to define the noun *place* first uses adjectives: *latitudinal, longitudinal, temporal, spatial, personal, political, layered, replete, human*. She tries nouns: *histories, memories, width, depth, connections*. Finally she shifts to four nominal clauses, *wysiwygs*, to round out her description:

> Place is latitudinal and longitudinal within the map of a person's life. It is temporal and spatial, personal and political. A layered location replete with human histories and memo-

ries, place has width as well as depth. It is about connections, *what surrounds it, what formed it, what happened there,
what will happen there.*
        Lucy R. Lippard, *The Lure of the Local*, 7

This *wysiwyg* clause serves as the subject:

What really endures are artifacts, effigies, things that speak
about a time, place or civilization.
        Karim Rashid, "What's Really Important," 191

Below, a *wysiwyg* clause as direct object summarizes a chapter:

Mapping tells *why the image matters.*
        Edward Tufte, *Beautiful Evidence*, 45

Two *wysiwyg* clauses, one as subject of the sentence and one as
object of a preposition, apply to contemporary choices:

How we choose says something about *who we are*, to the present and to the future.
        Virginia Postrel, *The Substance of Style*, 191

In a talk in 1958, playwright Harold Pinter persuasively expressed
an argument that he later refined and reapplied. In the earlier statement, he used two pairs of nominal clauses as objects of prepositions:

There are no hard distinctions between *what is real* and *what
is unreal*, nor between *what is true* and *what is false*. A thing is
not necessarily true or false; it can be both true and false.
        Harold Pinter, home page

Some years later, in another talk, he qualified these statements,
astutely changing them to questions in applying them to political con-
duct instead of to an exploration of reality through art:

I believe that these assertions still make sense and do still
apply to the exploration of reality through art. So as a writer
I stand by them but as a citizen I cannot. As a citizen I must
ask: *What is true? What is false?*
        Harold Pinter, home page

Interrogations and aphoristic statements of this kind at times serve well in public speeches. Among the most memorable are from John F. Kennedy's inaugural address:

> And so, my fellow Americans, ask not *what your country can do for you* but *what you can do for your country*.

Aphorisms, maxims, adages, proverbs often carry an emotional content that depends on characteristic choice of both vocabulary and syntax. Authors of books (as well as public speeches) on occasion heighten the appeal of an opening or a conclusion by using nominal clauses of the sort described here, as in the following closing sentence of a book of essays:

> Maybe life doesn't get any better than this, or any worse, and *what we get* is just *what we're willing to find: small wonders where they grow.*
> Barbara Kingsolver, *Small Wonder*, 264

Dependent clauses can be eloquent, playful, distinctive, or they can sound pretentious or overly clever. Using them requires ingenuity and good judgment.

When Uncle Runkin came to visit he brought his coffin and
slept in it, laying it across a couple of sawhorses we carried
into the upstairs bedroom.
                    Fred Chappell

His black heart beating wildly, he rushed over to his
unconscious daughter and brought her to.
                    J. D. Salinger

Odious vermin, Henry Fielding called critics.
                    David Markson

Through the windows ajar on the side aisle came the sweetness
of blossom, of bruised grass, of river mud.
                    Robert Penn Warren

His was a book which never was intended to reside in
a library, but rather to remain in the pockets of travelers.
                    Eunice Howe

CHAPTER EIGHT

Sentence Openers and Inversion

After he ate, he left the house answers the question,
"What did he do after he ate?"; *He left the house after
he ate* answers the question "When did he leave the
house?" The climax expression comes last...

A group of Czech linguists refers to this tendency
of many languages to put the known first and the
unknown or unexpected last as "sentence perspective."
They point out that, in order to communicate the sentence dynamics that has been partially lost by the stiff-
ening of word order, English must resort to other
stratagems, and these are among the things that give
the language its distinctive syntactic appearance.

Dwight Bolinger, *Aspects of Language*, 119-20

W RITERS create "sentence perspective" when trying to decide
how to begin the next sentence on the page or screen. The opening
words of a sentence glance both backward and forward, establishing a
relationship with what precedes and then bringing into view the new
information.

Perhaps two-thirds of English sentences open with the subject, and
then move from what is known to what is unknown. About one-fourth
of our sentences open with an adverbial modifier like the prepositional
phrase above in "*After he ate,* he left the house," or some other adverbial
opener, such as an adverbial dependent clause, illustrated below:

When Uncle Runkin came to visit he brought his coffin and
slept in it, laying it across a couple of sawhorses we carried
into the upstairs bedroom.

Fred Chappell, *I Am One of You Forever*, 119

Apart from connecting the new sentence with what has come before it, and then disclosing new information, as does the sentence above, there is often logical justification especially in narrative prose for showing the "when, where, or how" of an action before revealing other details. Adverbial phrases of time, place, and manner are exemplified in order in the following sentence:

> *Early one morning, under the arc of a lamp, carefully, silently, in smock and rubber gloves,* old Doctor Manza grafted a cat's head on to a chicken's trunk.
> Dylan Thomas, *Adventures in the Skin Trade*, 120

Two adverbials of time open this paragraph from a memoir:

> *Not long ago, when I was in town on business,* I determined to test my memories against the reality and drove to my old block, my old school, the homes of my closest friends, sure that I had inflated it all in my mind. But the houses were no smaller, the flowers no less bright.
> Anna Quindlen, *How Reading Changed My Life*, 3

When *time* is a vital aspect of the subject under discussion, prepositional phrases can become sturdy adverbial openers as in the two sentences below that introduce a paragraph:

> In her 1978 book *Silences*, Tillie Olsen documents the history of women writers and points out the relative silence of women as literary voices. In the twentieth century, only one out of twelve published and acclaimed writers is a woman.
> Mary Field Belenky, Blythe Clinchy, Nancy Goldberger and Jill Tarule, *Women's Ways of Knowing*, 17

Much less frequent but nonetheless useful openers are verbal groups, and conjunctions long and short, especially *and* and *but*. The simple coordinating conjunctions–*and, but, for, so, or, nor,* and *yet,* as well as the longer ones–serve to connect or contrast the new sentence with its predecessors, and to reduce repetition. Longer connectors– conjunctive adverbs such as *consequently, nevertheless, accordingly, in that case, likewise, therefore, similarly*–appear as the initial word less frequently than the short coordinators and less in professional prose than in amateur writing. Rounding out the list of openers are various kinds of inversions, the most common probably being the familiar *there* and *it*.

In sentences that begin with the subject, the first word of the subject is most often *the*, but professional writers tend not to use too many *the* openers in a row. Also common are other determiners (among them *both, such, some, few*), demonstratives (*this, that, these, those*), or possessives (*his, her, its, my, your*), all of these often linking the sentence to something that has gone before. Besides a determiner, a noun phrase functioning as subject sometimes has adjectives or nouns as modifiers preceding the headword. The frequency of certain initial words in subject-opened sentences varies with the author, the kind of prose, and the subject, but the following counts in an essay by D. H. Lawrence are probably not unusual. Of 439 sentences, 50 open with the word *the*; 34 with *and*; 29 with *but*; 7 with *so*; 7 with *for*, and 3 with *yet*. Only 7 instances of the longer conjunctions or connectors occur in the 439 sentences: *hence* and *at the same time* twice; *in short, for this reason*, and *that is to say* once.

In a count made of four thousand sentence openers in the mid-twentieth century, Francis Christensen found that 24.5 percent of the sentences began with a structure other than the subject. He reported that in the first 200 sentences from selected works of 20 American authors, fiction and nonfiction, the writers opened with adverbials in 23 sentences in 100; verbal groups in one sentence in 85; inverted elements, one in 300, and coordinating conjunction such as *and* or *but* in 7 out of 100.[1] Such percentages will vary with the authors and kinds of works chosen, but the available variety in sentence openers, interspersed with subject-openers as a mainstay, provides an important resource to establish continuity in any kind of writing.

Verbals as openers

Since the opening verbal modifies before the fact its character is deliberately vague, unresolved, and even suspenseful. But its effect may be uncertain and confused, if not employed to hold or suspend the subject-reference up to a point, and then say something about it. Below,

---

[1] Francis Christensen, *Notes Toward a New Rhetoric* (New York, 1967), 46-47.

an opening participial construction builds up a syntactic expectation that is denied when the expected subject, *he*, does not appear. The participial construction is said to "dangle":

> *Coming out into the late night and walking round the building*
> *with the secretive grating roll of the stony path beneath his steps,*
> the evening throbbed back through him as blood thumps
> slowly, reliving effort, after exertion.
> Nadine Gordimer, *The Soft Voice of the Serpent*, 243

One could substitute "As he came" for "Coming" and "walked" for "walking." Removing the two *–ing* words, however, makes the sentence less poetic and less revelatory of the reciprocal motion. One might try opening the sentence with "As he was," or one could insert, after the comma, the words "he sensed how." By choosing correctness, one sacrifices the flow and emphasis of the author's original. Although sentences like the above occasionally turn up in the work of good writers, professionals tend to avoid the opening participle or they take care that the intended noun or pronoun is placed next to the participial opening. Elsewhere, with conventional syntax, the same author uses an opening participle, *Arguing*, that is soon followed in the normal way by the subject to which it refers, *they*:

> *Arguing about the model of car, the level of possession appropriate*
> *for her, they* left hers and took the steps to the terrace.
> Nadine Gordimer, *The Pickup*, 14

Another experienced writer opens a sentence with a dangling past participle. But here the meaning is perfectly clear, and the *I* who was *brought up* appears immediately in the next sentence. Adding three words, "Because I was," at the beginning would remove the dangler, but the words are implied in any case:

> Brought up without books, my passion for them was, if not
> directly forbidden, discouraged. At that time I knew nothing
> of First Editions and their special lure but I associated books
> with magic.
> Jeanette Winterson, *Art Objects*, 122

Winterson uses in the approved fashion a present participial phrase to open a sentence and follows it immediately with the appropriate headword:

> *Mulling over my new freedom from the gross weight of how to get from A to B, I* came across Gertrude Stein in the Humour section. I do not know why...
> Winterson, 155

It is clear that both of these talented writers know how *not* to dangle participles but on occasion choose to do it or simply do not notice. The next example of a verbal, this time from fiction, opens with a gerund phrase, that is, the *–ing* form of the verb functioning as a noun, here used as object of a preposition:

> *After having his tea* he unpacked and arranged his books; then he sat down and tried to read; but he was depressed.
> W. Somerset Maugham, *Of Human Bondage*, 189

Also in common use are participial modifiers where the present or past participle is used in an adjectival function:

> *Quickened by this spiritual refreshment*, it had a boom.
> Sinclair Lewis, *Babbitt*, 178

> *Brought up to command* respect, he is often slightly withdrawn and uneasy now that he finds himself in a world where his authority has lately become less and less unquestionable.
> John Osborne, *Look Back in Anger*, 77

These verbal openers use the progressive participle, undangled:

> *Sitting down behind many layers of glass in a sort of green leather conservatory*, we started to town.
> F. Scott Fitzgerald, *The Great Gatsby*, 64

> *Weeping, sobbing, pleading*, the woman in the customs line begged forgiveness.
> Anne Applebaum, *Between East and West*, 295

Constructions formed from *having* plus a past participle, tempting as they may be, sometimes sound amateurish. Yet they have long been prevalent in some journalistic styles:

> *Having seen his long series of pastel paintings last January in a museum exhibition in Rochester,* we invited the artist, J. Erwin Porter, to explain how he came to this singular study.
> Norman Kent, "The Erie Canal," 46

Infinitive openers are less versatile than the participles but still fresh and useful; they refer at times to something that has preceded, and they can provide a new insight, transition, and cohesion:

> But *to tell the truth,* if it had not been for Nick and his socialism I should never have bothered with politics at all.
> William Golding, *Free Fall,* 95

The nominative absolute as opener

Similarly, the nominative absolute as opener is not a source of confusion, although its unique cumulative effect usually makes it more valuable at the end of a sentence. Since it carries its own subject, any problems of subject-reference disappear:

> *His black heart beating wildly,* he rushed over to his unconscious daughter and brought her to.
> J. D. Salinger, *Nine Stories,* 55

Adjectives as openers

A series of adjective phrases opens the following balanced sentences from a biographical sketch, referring to what has been said in the preceding sentence, and what will be said in the one that follows, both about the duchess's desire for fame:

> Garish in her dress, eccentric in her habits, chaste in her conduct, coarse in her speech, she succeeded in her lifetime in drawing upon herself the ridicule of the great and the applause of the learned.
> Virginia Woolf, *The Common Reader,* 70

Prepositions and conjunctions as openers

In all kinds of prose, two groups of small words—prepositions and conjunctions—are surprisingly frequent and valuable as sentence openers. At the end of a book review, the first sentence, below, opens with a prepositional phrase, its syntactic precision and stress hinting at the *method* it describes. And the final sentence opens with the language's most frequent conjunction, the syntax itself suggesting, as the words do, that the conversation will continue:

> *For its method alone,* this vibrant study is bound to be noticed, quoted, and remembered. *And* in setting a new standard for commentary on an often intractable topic, it may even set off a revived—and revitalized—debate.
> Garrett Stewart, book review, 772

Inversion

We approach an English sentence with certain expectations, conditioned by our long acquaintance with basic patterns. We come expecting a subject first, or soon, and next—only then—a predicate. Although we hardly notice this order when we meet it, we do tend to notice anything that is radically out of place. If we come upon a question, an exclamation, an imperative, we readily exchange our normal expectations for a new set, with which we are also quite familiar. This is automatic. There are many other kinds of inversions, however, that are not tied so closely to special meaning or tone, yet often emerge in every sort of prose. In reading, we may actually fail to note the dislocation.

Emphasis is shifted, below, to the news of the sentence by placing in the opening position the clause that is the direct object:

> *Indoor mold can cause or exacerbate respiratory problems,* says a new report by the U.S. Institute of Medicine.
> Erik Stokstad, "Asthma Linked to Indoor Dampness," 1229

Some inversions can pass us quietly by without calling attention to their reconstructed syntax. They seem almost inevitable, the natural way of putting down the idea. This kind of inversion appears at the start and finish of the next sentence:

> *Bad as this article was*, and time has proved it to be utter non-
> sense, the second article he wrote was probably even worse,
> and *why I printed it I don't recall.*
> Charles Angoff, *The Tone of the Twenties*, 127

Inversions with "there" and "it"

Some of the less obtrusive inversions seem to derive from a kind of formula, like the use of *there* to postpone the subject:

> And instead of the nasty square buildings *there are yet nastier*
> *huts*. And instead of the rusty streaks on the concrete, *there*
> *is a limitless expanse* of rusty tin roofing.
> John Kenneth Galbraith, *The Triumph*, 12

These inversions may render a sentence somewhat less direct and active, but they permit emphasis on the subject and room to amplify it. *There* as a sentence opener is followed not only by forms of *be* but by *seemed, appeared*, and other verbs, sometimes with a preceding adverb:

> *Suddenly there appeared* in the path ahead of them a rude
> door put together from stout planks.
> Jean Speiser, *River in the Dark*, 16

> In a hole in the ground *there lived a hobbit.*
> J. R. R. Tolkien, *The Hobbit*, opening line

Others make a second inversion that tampers with the *there* placement itself:

> *Mansions there are*—two or three of them—but the majority
> of the homes are large and inelegant.
> John Barth, *The Floating Opera*, 53

The *it*-inversion is another such formulaic switch in syntax, useful in all types of prose and automatically filling the position of sentence opener with a structural word that enables postponement of the theme:

> *It* occurs to me that boredom and panic are the two devils the solitary must combat.
> May Sarton, *From May Sarton's Well*, 33

Again, the introductory *it* allows postponement of the assertion to a position that draws emphasis:

> *It* is a new trend to write short books on writers, thinkers, and artists.
> A. Richard Turner, "Reason to Smile," R6

Both *there* and *it* are almost semantically empty as they begin a sentence or clause, but combined with content words they can open out a series of sentences or clauses to provide effective parallel structures for details of comparison or contrast. Below, a deft series of three *there* constructions (and one *it* clause) finds a pivot in the repeated appositive *days*:

> *There were days when it seemed* as if no one could talk of anything that was not tragic, as if no one could remember anything without bitterness. But then *there were other days, days when* I would, quite unexpectedly, meet someone who saw the past not as a burden but as a forgotten story, now due to be retold; *there were days when* I would find an old house, an old church, or something unexpected like the cemetery in L'viv, which suddenly revealed the secret history of a place or a nation.
> Anne Applebaum, *Between East and West*, xx-xxi

Inversions with negatives

The first of two *there*-transformations below is itself inverted because of a negative opener:

> *Nor was there* any normal forage on the island, since it was inhabited only by fishermen and growers of grapes and *there was* nothing for the English soldiers to gather except "shreds of vine stalks."
> Marchette Chute, *Two Gentle Men*, 196

Besides the *nor* opener, other negatives can bring about inversion:

> *Neither* is this the whole truth, for the poet's spirit, tinged by melancholy, is not completely free-moving.
> Geoffrey H. Hartman, *Wordsworth's Poetry 1787-1814*, 6

Other unobtrusive inversions

Some other common and useful inversions that do not call attention to themselves are the subject-verb inversions (or front-shifted auxiliary verb) produced by certain initial prepositional phrases, adjectives, adverbs, numerals, comparatives, and the like:

> *Thus* began his lifelong association with Paris.
> Martin Esslin, *The Theatre of the Absurd*, 2

> *More important than* most of the dramatic production within the Surrealist movement was the work of some of its members produced after they had left, or been expelled from it.
> Esslin, 275

> *Equally* valuable are Schneider's painstaking examinations of the formative experiences of such figures as Moreau, Redon, Signac, Cézanne, and even such a lesser light as Albert Marquet.
> Sheldon Nodelman, "The Mastery of Matisse," 53

> *Around him* sat four or five of the younger guides.
> Jean Speiser, *River in the Dark*, 39

> *Beyond the edge of town*, past tar-covered poor houses and a low hill bare except for fallen electric poles, was the institution, and it sent its delicate and isolated buildings trembling over the gravel and cinder floor of the valley. *From there*, one day in the early spring, walking with a tree limb as a cane, came Balamir, walking with a shadow and with a step that was not free, to fall under the eye and hand of Madame Snow.
> John Hawkes, *The Cannibal*, 3

Inversions for emphasis

Attention is often subtly shifted by moving certain sentence elements to the front. We see this in an arrangement that puts adverbial information at the beginning of a sentence, follows it with the verb on which it depends, and then the subject:

> *Into this grey lake* plopped the thought, I know that man, don't I?
> Doris Lessing, *Children of Violence*, 264

> *Inside this room* sits a motionless macaque monkey.
> The monkey is strapped in a chair, staring at a computer screen... The monkey is directing the robot with its thoughts.
> Carl Zimmer, "Mind Over Machine," 48

> *On a handsome Jacobean sideboard* was ranged a double row of bottles and cut-glass decanters and what looked like a silver-plated ice-bucket.
> Kingsley Amis, *The Anti-Death League*, 153

Adverbials also introduce the next examples. Followed first by the verb, they help postpone the subject for final disclosure:

> On the pleasant shore of the French Riviera, about half way between Marseilles and the Italian border, stands a large, proud, rose-colored hotel.
> F. Scott Fitzgerald, *Tender is the Night*, opening sentence

> Secretly, far beneath the visible surface of the island, imprisoned by this watertight cap of rock, lay the purest, sweetest, most copious water in all the land that bordered upon or existed in the great ocean.
> James A. Michener, *Hawaii*, 10

In the next example, an adverbial structure (a phrase plus an embedded relative clause) introduces the *there*-transformation and helps prolong our wait for a subject that at last emerges like the design it names:

> *Out of the goings-on that ensue* there begins to emerge an interesting design.
> Frank Kermode, *Continuities*, 225

Adverbial ideas in the following example are carried by a relative clause standing as a front-shifted object:

> *Where the cluster fell*, none knew for certain, but on impact
> it had resolved into separate angry bees.
> John Barth, *Lost in the Funhouse*, 28

Direct objects often take this first position:

> *The turtles* he fought in a curious fashion.
> Edmund Wilson, *Memoirs of Hecate County*, 4

> *Life* he saw as a ceaseless and courageous contest.
> Jerry Allen, *The Thunder and the Sunshine*, 233

A predicate adjective (or participle) may also begin a sentence, sometimes followed by inversion of subject and verb. The first word is thus emphasized, and the arrangement opens out the sentence for additional details and possible links to sentences that will follow:

> *Gone* are the potted plants, the Christmas cheeses, the toys
> for the children that were regularly issued by the old Francis
> Cleary.
> Mary McCarthy, *Cast a Cold Eye*, 79

> *Absent at the wilderness banquet* are the wild animals–the
> birds, monkeys, lion, and deer–that in Eden coexist peace-
> fully with one another and with the solitary Adam and Eve.
> Bruce Lawson, "Unifying Milton's Epics," 203

Unusual emphasis falls on an objective complement brought to the front of a short sentence:

> *Odious vermin*, Henry Fielding called critics.
> David Markson, *Vanishing Point*, 60

Inversions to aid amplification

Inversions are also designed to relocate in a more convenient spot the syntactic element that is about to receive substantial modification. Adverbial openers help by leading into the verb while the subject is placed in a position where it can be easily amplified:

> From far away came the sound of the bugle, *clarified by*
> *distance and echoing in the woods with a lost hollow tone.*
> Carson McCullers, *Reflections in a Golden Eye*, 6

> Through distant streets wandered a timekeeper,
> *beating on a gong the hours as they fled.*
> John Hersey, *A Single Pebble*, 181

> Beneath him was the River Tweed, *a great wide sweep of*
> *placid silver, tinted by the low saffron smudge of autumn sunset.*
> Down the slope of the northern Scottish bank tumbled the
> town of Tweedside, *its tiled roofs a crazy quilt of pink and yel-*
> *low, masking the maze of cobbled streets.*
> A. J. Cronin, *The Keys of the Kingdom*, 1

Inversions to aid cohesion

Adverbial openers can also assist another helpful function of the inversion in general–its use to rearrange ideas for greater cohesion. The passage below puts the adverbial units of its two sentences nearest each other for a continuity possible only because of the inversion in the second sentence:

> Light fell *through the colors of the stained glass beyond the altar.*
> *Through the windows ajar on the side aisle came* the sweetness
> of blossom, of bruised grass, of river mud.
> Robert Penn Warren, *Flood*, 78

A different kind of inversion, a possessive pronoun as the opening of the second sentence, helps to link the sentence closely to what immediately precedes:

> The author was guided by his faith in firsthand observation and contact with actual sites, and he expected his readers to follow his example. *His was a book* which never was intended to reside in a library, but rather to remain in the pockets of travelers.
> Eunice D. Howe, *Andrea Palladio*, 46

Inversions for a literary effect

These deliberate rearrangements, with syntax altered for clearer modification or for cohesion, often include use of the passive verb, as has been seen earlier. But the inversion's unique contribution to syntax as style often resides slightly apart from this, in the way an inversion may seem to show itself off. True, most of the inversions so far might have slipped past us in context without registering as unusual syntax. Some inversions, however, have a decidedly literary turn. When the context wants this kind of effect, these inversions can offer a stylistic flair that no other grammatical device is so well equipped to provide. Some examples:

> They came out on a bare hilltop *where stood the dark figure* of the ruined windmill.
> D. H. Lawrence, *Sons and Lovers*, 327

> An ecstasy of flight *made radiant his eyes* and *wild his breath* and *tremulous and wild and radiant his windswept limbs*.
> James Joyce, *A Portrait of the Artist as a Young Man*, 169

> But *go you down*, past the Quincunx, Amaryllis, as you wind your long way home, and you might see a newly varnished punt, looking bright upon the water of the lake.
> T. H. White, *Mistress Masham's Repose*, 255

The more dramatic inversions often direct particular attention to the out-of-place, front-shifted element, respectively in the following examples an appositive noun cluster and a string of adjectives:

> *A woman once of some height,* she is bent small, and the lingering strands of black look dirty in her white hair.
>   John Updike, *Rabbit, Run,* 111

> *Tall, powerful, barefoot, graceful, soundless,* Missouri Fever was like a supple black cat as she paraded serenely about the kitchen, the casual flow of her walk beautifully sensuous and haughty.
>   Truman Capote, *Other Voices, Other Rooms,* 54

The success of the inversions above lies in the peculiar skill with which the author weaves the rest of the sentence into an elaboration of the front-shifted element. Semantically, such sentences sometimes assume an almost circular pattern, with the end of the sentence suggesting an image closely related to the one at the very beginning. Additional illustration is seen below. Here the inverted elements have been lifted from the predicate. The first sentence opens with an adverb and verb, and the second with the direct object:

> *Fantastically whirled* the professionals, a young man in sleek evening-clothes and a slim mad girl in emerald silk, with amber hair flung up as jaggedly as flames.
>   Sinclair Lewis, *Babbitt,* 144

> *Saccharine melodies* she played, from memory and in the current mode, that you might hear on any vaudeville stage, and with a shallow skill, a feeling for their oversweet nuances.
>   William Faulkner, *Sartoris,* 194

The ultimate effect of the more striking inversions is to call attention, not to any sense unit within the sentence, but to the self-conscious style itself. What came to be known as the TIME style of some years ago has often been parodied, and rightly so:

> *Complained he* to Kennedy: "You are being extremely unfair..."

I feel—and the anxiety is still vivid to me—that I might easily have failed before I began.

V. S. Naipaul

The rats moved in the shape of a mob, a herding mass, with rat trying foolishly to pass rat, some not passing, some falling back, some climbing past the others.

Robert Sullivan

The crowd was in the cafes and the dancers came in, too, and sat, their tight-wound white legs under the tables, shaking the water from their belled caps, and spreading their red and purple jackets over the chairs to dry. It was raining hard outside.

Ernest Hemingway

CHAPTER NINE

Free Modifiers: Branching Sentences

> The stream of sound is not continuous, but is produced
> and interpreted (though seldom consciously) as a series
> of separated word-groups.... It is segmented into minor
> syntactical units, each of which has superimposed upon
> it a pattern of stress and intonation.
>
> Ian Gordon, *The Movement of English Prose*, 19, 21

Words flow in clustered, continuous, patterned segments. In speech, segments are indicated by pitch, stress, juncture. In writing, they are indicated by arrangement of words in phrase patterns and by punctuation. Speakers and readers pause at punctuation marks and observe word-groups set off by commas, dashes, semicolons, colons, parentheses. Rather than focusing on one word at a time, we read by making sense of segmented patterns. Segmentation is a basic resource of English syntax, often achieved by *nonrestrictive,* or *free, modifiers.*

Free modifiers are set off from a base clause, usually by commas or dashes. Free branches may modify the entire base clause or a single word. Begin with a base clause:

I watched him warily.
base clause

Then attach a free modifier in front, creating a *left-branching* sentence:

Sensing a possible rival,　　I watched him warily.
left branch　　　　　　**base clause**

Or, place a free modifier at the end of the base clause, an arrangement that yields a *right-branching* sentence:

> I watched him warily,   wondering who he was.
> **base clause**   **right branch**

Then, a base clause with both left and right branches:

> Sensing a possible rival, I watched him warily, wondering who he was.
> **left branch**   **base clause**   **right branch**

And that is how Ralph Ellison wrote the sentence, a base clause with branches left and right:

> Sensing a possible rival, I watched him warily, wondering who he was.
> *Invisible Man,* 315

The sequence surely makes a difference. With both branches at the left, the meaning changes since the sequence of actions changes:

> Sensing a possible rival,
> wondering who he was,   I watched him warily.
> **left branches**   **base clause**

Both free modifiers could be inserted as *mid-branches*, interrupting the base clause. This upsets the rhythm and mixes up the intended sequence of actions:

> I,   sensing a possible rival,   watched him warily.
> **base clause**   wondering who he was,   **base clause**
>   **mid-branches**

Finally, placing both free modifiers at the end of the sentence makes ambiguous *who* is sensing a possible rival:

> I watched him warily,   sensing a possible rival,
> **base clause**   wondering who he was.
>   **right branches**

If there is a chance for confusion, as is the case with participial phrases, a branch should be kept near the noun phrase it refers to. Other kinds of free modifiers are more flexible in the positions they may occupy.

Below this complicated but clear sentence uses branches (here in italics) both left and right. It is not a sentence to imitate in its entirety, but it serves to show the many syntactic structures and details that can be crammed into free modifiers, branching to the left and right from a short base clause:

> *During the slow journey from Winton,* she had gazed out of the win-
> *seated opposite me in the*
> *third-class compartment, wearing a shabby grey dress pinned with*
> *a large cairngorm brooch, a thin necklet of fur, and a black-winged*
> *hat which drooped over her ear,* she had gazed out of the win-
> dow, *her head to one side, her lips moving as she maintained a*
> *scient yet emotional conversation with herself, from time to time*
> *touching the corner of her eye with her handkerchief as though*
> *removing a fly.*
>
> A. J. Cronin, *The Green Years*, 3

Here is a sketch of the branches and base:

> *During the slow journey from Winton*
> *seated opposite me in the...compartment*
> *wearing a shabby...dress...fur...hat...*
> **left branches**

she had gazed out of the window
base clause

her head to one side
her lips moving as she maintained...
from time to time touching her eye...
right branches

These branching modifiers consist of prepositional phrases, past and present participial phrases, dependent clauses, and nominative absolutes. The syntactic sketch above shows that the branches might be moved or entirely lopped off without destroying the syntactic completeness of the sentence. Cronin's sentence is more than a syntactic feat. The subtlety of its content, the choice and arrangement of details, the rhythms the author is able to create with modifiers of this type, the particular observations the author saves for the last two branches—perhaps it all was occasioned by the sheer availability and roominess of the language's syntactic resources.

Left-branching Sentences

Cronin's long sentence is easy to decode, and the reader does not get lost in its left branches while searching for the subject of the entire sentence. In many successful left-branching sentences, there is a temporal or logical development of the expressed idea that invites the delayed disclosure of the left-branching arrangement. The material that comes first seems natural and appropriate, and the anticipated material that concludes the sentence makes an almost inevitable point:

> *So that, at the age of thirty-four, after she had been given three children and had one taken away, when she had a futile husband and had been fated a young and demanding lover, when for the first time she could not wait for the future to be revealed but had to make it for herself,* she was as startled by her own agency as an infant who waves a clenched fist and strikes itself upon the eye.
>
> Monica Ali, *Brick Lane*, 4

> *Now that the sad cycle of boom and bust has been tamed, now that many Americans have the means as well as the wish to diffuse prosperity and amenities throughout the community,* the challenges to public policy have taken a new turn.
>
> Robert Lekachman, *The Age of Keynes*, 4

> *The afternoon after the night at the tavern, while O's were being taken out of books and out of signs, so that the cw jumped over the mn, and the dish ran away with the spn, and the clockshop became a clckshp, the toymaker a tymaker,* Black issued new searching orders.
>
> James Thurber, *The Wonderful O*, 9-10

The following left-branching sentence describes the dependence on *each other and outsiders* by a group of senior citizens:

> *Lacking assurance that their way of life would continue, finding no consolation that a God would remember their name, unable to draw upon their own body for evidence of continuing vitality,* they turned to each other and outsiders to serve as willing or unwilling witness to their drama of existence.
>
> Barbara Myerhoff, *Number Our Days*, 144

Very long left branches, if well-crafted, may still be readable. In the first example, the dashes and the parallelism help:

> *With the exception of a three-act sex farce I composed when I was*
> *twelve—the action of which occurred aboard an ocean liner, the*
> *characters of which were, for the most part, English gentry, and*
> *the title of which was, for some reason that escapes me now,*
> *Aliqueen—*with the exception of that, *The Zoo Story* (1958),
> *The Death of Bessie Smith* and *The Sandbox* (both 1959), are
> my first three plays.
>   Edward Albee, *The Zoo Story*, 7

The next example pushes the length of its left branch to its limits:

> *If we were to conceive of Hemingway offering us his heroic choice*
> *and his disenchantment with the hollow idealism of modern life*
> *in a language which was sufficient to propagate a doctrine but no*
> *more than that, which failed to be its own quintessential comment*
> *on the modern world and which exposed us to the crude manipula-*
> *tions of ideology without those areas of retirement and indecision*
> *and even discordance which are so perfectly re-created for us in*
> *the subtle tones and rhythms of Hemingway's best writing—*this
> would approximate Mailer's situation as a novelist.
>   Diana Trilling, *Claremont Essays*, 201

In the first sentence below, difficulty occurs in a front-heavy clause that opens the second and much the larger half of a compound sentence. The second example has one main clause, to which has been grafted an unusually awkward left branch:

> They admired the poetry of previous generations, very
> rightly, for the taste it left in the head, and, *failing to realize*
> *that the process of putting such a taste into a reader's head*
> *involves a great deal of work which does not feel like a taste in*
> *the head while it is being done, attempting, therefore, to conceive*
> *a taste in the head and put it straight on to their paper,* they
> produced tastes in the head which were in fact blurred,
> complacent, and unpleasing.
>   William Empson, *Seven Types of Ambiguity*, 17

So, when family-life in Oak Park in that spring of 1909, conspired
against the freedom to which I had come to feel every soul entitled
and I had no choice would I keep my self-respect, but go out,
a voluntary exile, into the uncharted and unknown deprived of
legal protection to get my back against the wall and live, if
I could, an unconventional life–then I turned to the hill in
the Valley as my Grandfather before me had turned into
America–as a hope and haven–forgetful for the time
being of grandfather's "Isaiah."
      Frank Lloyd Wright, *Frank Lloyd Wright*, 173

These examples show the disadvantage of the left-branching sentence
compared to the *cumulative* or right-branching sentence. There are
many difficulties within the front-heavy section that make for problems wherever the section was placed. Nevertheless, reading is rarely
impaired by the reader's coming first to the subject of a given sentence
and then to its elaboration–by the reader's knowing, literally, *what* the
author is talking about. When there is no reason for constructing left-
branching sentences, then a good way to begin is with the subject and
its main clause. Short left branches are easy to write and are useful;
long left branches are a challenge.

Mid-branching sentences

The term mid-branching describes a sentence that is interrupted mid-
stream by an insertion of parenthetical, or at least syntactically extrane-
ous, material serving to postpone the grammatical conclusion of the
sentence. In the two examples below, the mid-branch is set off by dashes:

I feel–and the anxiety is still vivid to me–that I might
easily have failed before I began.
      V. S. Naipaul, *Literary Occasions*, 195

As she often says to herself–though never aloud, for she
knows how unpleasant it would sound–why shouldn't
she look out for herself? Nobody else will.
      Alison Lurie, *Foreign Affairs*, 5

In some mid-branching sentences, the delayed conclusion creates
a kind of suspense, but more often the device serves to allow a variety
of expansive materials:

> Taking out my pen, I did, *in blue, on a bare patch between
> two seraphic swirls of lipstick*, dare set my name.
> John Updike, *Assorted Prose*, 221

Mid-branching sentences like the one above, interrupted between the
auxiliary verb and the main verb (*did...dare set*), are rare. Usually the
interruption occurs between the subject and the predicate. Indeed, the
more extreme forms may seem almost perverse in the demands they
make on the reader, who must hold in mind the necessary grammatical parts until completed by others at the end of the sentence, and at
the same time must attempt to assimilate the internal elaboration. The
next example consists of a kernel as base clause, interrupted by free
modifiers in the middle of an awkward construction:

> Anne, *sticking entertainment-tax stamps on to green and orange
> tickets, listening to her mother's rich lazy ironical voice*, frowned.
> Christopher Isherwood, *The Memorial*, 11

In a longer sentence, dashes can provide visual clarification:

> Obviously the experiences of Negroes–slavery, the grueling
> and continuing fight for full citizenship since emancipation,
> the stigma of color, the enforced alienation which constantly
> knifes into our national identification with our country–
> have not been those of white Americans.
> Ralph Ellison, *Shadow and Act*, 24

Unlike left-branching and right-branching sentences, which place
elaboration in one direction from the essential grammatical base, the
mid-branching sentence begins and ends with grammatically relevant
materials and gathers the modifiers internally. The arrangement can be
extremely useful. For instance, if a mid-branching sentence begins with
the subject and is then arrested by some inserted elaboration, the
motion of thought is accelerated toward those anticipated elements

that will complete the idea whose subject has been disclosed. When these appear, the thought is quickly redirected toward the subject in order to bring the entire idea, elaboration included, into focus. The effect is to compress the sentence unit from both ends, to provide a useful tightening of expression appropriate to a highly controlled, logically organized style.

The mid-branching sentence is organized before the modification is begun. It suggests that its author has begun to say what is intended, has paused to elaborate *in advance* as necessary, and has then added the required grammatical conclusion, all without the need of a cumulative afterthought:

> The bronze-trimmed doors flashed in and out, and all these little bodies, *redolent of milk and pee, blessed heads of all hues, shapes, the promise of the world to come, in the eyes of the benevolent Herzog, its future good and evil*, hurried in and out.
> Saul Bellow, *Herzog*, 334

Moving the elaboration to the end creates a cumulative sentence, although here there is a loss of rhythm and balance:

> The bronze-trimmed glass doors flashed in and out, and all these little bodies hurried in and out, *redolent of milk and pee, blessed heads of all hues, the promise of the world to come, in the eyes of the benevolent Herzog, its future good and evil*.

Mid-branching sentences can be expanded internally with repeated identical interruptive structures. The modification position is often filled by appositive noun or adjective clusters. Here we see a pair of appositive nouns, each with added details:

> Of course it was a hell of a nerve for an instructor with so little experience in a college, *an Easterner not long in the West, until recently a stranger to most of his colleagues*, to ask them to elect *him* head of department.
> Bernard Malamud, *A New Life*, 289

In this mid-branching sentence, an appositive phrase set off by dashes follows the subject, and the appositive in turn is followed by a relative clause before the arrival of the predicate verb "came prepared":

> Thousands of mothers, fathers, grandparents, students, assembly-line workers and CEOs–*Americans of all ages, races, and walks of life–who yearned to talk about their personal dreams and their concerns for our nation*, came prepared with questions, speeches and sometimes requests for help.
> Hillary Rodham Clinton, *Living History*, 530

The appositives below, set off by dashes, form an effective mid-branch, as three parallel prepositional phrases carry significant details:

> A young man from a small provincial town–*a man without independent wealth, without powerful family connections, and without a university education*–moves to London in the late 1580's and, in a remarkably short time, becomes the greatest playwright not of his age alone but of all time.
> Stephen Greenblatt, *Will in the World*, 11

Parentheses may also be used to set off prepositional phrases, appositives, or other structures when they function essentially as free modifiers:

> When, in *Changing Places* an untenured professor plays this game with important colleagues and gets caught up in the desire to win, he is indeed humiliated by revealing that he has not read key primary texts in his field and he must ultimately leave his job (for a smaller school in Canada) to escape ridicule and a sense that he might be a fraud. Reading PMLA, I confess to feeling on occasion that I might be in a similar game. I think of myself as pretty well informed, but I am often reading (or not really reading, of course) about authors I do not know and have sometimes not heard of; presented to me in terminology (jargon?) I often do not fully understand.
> Charles S. Adams, "The Real Small World(s)," 161

> The 5-foot-2-inch dynamo ("I act tall," she says) has piloted her career with dazzling audacity.
> Anne Stockwell, "Salma Hayek," 33

Parentheses and dashes setting off the free modifiers give more freedom for punctuation within the free modifiers themselves, as demonstrated by the question mark after *jargon?* and the quotation marks around *"I act tall."*

Verb clusters, common sources of expansion, are usually set off by commas, especially where a participle functions as an appositive adjective:

> His glasses are thick, *magnifying*, and his eyes, *puffed and swimming*, seem not to miss a thing.
> Lorrie Moore, *Birds of America*, 51

> The Grandmother, *muffled* down in the back seat in the corner of the old carryall, in her worn sealskin pelisse, *showing* coffee-brown at the edges, and her eyes closed, her hands waving together, had been occupied once more in losing a son, and, as ever, to a girl and a family of which she could not altogether approve.
> Katharine Anne Porter, *Leaning Tower and Other Stories*, 44

Participles are not the only verbal structures found in this internal position, as seen above in the two absolute constructions, *her eyes closed, her hands waving together*, included as sentence modifiers in the elaborative section. In the example above, the final sixteen words of the sentence—"and, as ever, to a girl and a family of which she could not altogether approve"—although grammatically related to the base sentence, are not actually grammatically essential. We have seen the mid-branching sentence as concluding usually with grammatically necessary parts, but in practice the mid-branching sentence often receives additional expansion after the base clause. The following mid-branching sentences are carried beyond grammatical sufficiency by, respectively, a compound predicate and a subordinate clause:

> This audience, though often baffled by difficulties in his thought and manner, as is apparent from the eagerness with which it buys books expounding the poems, has no doubt of his poetic greatness, *and feels a desire to understand more fully both what he says and why he says it the way he does.*
> Helen Gardner, *The Art of T. S. Eliot*, 1

The lack of team spirit alone, the fact that the Brodie set preferred golf to hockey or netball if they preferred any-thing at all, were enough to set them apart, *even if they had not dented in the crowns of their hats and tilted them backwards or forwards.*
    Muriel Spark, *The Prime of Miss Jean Brodie*, 36

Mid-branches often figure in inversions of one sort or another, tending to suspend the subject and thus to postpone logical completion until late in the sentence. Examples here are of an *it*-inversion and a left-branching sentence with front-shifted adverbial modifiers, both with internal, mid-branching interruptions designated by italics:

It is quite natural and inevitable, then, and only superficially paradoxical, that the neoclassic age, *instead of yielding a harvest of mythological poems*, is almost completely barren, at least of good ones.
    Douglas Bush, *Mythology and the Romantic Tradition in English Poetry*, 5

Here at the far end of the hall, through windows exteriorly screened against vandalism, light from outdoors entered the school and, *unable to spread in the viscid, varnished atmosphere*, remained captured, like water in oil, above the entrance.
    John Updike, *The Centaur*, 10

The highly suspensive style of William Faulkner withholds reso-lutions, from that of oxymoronic verbal couplings to the overall psy-chological theme; the mid-branching sentence is especially appropriate to enforce and amplify this pervasive, calculated suspensiveness. Many of Faulkner's sentences make use of mid-branches that run to a page or more. These long ones, as well as those of moderate length, are often juxtaposed with very short sentences. Below are some of his shorter mid-branching sentences. The first mid-branch is a nominative absolute, the second a long clause that is the object of a preposition:

So he didn't move. He lay with his eyes closed, *his breathing gentle and peaceful*, and heard them one by one leave the tent.
    William Faulkner, *Delta Autumn*, 725

Because it was his land, although he had never owned a
foot of it. He had never wanted to, *not even after he saw plain
its ultimate doom, watching it retreat year by year before the
onslaught of axe and saw and log-lines and then dynamite and
tractor plows*, because it belonged to no man. It belonged
to all; they had only to use it well, humbly and with pride.
William Faulkner, *Delta Autumn*, 724

A noun appositive is elaborately expanded in Faulkner's long sentence:

And no tears, *no bereavement this time too, whether or not it was
because she had no time to mourn since she ran the store herself
now until she found a buyer for it, not keeping it open but carrying
the keys to it in her apron pocket*, hailed from the kitchen or the
garden or even from the field.
William Faulkner, *Absalom, Absalom!*, 186

Right-branching (cumulative) sentences

The distinguishing feature of the *right-branching*, or *cumulative*, sentence is the accumulation of material after the base clause is grammatically complete. Left-branching material in awkward sentences can
often be satisfactorily regrouped in a cumulative arrangement at the
end of a sentence.

In the following examples of right-branching noun and adjective
additions, their *appositive* characteristics usually redefine or elaborate
the basic idea, adding descriptive rather than narrative materials. Only
the headwords of each right branch are italicized:

Nothing would remain at last except the name itself, *itself
a legend* beautiful and talismanic, *a sound* of magic and of
recollection, *a phrase* of music and of strangeness—*Raintree
County*.
Ross Lockridge, Jr., *Raintree County*, 54-55

The air was thin and clear, *stringent* with wood smoke and
the tang of fallen apples, *sharp* with the hint of early frost.
A. J. Cronin, *The Keys of the Kingdom*, 3

A vigorous narrative impact is conveyed by verb phrases, such as present participles with a quality of an ongoing feeling or process:

> Their trim boots prattled as they stood on the steps of the colonnade, *talking* quietly and gaily, *glancing* at the clouds, *holding* their umbrellas at cunning angles against the few last raindrops, *closing* them again, *holding* their skirts demurely.
> James Joyce, *A Portrait of the Artist as a Young Man*, 216

> She had left him, really, *packing* up suddenly in a cold quiet fury, *stabbing* him with her elbows when he tried to get his arms around her, now again *cutting* him to the bone with a short sentence expelled through her clenched teeth.
> Katharine Anne Porter, *Flowering Judas and Other Stories*, 95-96

Present participles join with predicate verbs to depict alternately the rats moving *in the shape of a mob* and the three human beings standing back, frozen and quiet. In the third and fourth sentences, the action is incorporated in right branching free modifiers (shown in italics):

> I was nodding, and looking down at my feet. I was trying to simultaneously count the rats and stand still and stay out of the rats' way. The rats moved in the shape of a mob, *a herding mass, with rat trying feverishly to pass rat, some not passing, some falling back, some climbing past the others*. Matt and Dave and I gathered close together, *as if we were about to be burned at a stake*, and we watched in panic-stricken amazement, *deciding instinctively, I think, that it was better to stand very still than to run.*
> Robert Sullivan, *Rats*, 57

Below, the ideas expressed earlier in the sentence are developed in more detail in a right-branching series of prepositional phrases with clauses as their objects:

> This house, itself a chaotic museum of its master's lifetime of inventions, was, it seemed to them, the perfect manifestation of Picasso's self-containment, *of the way he demonstrated the complete autogenesis of the creative act, of the way painting comes from Painting, of the way Midas never had to leave his palace to turn everything to gold.*
> Rosalind E. Krauss, *The Optical Unconscious*, 198

Added for either descriptive or narrative purposes, or both, the nominative absolute is prevalent in cumulative sentences and is the chief form of expansion in the next examples. Because of its unique grammatical independence from the base sentence, the absolute construction is often described as a sentence modifier:

> He went to speak to Mrs. Bean, tiny among the pillows, *her small toothless mouth open like an "O," her skin stretched thin and white over her bones, her huge eye-sockets and eyes in a fixed, infant-like stare, and her sparse white hair short and straggling over her brow.*
> Muriel Spark, *Memento Mori*, 173

> They finally crossed the street at a cautious pace, *the colors of the street lights brighter as darkness descended, a stereo store blaring music from two huge, bleating speakers.*
> Helena María Viramontes, "The Cariboo Cafe," 63

Authors occasionally ignore a consistent pattern or smoothness of texture to take into account other special demands. Sentence additions also at times spread out in several directions rather than narrowing down from an initial idea, each expansion deflected further from the base sentence rather than directed back toward it as an additional elaboration:

> By summer term, the girls' favourite hours were spent unbrainfully in the gymnasium, *swinging about on parallel bars or climbing ropes up to the ceiling, all competing with agile Eunice to heave themselves up by hands, knees, and feet like monkeys climbing a tropical creeper, while the gym teacher, a thin grey-haired little wire, showed them what to do and shouted each order in a broad Scots accent interspersed by her short cough, on account of which she was later sent to a sanatorium in Switzerland.*
> Muriel Spark, *The Prime of Miss Jean Brodie*, 103

> Not bad, *considering that I didn't have an equivalent degree in the field; had never taught at the university level; didn't have the slightest clue how to put together a syllabus or actually "teach"; could unearth very little literature on the course topic that was appropriate for the classroom—and didn't have a clue about the special challenges I'd face in teaching a student body consisting mostly of international students.*
> Mitchell Friedman, "Among Our Key People," 6

This is not to suggest that these last sentences are not proper *cumulatives* although an alternate designation for the kind of syntactic arrangement we have been examining, the *loose* sentence, may seem more appropriate, especially for the last example. Nor are these sentences to be dismissed as inferior prose. It is this type of ultraloose cumulative in which Faulkner delights, for instance, and they are well used elsewhere for various special effects. The only tenable reservation concerning this type of *loose* sentence is that it seems best in fiction or informal prose. Sentences that appear loose are often highly contrived, with free modifiers at beginnings, middles, and ends.

Loose sentences can serve well. Controlled sentences with a variety of free modifiers, especially well-organized cumulative structures, can be called upon when complex, logical development is needed.

Good prose rhythm can be achieved by the controlled cumulative sentence, marked by regularity and balance but not calling attention to itself. When used in nonfiction, right branches are often short and limited to one or two. The opening of the sentence may be brief or include short left or mid branches. Often the right branch consists of one or more appositives containing significant details.

Many cumulative sentences in fiction, although neatly patterned, nevertheless have a rambling and elusive rhythm, generated by the very fact of accumulation and capable of being sustained over a long passage. Here the author, working in his distinctive style, relies on the cumulative sentence to stay controlled and artful while sounding perfectly natural and at ease:

> The covered seats of the bull-ring had been crowded with people sitting out of the rain watching the concourse of Basque and Navarrais dancers and singers, and afterward the Val Carlos dancers in their costumes danced down the street in the rain, *the drums sounding hollow and damp, and the chiefs of the bands riding ahead on their big, heavy-footed horses, their costumes wet, the horses' coats wet in the rain.* The crowd was in the cafes and the dancers came in, too, and sat, *their tight-wound white legs under the tables, shaking the water from their belled caps, and spreading their red and purple jackets over the chairs to dry.* It was raining hard outside.
>
> Ernest Hemingway, *The Sun Also Rises*, 170-171

The preceding examples show some of the variety possible with the right-branching sentence, and demonstrate its value in several kinds of prose. The logic of addition, the natural and effortless accumulation that is its definitive feature and its chief recommendation, makes it useful for those specialized prose effects known as *syntactic symbolism* (chapter 14). Much more broadly, the cumulative sentence is a basic tool of professional writers in today's fiction.

Free modifiers working together

In both fiction and nonfiction, free modifiers of all three kinds fit naturally together, in a single sentence or in a sequence of sentences. In the example below, from a novel, in the first sentence an adverbial left branch and a mid-branch that is a noun appositive are set off by dashes. In the sentence that follows, a right branch noun appositive also is punctuated by dashes:

> On the way home, the blue car with the Silver family inside –
> a car not so much like an egg as like a nest equipped with
> seats – runs into bad weather. Wind and rain lash the car, and
> Stella's mother sings "La Cucaracha" and "Frère Jacques"
> to keep their spirits up, but Stella wishes they were home
> sitting on the worn red rug singing while Mama played
> the piano – or even just played her own music – Chopin
> and Mozart.
>   Sena Jeter Naslund, *Four Spirits*, 11

The next example is from a science journal. The italicized segments are, in order, a left branch, a right branch, and finally a mid-branch:

> *Before the first ship sailed into the Galapagos archipelago in 1535,*
> it was home to at least 14 distinct populations of giant tor-
> toise (*Geochelone nigra*), *isolated from each other on different*
> *islands or on volcanoes separated by impassable lava flows.* But
> heavy exploitation at the hands of eighteenth- and nine-
> teenth-century whalers, *along with competition from introduced*

animals such as goats, pigs and rats, caused four of these subspecies to go extinct and has earned the remaining eleven a place on the World Conservation Union's list of threatened species.

Henry Nicholls, "One of a Kind," 498

The variety in length and arrangement of sentences with free modifiers helps them to combine well and contribute to texture and density of meaning. Neatly constructed, with short segments or long, such sentences find a place in almost any kind of prose.

There's nothing there, nothing contained in nothing. Nothing at all.
T. Coraghessan Boyle

They drove up the coast, the incomparable coast, they visited gardens, and climbed Table Mountain and drove through vineyards.
Doris Lessing

The desire to move on, to metamorphose—or perhaps it is a talent for being contemporary—was given to me as life's inevitable and rightful condition. To keep becoming, always to stay involved in transition.
Arthur Miller

CHAPTER TEN

The Appositive

Lou introduced me to Jack Dempsey, the great boxer.
Bob Dylan, *Chronicles*, 3

I N Bob Dylan's sentence, *the great boxer* is an appositive, one of the most versatile syntactic structures, useful in almost every kind of writing to rename or add information, details, opinion, drama, texture in a natural and easy way. The most common appositive is a noun phrase that closely follows another noun phrase and renames it. This chapter considers the term more widely as any part of speech that renames an antecedent and will substitute for it. Also discussed are *appositive adjectives*, modifiers of a noun that are usually placed after it, but do not substitute for the antecedent.

Noun phrases as appositives appear in many different positions in the sentence:

> Carmen, *the tragic story of a fascinating bohemian*, continues to lure artists and audiences alike since its original appearance in Prosper Mérimée's novella of 1845.
> Evelyn Gould, *The Fate of Carmen*, 1

> Over the last decade William Langewiesche has been fascinated by the modern-day frontier—*those wild places that stubbornly defy all efforts of control.*
> Nathaniel Philbrick, "Waterworld," 5

But there was another element in the painting, *the equilibrium of the pulley itself, lifting the immense stone pillar on a steel thread, as if the stone were a feather.*
    May Sarton, *Writings on Writing*, 21

There's nothing there, *nothing contained in nothing. Nothing at all.*
    T. Coraghessan Boyle, *Stories*, 691

In these examples above, the appositives are free modifiers, sometimes called loose or nonrestrictive appositives, set off from the rest of the sentence usually by commas or dashes but sometimes by parentheses or at the end of a sentence by a colon. Another occasional mode of punctuation is to isolate an appositive as a sentence fragment, as in Boyle's sentence above.

Below, *rituals* is the antecedent for a series of appositives punctuated as fragments, four free modifiers each consisting of a fairly long noun phrase that begins with a gerund (italicized):

A seductive aspect of gardening is how many rituals it requires. *Uncovering* the garden in the spring, for example. *Replacing* a broken-down metal gate with a burly wooden one. *Transplanting* rhododendrons to a sunnier spot. *Moving* the holly bushes to the side of the garage, to hide them from the deer, who nonetheless find and eat them, prickles and all.
    Diane Ackerman, *Cultivating Delight*, 1

In contrast to the free-modifying appositive, is the *close* or *restrictive* or *bound* appositive noun phrase, not set off by punctuation –expressions such as *the river Thames, the composer Chopin, the volcano Popcatepetl, Frederick the Great, my Aunt Jane.* The close appositive functions with its principal as a single syntactic unit, as in this striking first sentence of a novel:

Ten days after the war ended, my sister Laura drove a car off a bridge.
    Margaret Atwood, *The Blind Assassin*, 1

The free-modifying appositive, not the bound appositive, serves best for renaming, defining, exemplifying, clarifying, adding facts or details, comparing, contrasting, emphasizing key words, and enlarging or narrowing the focus. *Apposition* is a matter of word placement. As the root of the word indicates, apposition is juxtaposition, placing one thing beside or near another. Placement is what distinguishes the *appositive adjective*. Adjectives are given space adjacent to the modified noun phrase, and are set off by commas or other punctuation. Often appositive adjectives follow a noun appositive, come in pairs or triplets, and are accompanied by adverbs:

> Baby Bertie, the younger sister, *beautiful and innocent but inevitably exploitable*, never is able to forget her fate.
> Yaffa Draznin, *My Other Self*, 35

Appositive as a label is in contrast to the term *attributive*, which refers to closely modifying adjectives that precede the noun:

> The *slim, taut* body and *alert leonine* head unite the *natural and supernatural* forces she represents.
> Lorna Price, *Masterpieces from the Los Angeles County Museum of Art Collection*, 26

Appositives as reiteration

In one of its highly useful forms, the appositive is simply a *reiteration* of the principal. Repetition gives a special emphasis to the repeated word and its modifiers, or it may enable the writer to take a fresh start, with a handy new peg on which to hang additional details. The reiterated appositive is at home in expository prose, fiction, or memoir:

> The sound of it belongs to *another era, the era of radio plays,* when audiences relied on exposition and the externalization of a character's inner drama to keep the story moving.
> Hilton Als, "The Theatre," 88

> The Antigua that I knew, *the Antigua in which I grew up*, is not the Antigua you, a tourist, would see now.
> Jamaica Kincaid, *A Small Place*, 23

His *rage* passes description—*the sort of rage* that is only seen when rich folk that have more than they can enjoy suddenly lose something that they have long had but have never before used or wanted.
    J. R. R. Tolkien, *The Hobbit*, 208

And at those times there would come *a hush*—
a hush quivered by voiceless words.
    Carson McCullers, *The Member of the Wedding*, 149

They drove up *the coast, the incomparable coast*, they visited gardens, and climbed Table Mountain and drove through vineyards.
    Doris Lessing, *The Grandmothers*, 310

Here is *a jug, a beautiful black milk jug*—the dairyman left it years ago when it was cheaper to make your own ice-cream.
    F. Scott Fitzgerald, *The Crack-Up*, 61

All of the foregoing are noun phrase appositives, but the device of repetition is used also with other parts of speech. Below, again from Fitzgerald, the word *open*, a predicate adjective in a nominative absolute, serves as the principal and is twice repeated in an appositive:

We loved the temperate shapes of Nassau Hall's old brick, and the way it seems still a tribunal of early American ideals, the elm walks and meadows, the college windows *open* to the spring—*open, open* to everything in life—for a minute.
    The Crack-Up, 48

In the next example, two appositives repeat the principal, the participle *known* and the noun *secret*:

People feel that if the terrible event is *known, fully known*, down to the least detail of who stood where, what this one wore, and what the other one thought, that day in Dallas will then deliver its *secret, the secret* that everyone believes it has, must have.
    James Dickey, *Spinning the Crystal Ball*, 2

In this 110-word sentence that opens a short story, the repeated appositives *late* and *a driver* carry vital and poignant modifiers:

> My daughter is walking along the roadside late at night—too late, really, for a seventeen-year-old to be out alone even in a town as safe as this—and it is raining, the first rain of the season, the streets slick with a fine immiscible glaze of water and petrochemicals so that even a driver in full possession of her faculties, a driver who hasn't consumed two apple martinis and three glasses of Hitching Post pinot noir before she gets behind the wheel of the car, will have trouble keeping the thing off the sidewalk and out of the gutters, the shrubbery, *the highway median*, for Christ's sake.... But that's not really what I want to talk about, or not yet, anyway.
>
> T. Coraghessan Boyle, "Chicxulub," 133

The first appositive is elaborated to provide information about the central character—her age, the time, the place, the scene. The second grips the reader with its devastating detail and heart-rending exclamation that intimates what is to come.

Appositives as synonym—at end of sentence

Most often the appositive is a *synonym*, not a repetition of the antecedent. Sometimes the appositive is a more important word semantically. The base clause may have as its subject a relatively empty word such as "it" or another pronoun, and the semantic subject of the sentence is developed in an appositive, postponed often to final position in the sentence, permitting generous expansion without interrupting or delaying the basic clause structure:

> He lumbered into the city room, *a big guy in his middle twenties, wearing a suit too dark for the season, and the disconsolate frown of a hunter who has seen nothing but warblers all day.*
>
> James Thurber, "Newspaperman," January 5, 1952

Here the principal is the pronoun *he*, and the appositive is the noun cluster that has *guy* as its headword. Obviously in this sentence, as in the preceding examples, the appositive does more than rename; it defines and expands, with successive levels of detail making the picture more exact.

The base clause may have relatively little semantic content. Below, it is an equative clause, in which both the subject *theme* and the predicate nominative *that…* are relatively empty words; the appositive carries most of the message:

> The theme is that of all Robin Hood ballads, *the setting of the fair, free, honest forest life against that of the town, the law, and the church.*
> Evelyn Kendrick Wells, *The Ballad Tree*, 21

In both fiction and nonfiction, the appositive at times is in apposition to a principal that leads to subtle revelation, an opening out at the end of a sentence:

> He seemed very nice, *whoever he was.*
> Maggie Alderson, *Pants on Fire*, 5

Double and triple appositives

Repeating a construction often adds additional insights or information. Here two synonymous appositives follow the principal, *redemption*:

> The songs caressed her, and while she tried to hold her mind on the wages of sin, her body trembled for redemption, *salvation, a mysterious rebirth that would simply happen, with no effort on her part.*
> Toni Morrison, *The Bluest Eye*, 62

Three noun phrases are in apposition to the principal, *my own car*:

> Now I drive my own car, *a 1998 Toyota Camry, the best-selling automobile in the United States*, and therefore *the one most often stolen.*
> Sherman Alexie, *The Toughest Indian in the World*, 24

Chains of appositives

Occasionally writers form a chain of principals and appositives, creating a series in which a noun from an appositive phrase becomes the principal for another appositive that itself becomes the principal for yet another appositive. The syntax is particularly appropriate to the subject here:

> It also traces Smithson's fascination with entropy—nature's tendency to increasing disorder—and with the entropic landscape, from the barren apocalyptic horizon found in his 1960's poetry to his choice of *Rozel Point, the site of his most famous work, Spiral Jetty, a dramatic rock coil that extends out into the Great Salt Lake in Utah.*
> Connie Butler, "Robert Smithson," 4

Final appositives, single or multiple, are relatively easy to compose. And the terminal appositive is an important feature of the very useful right-branching or cumulative sentence.

Inverted appositives

Another placement of the appositive, not frequent in the works of professional writers, is at the beginning of the sentence. Initial appositives are difficult to use successfully. An opening appositive needs to be semantically related to the clause that follows, as in the sentences below. One would *not* write, "A lonely boy, Coleridge was born in 1772."

> *A lonely boy*, Coleridge retreated into books—
> he read *The Arabian Nights* at six—and fed his mind
> with adventures so wild and fancies so morbid that
> he often feared the coming of the night.
> Louis Untermeyer, *The Lives of the Poets*, 345

> *One of the greatest poets*, Milton is also one of the least read.
> Untermeyer, 189

And this successful sentence features an elaborate catalog of appositives around the principal *he*, in an arrangement that places the most general item in front of the principal and the others at the end of the base clause:

> *A truly Byronic figure*, he was strikingly handsome and flamboyantly reckless, *an aristocrat who lampooned his class, a physically handicapped and psychologically maimed youth who triumphed over every disadvantage, an audacious rebel who loved liberty and could not refuse a folly, a dreamer courting disaster, an irresistible lover, and an irresponsibly shocking genius.*
> Untermeyer, 383

Like other left branches, an inverted appositive can give force to the subject matter if kept short and related closely to what follows:

> *A persuasive advocate on many levels*, Pat made a convincing case for the university's commitment.
> Mary Livingstone Beebe, "Introduction," 13

An initial appositive opens the following sentence. A neat pattern provides a definition at the end in an appositive preceded by a colon:

> *An update of curator Darrell Frost's 1985 reference book*, the site encompasses more than 5500 species of frogs, toads, salamanders, and caecilians: legless burrowers found in the tropics.
> Mitch Leslie, "Range of Newt and Name of Toad," 1087

Catalogs of appositives are sometimes used successfully in the initial position. Below, the second is less formulaic than the first:

> *Fertility, fecundity, lushness, abundance*–these were the hallmarks of the New World.
> Richard M. Dorson, *American Folklore*, 14

> *Overcommercialization, overly loud commercials, heavily biased program content, secret changes of station ownerships, or neglect of local news, public affairs, religion or agricultural interests*– those are some of the legitimate grounds for opposing the renewal of a broadcaster's three-year license.
> *Consumer Reports*, October 1968, 535

Appositives in the middle of the sentence

Usually punctuated by dashes or parentheses, medial appositives take many shapes:

> Mr. Somervell–*a most delightful man, to whom my debt is great*–was charged with the duty of teaching the stupidest boys the most disregarded thing–*namely, to write mere English.*
> Winston Churchill, *A Roving Commission,* 16

Both a medial appositive and one at the end of the sentence appear in the sentence above. A similar effect is seen in the pair of sentences below, the first with a medial appositive, and the second with one at the end:

> Actually the idea of environmental art–*that of a 'surround' providing us with numerous sensory stimuli*–is not all that new. The concept was well expressed, it could be argued, in the great cathedrals of the Middle Ages–*actual mixed-media works that appealed to the senses via lighting effects, music, art, tactile, spatial, and olfactory stimuli.*
> Grace Glueck, "The Kinetic Eye," 137

Dashes mark off this medial appositive– *orchestra, conductor, audience*– that opens out the sentence to an eloquent conclusion:

> Gehry has described the interior as a type of sanctuary, and I think of the long slice of mankind–orchestra, conductor, audience–brought together here, floating in space, to share an experience, isolated from everything else in the world.
> Esa Pekka Salonen, "Variations and Traditions," 121

Verbs as appositives

Although nouns are most common, other structures and word classes also serve well as appositives. Juxtaposed verbs that are synonymous or subtly different in meaning are seen often and sometimes appear with nominal appositives:

> His temperament is fixed, *set.*
> J. M. Coetzee, *Disgrace,* 3

And now surely these four remaining, the women and
their sons, should say something, *elucidate, make things clear?*
    Doris Lessing, *The Grandmothers*, 9

Between the last paragraph and this, just over two and
a half months have gone by, *elapsed.*
    J. D. Salinger, *Seymour–An Introduction*, 149

And she remembered how, time and again, he had given
away, *"loaned,"* to the first person who asked him the favor,
money or food or things which were desperately needed…
    James Agee, *A Death in the Family*, 44

At the time of their encounter she was odd-jobbing
in Cornwall–*trimming hedges, digging gardens and so on,
traveling from place to place on her motorcycle.*
    Norman R. Baldwin, "Island Cottage," 381

Both the opening and closing of this passage contain verbs as
appositives. In between, a vivid series of nouns is a medial appositive
to the principal *real things*:

My artistic initiation coincides with having been in some
ways enchanted, *put under a spell.* Once when I was seven
years old in Molise, where I was born, I happened to see a
woman painting a landscape in the open air, from life, and
I was so struck by the way she was able to reproduce real
things with her brushes–a donkey passing, a green curtain
being blown out of a window by the wind, the sky, the
trees, and the clouds–that since that day I have never ceased
to have something to do with art, *never stopped thinking
about creating.*
    Gino Marotto, "Uncontrollable Curiosity," 54

Adverbial, adjectival, and prepositional phrases as appositives

The *adverbial phrase*, a common appositive, provides descriptive and
explanatory detail without drawing attention to itself:

The church was not very far away, *four blocks up
Lennox Avenue, on a corner not far from the hospital.*
    James Baldwin, *Go Tell It on the Mountain*, 4

The Grimes family arrived in a body, always a little late,
usually in the middle of Sunday school, which began at
nine o'clock.
Baldwin, 6

Adjectivals, similarly used, attract little notice:

It's cold—*just above freezing* everywhere below the surface
zones.
Clement S. Pepper, "Electronics Put to Sea," 27

Prepositional phrases are frequently used as appositives in constructions of this kind:

Just before Race Rocks, *about 15 miles from the finish,*
Diamond Head blew out a second spinnaker.
Yachting, "This Month in Yachting,"30

She was associated in his mind with flame; *with fiery leaves*
in the autumn, and the fiery sun going down in the evening over
the farthest hill, and with the eternal fires of Hell.
James Baldwin, *Go Tell It on the Mountain,* 152

Appositives can advance the argument. Five prepositional phrases in a
string (two of which include additional prepositional phrases) serve as
multiple appositives to the adverb *everywhere,* making specific the sorts
of places *everywhere* includes:

Although the brands seem to be everywhere—at kids'
concerts, next to them on the couch, on stage with their
heroes, in their on-line chat groups, and on their playing
fields and basketball courts—for a long time one major
unbranded youth frontier remained: a place where young
people gathered, talked, sneaked smokes, made out,
formed opinions and, most maddeningly of all, stood
around looking cool for hours on end. That place is
called school. And clearly, the brands had to get into
the schools.
Naomi Klein, *No Logo,* 87

Clauses as appositives

An entire clause sometimes functions as an appositive:

> Modern houseboats being what they are–*sinfully luxurious*
> *is what they are*–it ought to be enough to run them lazily
> around back rivers and bayous. The last thing anybody
> really needs is a national championship houseboat race.
> Hugh D. Whall, "A House Is Not a Hot Rod," 14

> Frinton has had an appalling press–*it has been called*
> *"the snootiest town in Britain," "Nannie Town-on-the-Sea,"*
> *and "Westminster Abbey-with-Sand."*
> Corin Hughes-Stanton, "Beside the Same Seaside," 20

Enlarging, narrowing and renaming

Sometimes, as in the following sentences, the appositive enlarges or narrows the field set up by the principal, designates particular parts or aspects, or simply renames the principal:

> In Viking times Norwegians had no tables as we know them.
> Men dipped their porridge from a common kettle and ate
> from wooden trays, *often round ones*, which they held on their
> knees wherever they chose to sit.
> Janice S. Stewart, *The Folk Arts of Norway*, 32

> Outpost of Up-Island is Gay Head, with its precipitous,
> colorful clay cliffs rising 150 feet to 200 feet above the
> ocean in a striped array of brilliant color–*red, orange,*
> *yellow and brown.*
> Marcia Wiley, *Yachting*, 58

> The Diz–the Walt Disney Concert Hall–is irresistible.
> Patt Morrison, "Flirting with Urbanismo," 135

Appositives to convey key words and concepts

Especially in descriptive passages, professional writers at times place key words and concepts in the appositive construction. In the first thirty sentences of what he called a "nonfiction novel," the author set the scene, moving gradually toward a particular time and place. When he reached this point, in the last two sentences of the introductory section, the author placed the key words, not in the base clause, but in two appositives. In both instances, the climactic words are in apposition to the relatively empty word *them*:

> At the time not a soul in sleeping Holcomb heard them—*four shotgun blasts* that, all told, ended six human lives. But afterward the townspeople, theretofore sufficiently unfearful of each other to seldom trouble to lock their doors, found fantasy re-creating them over and again—*those somber explosions* that stimulated fires of mistrust in the glare of which many old neighbors viewed each other as strangers.
> Truman Capote, *In Cold Blood*, 5

As a dramatic device, the appositive enables a writer to delay until the end of a sentence or passage its most momentous words, providing the space also to hone them and add to the intensity.

Appositive adjectives

In their positioning, appositive adjectives, like the noun-headed appositives, often add details and even drama. Here appositive adjectivals occur in terminal or medial position; less frequently, they occur at the beginning of the sentence:

> The house was a real family house, *large and sprawling.*
> Katharine Graham, *Personal History*, 209

> He was a young farmer, *in his late twenties or early thirties, thin as a grasshopper.*
> John Hersey, *White Lotus*, 317

> Far behind the farthest unmoving line of standing starers, a few village women, *white and scriptural*, move, or seem to glide in the quivering sunlight, *serene and unperturbed*, about their business.
> Dylan Thomas, *The Beach of Falseá*, 64

Appositive adjectives and noun-headed appositives often work together effectively in the same sentence:

> Even in their absolute immobility, *complete as that of the morning,* she felt a purpose, *a working over something, a direction, an act of creation different from any she had known.*
> F. Scott Fitzgerald, *Tender Is the Night,* 19

> All was moonlit, *all silver, too beautiful to describe.*
> T. H. White, *The Once and Future King,* 21

And here, five appositives fall comfortably into place in a context that illustrates the unmannered efficiency of this syntactic structure:

> Plants change according to their surroundings in remarkable ways. It is almost impossible to grow the delightful autumn-flowering gorse *Ulex gallii* in gardens, because any but the poorest soil makes it grow out of character—*tall and lanky instead of neat and compact.* But W. Elcock, of Fleet in Hampshire, finds that garden conditions have the opposite effect on a new Eryngium (*sea holly*) species he collected on the slopes of the volcano *Popocatepetl* in Mexico. It has a more refined flower under cultivation than in the wild—*a delicate arrangement of petals and fronds like a silver ornament fashioned by a craftsman with infinite patience.*
> John Street, "Here's Flowers for You," 362

Below, a close or restrictive appositive, *her mother's cousin Oliver Huston,* is followed by a free-modifying appositive *a family historian...* that brings with it fascinating details. Additional appositives (with their principals) are *occasion...presentation,* and *artifacts...potato masher:*

> My mother was sent the photograph of this marker by her mother's cousin Oliver Huston, a family historian so ardent that as recently as 1957 he was alerting descendants to "an occasion which no heir should miss," the presentation to the Pacific University Museum of, among other artifacts, "the old potato masher which the Cornwall family brought across the plains in 1846."
> Joan Didion, *Where I Was From,* 5

Complex, artful, and unpretentious, the appositives below exemplify the flexibility of the structure in a literary artist's hands. The first two italicized segments are in apposition to all or part of the opening phrase. The italicized fragment that follows the first sentence serves as an appositive to the sentence opener or to the words that immediately precede the fragment, or to the *it* or the *all* in the sentence that follows. Ingenious writers use fragments especially well by integrating the syntax of the fragment with that of nearby sentences:

> The desire to move on, *to metamorphose*–or perhaps it is
> *a talent for being contemporary*–was given to me as life's
> inevitable and rightful condition. *To keep becoming, always*
> *to stay involved in transition.* It was all she and my father
> had ever known.
> Arthur Miller, *Timebends: A Life*, 4

And finally, in a display of the appositive's merit and versatility, in an author's expressive story of his remarkable father, is a generous and unrestrained use of appositives–nouns, verbs, and prepositional phrases–that give *shape and form and color* to the author's memories:

> Someone, *perhaps my mother, perhaps I,* had taken the camera
> away from him–*a rare occurrence in itself*–and made him
> stand still for a shot. His face was square and large, with
> wide-set eyes and a shock of dark hair across his broad fore-
> head. The smile seemed to consume the face, *seemed to be*
> *him, rather than part of him*...

> For hours I watched those slides that evening, and for the
> next few days I continued to project and study and take
> delight in all those images out of my past. They helped
> create a special picture of my father–*my gossamer memories*
> *suddenly given vivid shape and form and color*...

> His country was vast ranges of mountains, *of dawn making*
> *a jagged black line out of distant peaks; of a white lake of tufted*
> *clouds floating below us as we stood lords of a summit; of a streak*
> *of wind-whipped rain racing over the shine of an icy mountain*
> *lake; of mist-wrapped mountainsides; of cold blue days when*
> *the wind took the few white cloud balls over the mountains like*
> *missiles, making the cloud shadows race over the peaks, sudden*
> *fleeting eclipses of silver.*
> Philip B. Kunhardt, Jr., *My Father's Country*, 48

Shakespeare left behind no diaries or letters. His name appears in some parish records and legal papers and in the commentaries of a few contemporaries. The rest is silence. Or is it?

Richard Lacayo

Imagine. I had been teaching and writing about wine for nearly twenty years before I discovered that Mexico has a burgeoning wine industry, and that it was just over the border in Baja, California.

Ralph Amey

Night, said Mado, more and more angrily, night, night, night, night, night.

A. S. Byatt

Avidly, ardently! As if my life depended upon it.

Joyce Carol Oates

CHAPTER ELEVEN

Interrogative, Imperative, Exclamatory

> I feel very strongly about putting questions; it partakes
> too much of the style of the day of judgment. You start a
> question, and it's like starting a stone. You sit quietly at the
> top of the hill; and away the stone goes, starting others.
> Robert Louis Stevenson, *The Strange Case of
> Dr. Jekyll and Mr. Hyde*, 10

THREE common reshapings of the basic declarative sentence are the *interrogative*, *imperative*, and *exclamatory*. All three make demands. A question calls for an answer, an imperative calls for an action, an exclamation calls for experiencing an emotion.

Interrogatives, imperatives, and exclamations can set an expressive tone, accent a point, serve as summary or transition, create a structure for a paragraph, and function in parallel to structure several paragraphs.

The interrogative

Here, the immediacy of the direct questions imparts an urgency to the narrative, serving to raise the dramatic pitch and to heighten the suspense of the story:

> What was the good of yet another delaying lie?
> He wondered what Wilson had said to her. Could he
> go on lying week after week, finding some reason
> of work, of health, of forgetfulness, for avoiding the
> issue at the altar rail?
> Graham Greene, *The Heart of the Matter*, 246

> What, I asked myself, was I frightened of? Thirty-one
> years old, healthy and whole, married to a fourth husband
> (why four?) who loved me, with a bodyguard of children
> (why so many?)–what was I frightened of?
>
> Not of Philpot, surely, Oh no, not in the slightest of Philpot.
> Of whom, then? Of what?
>   Penelope Mortimer, *The Pumpkin Eater*, 30

Even this mild suspense helps to keep a story going, tying loose ends together and focusing attention on the unresolved question at hand. This technique is also useful for nonfiction writers. Here the interior question direct readers toward an answer:

> Now, in the middle of the twentieth century, what is left
> of this towering reputation?
>   Kenneth Clark, *Ruskin Today*, xiv

> Nashe used them; Lodge used them; did Spenser?
>   Rosemond Tuve, *Allegorical Imagery*, 81

> Why did a play of the supposedly esoteric avant-garde
> make so immediate and so deep an impact on an audience
> of convicts? Because it confronted them with a situation
> in some ways analogous to their own?
>   Martin Esslin, *The Theatre of the Absurd*, xvii

Below, three questions bring into perspective what has preceded and signal that the author is about to provide answers:

> Perhaps we should end where we began, in Columbia
> University's Low Library, where, in 1932, Alice Pleasance
> Liddell Hargreaves came to receive her honorary doctorate
> for having inspired Lewis Carroll. Decorated with white
> flowers, the rotunda was crowded with people, some of
> whom must have been obliged to suppress an attack of
> anxious laughter when university president Nicholas Murray
> Butler confidently parked himself on the flowered throne
> meant for Alice. *Who were these people? What could they have
> thought? And how much did they know or care about the elderly,
> self-possessed woman who stood before them?*
>   Francine Prose, *The Lives of the Muses*, 369

Sometimes questions make statements:

> The main problem might be stated, How do we make
> long-term thinking automatic and common instead of
> difficult and rare? How do we make the taking of long-
> term responsibility inevitable?
> Stewart Brand, *The Clock of the Long Now*, 2

Here the author asks questions and answers them:

> The question needs to be asked: If this book is so flat, so
> full of stereotypes and Mason jars, why even review it?
> Why read it at all? The answer is that these are stories of
> lives being led, honest tales of human existence. In Arthur
> Miller's words, attention must be paid. If cooking and pray-
> ing and doing chores are your life, then that experience
> must be recorded. If something terrific happens, if your
> house survives a fire or you get to run on a champion cross-
> country or relay race team, that should be recorded too.
> Carolyn See, "Sisters of a Kind," R2

This guiding of the reader toward an anticipated assertion or discussion, in answer to previous interrogation, is often done very directly:

> Five years she has been married to him, she has had two
> children by him, she has known a long and important period
> (important because she is still very young) of domesticity
> and marital tenderness and motherhood. How does she tell
> us of these matters?
> Dorothy Van Ghent, *The English Novel*, 37

A commonly held opinion or assertion the writer intends to challenge
is sometimes followed by a question:

> Common sense tells us that the definition is foolproof.
> Or is it?
> Marjorie Perloff, *The Futurist Movement*, 189

> Shakespeare left behind no diaries or letters. His name
> appears in some parish records and legal papers and in the
> commentaries of a few contemporaries. The rest is silence.
> Or is it?
> Richard Lacayo, "Shakespeare," 59

Below, a question to be explored is inserted in the middle of a sentence:

> The issue – Is painting dead? – was seriously debated in
> the late sixties and remained a topic of contention during
> the following two decades.
> Irving Sandler, *Art of the Postmodern Era*, 24

Interrogatives are further used to lend unity that a single question provides in chapter titles like "What Is Minor Poetry?" and "What Is a Classic?" in T. S. Eliot's *On Poetry and Poets*, and in entire volumes like Jean-Paul Sartre's *What Is Literature?*

Too many questions in a row may get out of hand. By asking a question and urging an answer, interrogatives demand more from readers than declaratives. An extended repetitive parallel series of questions may become tiring, especially if the answers are complex:

> Does the university have the right to require that faculty
> members guide student groups and approve their action
> in inviting off-campus speakers? Does the university have
> the right to require that one view presented on campus be
> balanced by another? Does the university have the right to
> require that questions be allowed at meetings? Does the
> university have the right to require that faculty members
> chair meetings? Does the university have the right to decide
> where in the university a meeting shall be held, thus limiting
> effectively the size of the audience? Does it have the right
> to require student groups to pay for police protection, if
> the off-campus speaker is so controversial that disorder or
> violence may be feared? Must the university provide loud-
> speakers for the speaker? May the university deny the most
> prominent locations on the campus to the speaker?
> Nathan Glazer, "Student Politics in a Democratic
> Society," 204

Two common interrogative forms are the *leading question*, designed to imply and to elicit the answer it intends, and the *rhetorical question*, formed strictly for effect and thereby making any answer at all superfluous. If the interrogative is employed to direct us specifically toward the resolution of some problem, the leading question takes us directly there. Indeed, it leads us straight to this resolution along the length of its own sentence, which itself includes the answer, sometimes in the form of "Isn't it so that...?" The rhetorical question is what might be called a question after the fact, an announcement that we have arrived at an answer. It celebrates that forming a question in the face of such certainty is simply for ironic emphasis.

These leading questions assume the desired answer and leave room for little else:

> To have created love like that out of absolutely nothing–
> it was a sort of miracle, wasn't it?
> Marianne Wiggins, *Evidence of Things Unseen*, 381

> Had Marilyn Monroe not been enough punished in child-
> hood to insure her against future misfortune?
> Diana Trilling, "The Death of Marilyn Monroe," 233

These rhetorical questions reveal the characteristic indifference to the answer:

> The Spaniards, Hemingway adds, are not preoccupied by
> death. "It has no fascination for them." Can the writer say
> as much for himself?
> Maxwell Geismar, *Writers in Crisis*, 57

> But what–what would be more human? Some great force
> has swallowed up your brother, no reason, he's just
> gone–why the hell *not* smash all the windows? Is this a time
> to be reasonable?
> Martin Green, "The Image-Maker," 283

The imperative

Schools for years taught that imperatives are commands and that the word *you* is an understood subject. This is a useful way to think about imperatives, for it emphasizes the relation of direct address they set up and in a sense their commanding nature, a suggestion that good writers have been quick to pick up. The imperative can be quite strong in continuous prose if used carefully and judiciously: carefully because such a strong form can soon become heavy-handed, and judiciously because its attention-getting effect derives from sparing use.

To organize the examples, the types of imperatives discovered most often in prose samples can be divided into five main groups, differing only in emphasis and effect.

1. The typical *command* forms, more common in speech than in writing, are usually written with an exclamation point: "Beware of the dog!" "Keep off the grass!" "RSVP" "Carpe diem!" and "Drop dead!" In fiction this type of strong command expresses a sense of urgency, usually taking a character in the narrative or the narrative voice itself as the understood *you*:

> Sometimes I thought, but this *is* your life. *Stop fighting it. Stop fighting.*
> James Baldwin, *Giovanni's Room*, 128

2. Unlike the above commands, milder *directives* more often occur in essay style, where for didactic purpose the writer usually understands the reader as the implicit "you":

> Regard yourself in the bathroom mirror.
> Robert Ardrey, *African Genesis*, 254

> Notice, in this book, how much a hair-do alone can transform her in person and mood; also how much severity is communicated by her profile in contrast with her fullface.
> Parker Tyler, "The Garbo Image," 9-10

Imperatives have a twofold effect, helping to lend grammatical variety and to bring the reader into a direct relationship with the writer:

> Take the word 'self-esteem.' Today, a low level of self-esteem is associated with a variety of emotional difficulties that are said to cause a range of social problems from crime to teenage pregnancy...Yet until recently not only was a lack of self-esteem not perceived as a problem, the term itself had no therapeutic connotations.
> Frank Furedi, *Therapy Culture*, 2-3

> Think of the times you have said: "I can't write," "I can't paint," "I can't run," "I can't shout," "I can't dance," "I can't sing." Since this was not literally true, you were really saying: "I can't meet some outside standard. I'm not acceptable as I am."
> Gloria Steinem, *Revolution from Within*, 176

Such direct advice may alternate with explanation or comment. The first two sentences, below, filled with directives, are made more friendly by the sentences that follow:

> Second, try to establish some contact with your listeners before you give your presentation. Converse with them, see what they're interested in, try to get to know them a little. This will help you think more about your audience and help prevent you from being paralyzingly self-conscious. And it will encourage you to use a more natural, conversational style of speaking.
> Leslie A. Olsen and Thomas Huckin, *Technical Writing and Professional Communication*, 381

This type of directive can also be successfully employed to set off quoted materials. See this in such a simple introductory imperative as the one below:

> Consider
> But we are old, and…
> William Empson, *Seven Types of Ambiguity*, 95

Or, an imperative following the quoted material:

> give to me o
> my cruel one.
>
> Compare this poem with almost any of the published poems in which he speaks of his beloved.
> M. L. Rosenthal, "The Poetry of Yeats," xxviii

Below, as the opening of a book, a directive single-word sentence becomes a gracious invitation in its address to the reader:

> *Imagine.* I had been teaching and writing about wine for nearly twenty years before I discovered that Mexico has a burgeoning wine industry, and that it was just over the border in Baja, California.
> Ralph Amey, *Wines of Baja California*, 1

3. The third is a less common type of imperative, a *formula* or *recipe* (resembling an "add a pinch of this and a pinch of that" expression). These imperatives usually assume an air of scientific certainty, implying a definite action and reaction by which given steps obtain given results; they can therefore be used effectively to underscore the inevitability of a statement:

> Add to these the parade of further commentators and of characters in positions analogous to Jim's, all made available to us by Marlow, and we have a brilliant series of variations upon a theme.
>
> Murray Kreiger, "Afterword," 314

> Roughly calculate the mass of public conveyances, taxicabs, buses, private cars and trucks that success will bring to any overgrown village consisting of one hundred thousand to several million people: add half that number of private cars and add, perhaps one twenty-fifth as many delivery machines; add one fiftieth as many buses to displace street-car tracks and carry children to school; and add unwholesome subways. You will find that...
>
> Frank Lloyd Wright, *Frank Lloyd Wright*, 259

4. The next class of examples is the imperative of *permission*, which employs the verb *let* and which may take as its object the first person singular:

> Let me change the subject and say...
>
> J. D. Salinger, *Seymour–An Introduction*, 108

Or, more often, it is used in the plural:

> Let us turn for a moment to a brief survey of the conditions of modern society.
>
> Richard M. Kain, *Fabulous Voyager*, 8

More an imperative of invitation than of permission, *let us* is a common device for essay writing; in its facile effort to direct the reader's attention, however, it can be easily overdone. Nonetheless these imperatives can be effective in formal style, as in the following passage where invitation becomes injunction and the imperatives accumulate in a peroration at the close of the essay:

Be it ours to shed sunshine on their path, to light their
sorrows by the balm of sympathy…Let us not weigh in
grudging scales their merits and demerits, but let us think
only of their need…let us remember that they are fellow
sufferers in the same darkness, actors in the same tragedy
with ourselves. And so, when their day is over, when their
good and their evil have become eternal by the immortality
of the past, be it ours to feel that, where they suffered,
where failed, no deed of ours was the cause…
> Bertrand Russell, *Why I Am Not a Christian*, 111

5. The same *let* form is used in these final examples as a heighten-
ing device to create the *rhetorical* imperative:

Let him look at it—his beach, perverted now to the tastes
of the tasteless…
> F. Scott Fitzgerald, *Tender Is the Night*, 280

Let the poets and their defenders, he says, refute it
if they can, and we shall listen to them with respect.
> Northrop Frye, *Fables of Identity*, 41

Let the wind blow; let the poppy seed itself and the carna-
tion mate with the cabbage. Let the swallow build in the
drawing room, and the thistle thrust aside the tiles, and the
butterfly sun itself on the faded chintz of the arm chairs.
Let the broken glass and the china lie out on the lawn and
be tangled over with grass and wild berries.
> Virginia Woolf, *To the Lighthouse*, 208

Often derived from a biblical model, "Let there be light," this type of
imperative can yield prose that is both elevated and convincing. Yet, it
can be overworked (here, a few of the 34 imperatives on one page):

Break up the forms and melt the letters back. Let there be
no more legends on the earth. Let life live and death die, and
let there be no names for sorrowful recollection. Let there
be no words for the earth, for life, for death, for beauty and
piquant faces. Let there be no sorrow or recollection of life.
Let there be only the river and its odor of fish and flower, let
there be the river, the nameless river, flowing from distant
summer.
> Ross Lockridge, Jr., *Raintree County*, 970

The exclamatory

Almost any word, phrase, or sentence (with the exception of a very long sentence) may be written as an exclamation. Because an exclamation or interjection can stand alone, whatever precedes the exclamation point, or whatever *sounds like* an exclamation, can stand alone even if it is the single word *Ugh!* or *Wow!* (Heaven forbid!)

Certain grammatical filters or structural words often announce an exclamation. *What* snobs! *How* snobbish! *Such* snobbery! To compose these ideas in full exclamatory sentences requires an inversion: *They are snobs* and *They are snobbish* become *What snobs they are!* and *How snobbish they are!* The *exclamation inversion* often appears without an exclamation point:

> He thought: *How beautiful she is.*
> Graham Greene, *The Heart of the Matter*, 14

> *How light* the little package was now that it was
> on the table between them.
> Greene, 222

No introductory structural word appears below but an inverted object as opener and its fivefold repetition create a striking exclamation:

> Night, said mad Mado, more and more angrily, night, night, night, night, night.
> A. S. Byatt, "The Pink Ribbon," 236

The particular effect an exclamation produces is emotional emphasis, and, not seeking this emphasis, most essay writers characteristically lack, or regularly conquer, the impulse to exclaim. In fiction the exclamation is usually limited to direct quotation. Novelist Edward P. Jones has remarked, "I don't like to use a lot of emotions or what I call 'neon-lighting' because almost all the time whatever I'm writing about has enough emotion in it, and all I have to do is tell the story."

On occasion, however, exclamatory material can be appropriate. The exclamations below, varying in form, length, and complexity, make up only a fraction of the available examples in the single chapter from which they come. Together, in their context, these exclamations suggest the writer's personal commitment to the material and help to give the prose a lively and engaging flavor:

> A magnificent fragment!
> Maxwell Geismar, *Writers in Crisis,* 191

> Memory and desire: what power resides in these attributes of the human temperament, and especially when they are denied their realization by the facts of our life!
> Geismar, 201

The strong feeling that characterizes exclamations is sometimes seen in autobiographies and memoirs. In an entirely appropriate gesture, the fragmentary exclamations that conclude the passage below make vivid the intensity of childhood emotions and motivations:

> Reading for children in our grade-school textbooks, was simple-minded in its vocabulary, grammar, and content; it was usually about unreal, improbably, or unconditionally fantastic situations, like fairy tales, comic books, Disney films. It might be amusing, it might even be instructive, but it was not *real.* Reality was the province of adults, and though I was surrounded by adults, as an only child for five years, it was not a province I could enter, or even envision, from the outside. To enter that reality, to find a way *in,* I read books.

> *Avidly, ardently!* As if my life depended upon it.
> Joyce Carol Oates, *The Faith of a Writer,* 8

Although the exclamatory can verge on the melodramatic, especially if overused, here it aptly expresses the child's sense of urgency and immediacy. Used with economy, the exclamatory can add genuinely dramatic emphasis in almost any genre.

Science is inherently open and egalitarian, and thrives on free speech; the military is inherently hierarchical and secretive.
Timothy Ferris

We mapped the traffic and the colors of the leaves in the fall and the fences. We mapped the graffiti made in wet cement and the street signs and the dollar value of the real estate, the colors of the houses and the number of stories and the number of steps from the sidewalk to the front porches, and where the wind chimes were and the clotheslines. We mapped everything we could figure out how to map.
Dennis Wood

We can no longer take refuge, or seek to escape, in the question of whether or not we can become truly human.

We can.

The question now is whether or not we will.
William Appleman Williams

CHAPTER TWELVE

Parallelism

> The matching of phrase against phrase, clause against
> clause, lends an unmistakable eloquence to prose.
> That, indeed, is one of the principal glories of the King
> James Bible... And, to some extent in reminiscence and
> imitation of the Bible, English prose all the way down
> to our time has tended toward balanced structure for
> the sake of contrast or antithesis or climax...
> Richard D. Altick, *Preface to Critical Reading,* 210

P ARALLELISM is saying like things in like ways. It is accomplished
by repetition of words and syntactic structures in planned symmetrical arrangements and, if not overdone, has a place in day-to-day writing. But the "eloquence" mentioned by Richard Altick makes parallel
structures most at home in ritualistic prose and public speeches:

> To every thing there is a season, and a time to every
> purpose under the heaven:
>
> A time to be born, and a time to die; a time to plant,
> and a time to pluck up that which is planted...
> Ecclesiastes 3: 1 and 2

> All this will not be finished in the first one hundred days.
> Nor will it be finished in the first one thousand days
> nor in the life of this administration, nor even perhaps
> in our lifetime on this planet. But let us begin.
> John F. Kennedy, *Inaugural address,* January 20, 1961

So I say to you, my friends, that even though we must face
the difficulties of today and tomorrow, I still have a dream.
It is a dream deeply rooted in the American dream, that one
day this nation will rise up and live out the true meaning of
its creed...I have a dream...I have a dream...
Martin Luther King, Jr., August 28, 1963

Such prose for ritual or for public occasions derives much of its
poetic quality from the artful use of repetition and balance. Similar
techniques, less dramatically applied, can be effective in fiction, biography, memoirs, book reviews, and essays. Often too, such structures
can serve everyday prose by simply sorting and characterizing items so
they can be easily understood or compared. Some varied examples:

The number of human beings now alive is around six
billion. The estimated number of humans who have ever
been alive is about one hundred billion. What is the number
of humans who *will* be alive? We owe the past humans our
existence, our skills, and our not-bad world. What do we
owe the future humans? Existence, skills, and a not-bad
world. Maybe even a better world.
Stewart Brand, *The Clock of the Long Now,* 8

I see the neighbor's mulberry tree whose branches hung
down so low you could duck right under them and hide
against the trunk, peeking out and staining your mouth
and cheeks and hands with mulberry juice. I see our rabbit
in his cage over the lettuce rows in the vegetable garden,
and the clothesline filled with sheets and tiny dresses, all
stuck on the line with wooden clothespins. I see the trees
lining the sidewalk in the front yard which bloomed in
masses of deep pink in the spring.
Joan Baez, *And a Voice to Sing With,* 19

Science is inherently open and egalitarian, and thrives on
free speech; the military is inherently hierarchical and
secretive.
Timothy Ferris, *The Universe and Eye,* 79

One role of parallel structures in guiding the reader is illustrated in the following 176-word sentence about Victorian daily life. Its six dependent clauses beginning with *that*, along with three long strategic parentheses, create a bumpy but negotiable path through a busy terrain:

> In contrast, by meticulously uncovering the daily life of their subjects, Gordon and Nair show *that* work and home and the public and private spheres were (especially within the professional class) in many ways far more intertwined than they are today; *that* many men and women prized female intellectual attainment; *that* the dominant religious ethos impelled some women toward an exclusively nurturing, domestic role, but others toward independence and a public role; *that* middle-class mothers' conception of their function—and, concomitantly, the amount of time they devoted to child-rearing—varied enormously; *that* men were intensely involved in raising and caring for their children, were "indulgent fathers," and were "home-loving, gentle and whimsical"; and *that* generally the middle class was far less somber (its members partied hard and regularly kept astonishingly late hours), and family and social relations far warmer and more informal than the stereotype allows (for instance, although Flanders devotes pages to the elaborate etiquette of "calling" as described in novels and prescribed in advice books, Gordon and Nair's scrutiny of how lives were actually led reveals that everyday, drop-in visits were much more common).
>
> Benjamin Schwarz, "New and Noteworthy," 113

Although most of us may not have occasion to write so full a sentence, it is perhaps singularly appropriate for Schwarz's account of the book's "meticulous uncovering" of the myriad aspects of daily life in nineteenth-century England.

We turn now to some grammatical conventions in the use of parallelism and to successful violations of those conventions by experienced writers. Before it has anything to do with style, parallelism is often a syntactic concern; in certain cases where conjunctions are used in the process of compounding, long-standing rules of parallelism insist that only like things, grammatically, can be joined: *shoes* and *ships* and *sealing wax*, all nouns, but not *shoes* and *high-heeled* and *run*, a noun, an adjective, and a verb. The conventions about parallelism extend also to phrases and clauses in series.

Deliberate faulty parallelism

For particular effects, professional writers occasionally indulge in deliberate faulty parallelism. Below is a rather extreme instance, in which the author succeeds in a lax, informal, almost slangy, effect appropriate to the character:

> Here was himself, *young, good-looking, snappy dresser,*
> and *making dough.*
> John Steinbeck, *Sweet Thursday*, 156

Few constructions so stridently ignore the rules. Most of those who appear to add a seemingly unparallel item to a series really mix grammatically similar elements, differing only enough to get a separate, individual emphasis:

> Is there any one period of English literature to which we can point as being *fully mature, comprehensive,* and *in equilibrium?*
> T. S. Eliot, *On Poetry and Poets*, 55-56

> The strangely shaped glands, and bones, the transparent
> lungs, the madly dense tangle of cells in the brain hold
> worlds within worlds; and, *through it all* and *always,*
> streams the blood.
> Leo Vroman, *Blood*, IX

> *Religiously, politically,* and *simply in terms of the characters'*
> *efforts to get along with one another,* this incongruity is
> pervasive.
> Frederick C. Crews, *E. M. Forster*, 142

Prepositional phrases, for the most part, jarred the parallelism of simple adjectives and adverbs in the preceding examples. In the next four, first a past participle and then present participles break the expected parallelism:

> But it is, on the contrary, wonderfully *dramatic* and *picturesque* and *cast in heroic mold.*
>> Allan Nevins and Henry Steele Commager, *A Pocket History of the United States*, VI

> He can be diplomatic and yielding, yet at the same time he is one of the most undiplomatic persons imaginable, often *stubborn*, or *doing something just to see the fireworks.*
>> Erich Fromm, *Sigmund Freud's Mission*, 118

> Yet *two days ago*, and *remembering* to allow for the time change, no stars fell, no lightning flashed, no premonition ruffled the hairs on the nape of the neck.
>> Audrey Callahan Thomas, *Ten Green Bottles*, 15

> She is alternately gamin-like, sexy, mischievous, innocent, confident, insouciant, girlish, and *radiating warmth.*
>> Hollywood Bowl program, *An Evening with Barbra Streisand*

Ellipsis

Parallelism helps to make possible the device of ellipsis, the acceptable removal, because they are understood, of parallel items in a series. Because of the underlying logic of parallelism, the reader recognizes the common denominator of the series and can easily fill in the gaps. This shared item can appear at the end of the series, as in the next deliberately strained and unusual example:

> My Juvenal and Dante are as faithful as I am able or dare or can bear *to be.*
>> Robert Lowell, *Near the Ocean*, 9

Much more often, the common denominator, later understood and removed, comes just as the compounding gets under way. This happens in the next excerpts, the sentences tightened considerably by the omission of repetitive material in an elliptical concision made possible by the parallel arrangement. As above, italics indicate the removed material:

> For love *is stronger* than hate, and peace than war.
> Bradford Smith, *A Dangerous Freedom*, 362

> The walls of the town, which is built on a hill, *are* high, the streets and lanes tortuous and broken, the roads winding.
> Malcolm Lowry, *Under the Volcano*, 3

> For all the persons with whom I have been concerned *got* what they wanted: Elliott social eminence; Isabel an assured position backed by a substantial fortune in an active and cultured community; Gray a steady and lucrative job, with an office to go to from nine till six every day; Suzanne Rouvier security; Sophie death; and Larry happiness.
> W. Somerset Maugham, *The Razor's Edge*, 343

Extended parallelism within the sentence

In a short story, a right-branching sentence by itself forms a paragraph developed in two sets of parallel layers. The opening words in the parallel segments are italicized:

> Lauren had learned the signs, and she thought she saw *what* there was to be gone through now, *what* price there was to be paid for the miraculous rescue—the *never* turning to go back to school or go near the hotel, perhaps *never* to walk in the streets at all, *never* to go out of the house in the two weeks left before the Christmas holidays.
> Alice Munro, *Runaway: Stories*, 228

Parallel additions stretch the sentence below to the limit:

> Yet it has long been assumed on the basis of his findings that
> distributed practice is better than massed practice; that short
> practice periods are better than long ones; that frequency,
> recency, and repetition favor the acquisition of knowledge –
> all this despite the personal experience of countless scholars
> who have found that they can achieve more when they
> have a whole day rather than half a day at their disposal,
> when they are trying to understand the material instead
> of repeating it by rote, when they have worked through
> a problem until it is solved, instead of toying with it for
> periods regularly distributed; and who also know that once
> understood a problem is mastered for good.
>> Magda B. Arnold, *Emotion and Personality*, 3

This parallel structure supports a careful, clear ordering of ideas into
measured units, with clauses most prominent. In this one sentence,
parallelism defines and frames a protracted structure that is consciously
balanced.

Balance and repetition

Balance is a term from rhetoric, and the various shadings and implications it contributes to prose style are, out of context, not always evi-
dent. Still, its essential characteristics are syntactic, and it builds on a
base of grammatical parallelism for which it is a most important complement in the ordering of sentence groups. Three examples of balanced configurations, two within and one between sentences, illustrate
the achievement of *syntactic balance* in short space:

> And he took the pain of it, if not happily, like a martyr,
> at least willingly, like an heir.
>> Edward Lewis Wallant, *The Pawnbroker*, 279

> Desirous, she chooses her aperitifs wisely, or content,
> she enjoys the caviare of potential power.
>> F. Scott Fitzgerald, *Tender is the Night*, 291

James was an artist, however tortured his sentences finally
became. Wells was a propagandist, however skillfully he
stated his sometimes complex ideas.
    Myrick Land, *The Fine Art of Literary Mayhem*, 85

Repetition helps create balance, but facile repetition, which tends
to exist in elementary parallelism, is not an effective technique for order
or cohesion over large verbal areas. On paper it may seem applied and
artificial, although it sometimes sounds better in a speech:

My thesis is that such a search demands total involvement
and maximum awareness, but that man is encapsulated.
By encapsulated I mean claiming to have the whole of truth
when one has only part of it. *By encapsulated I mean* looking
at life partially and proceeding to make statements concerning the whole of life. And *by encapsulated I mean* living partially because one's daily activities are based on a world-view
or philosophy of life which is meager next to the larger
meaning of existence. Thus, this book focuses its attention
on the dilemma of contemporary specialism in work.
I mean, in other words, the outlook that only certain views
are correct and that only certain people have the proper
background to have these views. *I mean* the narrowing down
of vocational tasks brought on by the industrial revolution
and resulting in twenty different "experts" making a shoe
rather than one master shoemaker. *I mean* the situation in
which a person dares not comment "outside his field" and
feels he must take a course in electrical engineering before
replacing a light bulb. *I mean* those policies which are promul-
gated as supra-national but are, in fact, nationalistic in intent.
I mean, in short, the fragmentary ethos of the 20TH century.
    Joseph R. Royce, *The Encapsulated Man*, 2

Although there is an attempt to shift the parallelism somewhat by varying the repetitions, this passage fails in its desired effect. It lacks real balance; the simple repetition is overdone, yet the functional parallelism
is insufficient. When effective grammatical parallelism combines with
careful balance, the two together can control a long and complex series
of thoughts, ordering them for concision and clarity, and turning out
neat, crisp, sentences as part of a closely worked exposition.

Alternation as a device for cohesion

The logical *alternation* of subordinate and main clauses is a common way of ordering expository material. This alternation uses a rather extended parallel pattern of *if...these* clauses:

> *If a good play* must have a clearly constructed story, *these* have no story or plot to speak of; *if a good play* is judged by subtlety or characterization and motivation, *these* are often without recognizable characters and present the audience with almost mechanical puppets; *if a good play* has to have a fully explained theme, which is neatly exposed and finally solved, *these* often have neither a beginning nor an end; *if a good play* is to hold the mirror up to nature and portray the manners and mannerisms of the age in finely observed sketches, *these* seem often to be reflections of dreams and nightmares; *if a good play* relies on witty repartee and painted dialogue, *these* often consist of incoherent babblings.
> Martin Esslin, *The Theatre of the Absurd*, xvii-xviii

The pattern of an "if" dependent clause preceding a main clause, as seen above and in later examples has precedent in the King James translation of the Bible with about a dozen uses scattered through the five chapters in the General Epistle of James. One example:

> If ye fulfil the royal law according to the scriptures,
> thou shalt love thy neighbor as thyself, ye do well...
> *James* 2:8

A twentieth-century novelist makes use of a series of such "if" clauses to open his novel and intersperses them throughout the story. The book begins with a series of "if" clauses as fragmentary sentences:

> If the mountain had not gleamed so white.

> If yonder, under the peaks, the snaggled line of the fir forest had not been so blue-black, against the white.

> If the sky above that glitter of snow on the Zelzsteinberg had not been heart-breaking with the innocence of new blue. If one puff of cloud, white as whipped cream, had not lounged high in that washed glitter of blue. If the world had not been absolute in beauty.
> Robert Penn Warren, *Wilderness*, 3

Throughout the novel, at least thirty times, the author uses the syntactic "if" pattern, harking back to his opening pages, marking the habit of mind of the protagonist of thinking in alternatives, and helping to establish the "novel's major movement."[1] In the final pages, the protagonist summarizes with an elliptical "if" clause:

> ... if necessary, he would do it all again. But then cried,
> in his inwardness: But, oh, with a different heart!
> 　　Warren, 309-310

The striking appropriateness of parallel syntax is exemplified by the apt use of the "if-then" syntactic phrase repeatedly in this essay of literary criticism. Here is the final paragraph:

> Do postmodern genres exist? If we wish to understand the proliferation of academic anthologies, journals, collections of critical essays, then we need names for such omnibus volumes and genre theory provides them. If we wish to study these kinds of writing with reference to the social environment of which they are a part, then genre study helps us relate institutions and economics to the production of texts. If we seek to understand the historical recurrence of certain kinds of writing, the rejection or abandonment of other kinds, genre theory provides the most adequate procedure for this inquiry. If we wish to analyze an individual text, genre theory provides a knowledge of its constituents and how they combine. Not only do these actions recognize the value of a genre theory in analyzing modernist writing, but they demonstrate that postmodern theorists, critics, authors and readers inevitably use the language of genre theory as they seek to deny its usefulness.
> 　　Ralph Cohen, "Do Postmodern Genres Exist?" 25

---

[1] Randy J. Hendricks, "Warren's Wilderness and the Defining 'If'," *The Mississippi Quarterly* 48 (Winter 1994-1995): 115-131.

Rhythm, chiasmus, and paired constructions

Balance implies a measure, something reasonably exact and static. But prose is not static, not meant to be measured but read; thus balance, when read, becomes rhythm. Certainly this is apparent in the long alternating constructions that illustrate balance, just as it can be seen earlier in this chapter, even in the examples of broken parallelism and ellipsis. Even imbalance, another kind of prose arrangement, has its own distinct rhythm, which can be combined with more obvious, regular patterns into a multiplicity of larger rhythms.

Rhythm is an unavoidable consideration for any prose writer, like metrics for the poet, and it is by no means limited to the use of parallelism. Wherever one notices and appreciates *syntax as style*, rhythm is likely to be a factor. It results from the way things are put together syntactically: prose structures, like poetry, create beat and cadence; syntax becomes rhythm. Rhythm is that peculiar quality of parallelism, hard to define or formulate, that helps explain its practicality and impact.

Two balanced rhythmic constructions—*chiasmus* and *paired constructions*—help produce narrowed but pronounced rhythms. *Chiasmus* is an inverse parallelism or grammatical mirror image, as a short syntactic pattern is reversed rather than repeated. In this example below, "It is criticism, not biography" is reversed:

> *Criticism it is, not biography*, that must establish the character of that point in mental space-time, determining what is conveyed, what kind of thing is expressed.
> Francis Noel Lees, "The Keys Are at the Palace," 107

Balance is a refinement of parallelism with equally weighted elements; chiasmus is inverted balance with symmetrical elements. Note the play with symmetry in the sentence below. Italics show the structure of interest:

> ...nor *was he* revived during his own lifetime *like Faulkner*, nor *like Hemingway has he* had much of his work handed over to the academicians.
> Richard Walser, *Thomas Wolfe*, 142

> The synagogues are flaming, and the first step has been
> taken in that tragic tale of *proscription* and *tallage, tallage*
> and *expulsion* which (it seems) must never end.
>> Eileen Power, *Medieval People*, 13

It is the habit of some writers, and the occasional decision of others, to organize a series of items into pairs, perhaps obtaining greater control than in a straightforward series, and certainly resulting in a more distinct rhythm:

> One might ponder the melancholy question whether it
> does *take misfortune and great tension, national agitation
> and even calamity*, to *arouse and inspire* film-makers to *dare*
> radical leaps ahead *and explode* devastating expressions.
>> Bosley Crowther, *The Great Films*, 10

> There are *institutions and bureaucracies, political habits and
> commercial systems*—all *developed and perfected, proliferated
> and entrenched, during the course of and in the service of* our
> transportation history just now ended.
>> George Fox Mott, *Transportation Century*, 6

Antithesis

Sometimes pairing seems rather arbitrary because it does not develop from the sense of the sentence. Other ideas seem to fall naturally into paired constructions, especially those that follow the logic of contrast. The next passages, although they move toward arbitrary pairs near the end of each (triplets in the third example), produce paired constructions that assume the natural rhythm of antithesis. Only the antithetical pairs are italicized here:

> Moving from the *known to the unknown*, proceeding as we
> must from *light toward dark*, and into the wild and watery,
> the untried and unshored, it is noteworthy that we start
> on Christmas Day.
>> Harry Levin, *The Power of Blackness*, 204

Like nature the whale is paradoxically *benign and malevolent, nourishing and destructive*. It is massive, brutal, monolithic, but at the same time protean, erotically beautiful, infinitely variable.

Richard Chase, *The American Novel and Its Tradition*, 110

At once *materialistic and moral, aggressive and religious, self-satisfied and self-critical*, the middle generation of Victorians enjoyed a special moment in English history.

David Thomson, *England in the Nineteenth Century*, 117

A similar effect is produced when the antithesis goes beyond the halves of a single pair to a trio of contrasts:

I go further, much further, than this, much further, and say *this is waking, that is a dream, this belongs to the body, that to the spirit, this belongs to space and distance, that to time and duration*. But space spills over into time, as the body into the soul, so that the one cannot be measured without the other.

Penelope Fitzgerald, *The Blue Flower*, 217

Language is finite and formal; reality is infinite and formless. Order is comic; chaos is tragic.

John Updike, *Assorted Prose*, 200

From a different context, and going beyond a single sentence, the opening of the following paragraph has three parallel sentences with the second half of each sentence in antithesis to the first half. Here the antithetic parallelism is established by the repeated structure and the repeated words *does not* and *but of course he wants*. In the final sentence, the author shifts, using only the last half of the pattern to continue the parallelism:

He does not go to banks but of course he wants to. He does not have a driver's license but of course he wants one. He does not have a phone but of course he wants one. He wants his family to be with him.

Dagoberto Gilb, "You Know Him by His Labors," B15

Writers, public speakers, and debaters often take advantage of the sense of contrast or antithesis, as well as the emotive appeal, that parallel syntax can convey in framing an argument. Below, balance and parallelism go beyond the individual sentence to provide structure for the argument setting forth what human beings *do not* do and what they actually do. The first three sentences briefly state both sides of the argument. The next five give instances to support the view being advanced, with *Poor people* opening four sentences, followed by *unimaginably poor* in the final item to pick up the thread. The paragraph's last sentences restate the argument and elaborate on it:

> Human beings do not wait for aesthetics until they have full stomachs and a roof that doesn't leak. They do not pursue aesthetic needs "only when basic needs have been satisfied." Given a modicum of stability and sustenance, people enrich the look and feel of their lives through ritual, personal adornment, and decorated objects. Poor people create bodily decoration that illustrates *National Geographic*. Poor people built the cathedrals of Europe and developed the sand paintings of Tibet. Poor people turned baskets and pottery into decorative art. Poor people invented paints and dyes, jewelry and cosmetics. Five thousand years ago, unimaginably poor Stone Age weavers living in Swiss swamps worked intricate, multicolored patterns into their textiles, using fruit pits as beads, work that archaeologists have found preserved in the alkaline mud. These artifacts do not reflect societies focused only on "lower-order" needs. Aesthetics is not a luxury, but a universal human desire.
>
> Virginia Postrel, *The Substance of Style*, 4

Individuality of effect

The straightforward parallelism, like the terse imperative verbs–*use, omit, broil, grill, serve*–in the directions below for modifying a recipe, has an uncluttered economy and directness:

> *Grilled or Broiled Eggplant Slices with Miso Dressing* Use canola or other neutral oil in place of olive oil, and omit the garlic. Broil or grill the eggplant, and serve with a dressing made by mixing together 4 tablespoons miso; 1 teaspoon sugar; 1 tablespoon mirin (or ½ tablespoon honey, thinned with water); and rice or other mild vinegar to taste.
>
> Mark Bittman, *How to Cook Everything*, 568

Economy of a different sort, however, although still suggestive of a list of items, is seen in the repeated subjects and terse clauses of the next examples, each highly individual in its impact:

> I want to introduce, I want to describe, I want to distribute mementos, amulets, I want to break out my wallet and pass around snapshots, I want to follow my nose.
> J. D. Salinger, *Seymour – An Introduction*, 107

> We mapped the traffic and the colors of the leaves in the fall and the fences. We mapped the graffiti made in wet cement and the street signs and the dollar value of the real estate, the colors of the houses and the number of stories and the number of steps from the sidewalk to the front porches, and where the wind chimes were and the clotheslines. We mapped everything we could figure out how to map.
> Dennis Wood, "Two Maps of Boylan Heights," 104

> Commercials are infuriating. They are also irresistible. Commercials are an outrageous nuisance. They are also apt to be better than the programs they interrupt. Commercials are the heavy tribute that the viewer must pay to the sponsor in exchange for often dubious pleasure. They are also an American art form.
> "…And Now a Word about Commercials," TIME, 55

Predicate adjectives and predicate nouns arranged in a string, with intervening qualifiers and other adverbs, here organize and create meaningful parallel structures:

> There was something rather "doggy," rather smart, rather acute and shrewd, something warm, and something slightly contemptible about him.
> D. H. Lawrence, *Sons and Lovers*, 103

Below, in a different context, a predicate nominative is expanded by a string of parallel prepositional phrases:

> The chief occasions were those of the investiture of an heir, of marriage, and of acquisition and demonstration of religious powers, of mourning, of warfare, and of accident.
> Ruth Benedict, *Patterns of Culture*, 201

Heavy repetition in the next example sets up a kind of rhythm of persistence, where the returning syntactic pattern imparts the same feeling of stability and endurance that the statement literally conveys:

> The vision of science may go unappreciated, *but it is there.* It may be reduced by a plodding soul to mere dots on a photographic plate, *but it is there.* It may be drained of juice and pounded into flat phrases, *but it is there.*
> Isaac Asimov, *From Earth to Heaven,* VII

Describing a period of rapid changes, a newspaper columnist speeds up the syntax with three parallel uses of *from young women ... to older women* (or *older ones*), echoing the idea of things happening fast:

> From young women playing quarterback on high school football teams to older women trading in their empty nests for city council seats, from young women trying new methods of contraception to older ones refusing hormone replacement therapy, from young women insisting they could be sexual beings and still be treated seriously to older women saying the same: Things happened so fast you almost got history whiplash.
> Anna Quindlen, *Loud and Clear,* 141

Parallel structures are used at times to set off and emphasize an abrupt departure from them; in the following paragraphs, the repeated patterns build toward a climax that breaks with the parallelism:

> According to the Almanac, Mae West was born in 1893.
> According to Mae West, Mae West is 28 years old.
> The Almanac lies.
> Burt Prelutsky, "At Home with Mae West," 4

> The man who thus called upon a saint was later to repudiate the cult of the saints. He who vowed to become a monk was later to renounce monasticism. A loyal son of the Catholic Church, he was later to shatter the structure of medieval Catholicism. A devoted servant of the pope, he was later to identify the popes with Antichrist. For this young man was Martin Luther.
> Roland H. Bainton, *Here I Stand: A Life of Martin Luther,* 15

Below, fluctuating repetitions collect into a loose pattern from which the last word, in its adjusted meaning rather than its form, is an important displacement:

> But we now confront these possibilities as real choices. We *can* provide ourselves with the material basis for a truly human life and also produce enough to help other human beings achieve the same position. We *can* do so, moreover, while simultaneously decentralizing our economic and political institutions, so as to enable us to live at the scale, and in the kinds of relationships with ourselves and each other, appropriate to our nature.
>
> We *can* no longer take refuge, or seek to escape, in the question of whether or not we *can* become truly human.
>
> We *can*.
>
> The question now is whether or not we *will*.
>   William Appleman Williams, *The Contours of American History*, 9

Variations in an expected parallel pattern can have still subtler results. The contrast between an outer and an inner world in the next passage is caught in the syntax itself as the abruptly punctuated series *senescent, disintegrating, despairing*, relaxes instead into the easy coordination of *soft and warm and linen-sheeted*:

> Outside 43 Spadina Road the world was senescent, disintegrating, despairing, and everyone was on his way to a breakdown. Inside, it was soft and warm and linen-sheeted, and everyone was in the pink of mental health.
>   Michael Frayn, *Against Entropy*, 46

There is a continuity in the balanced accumulations of the next right-branching sentence, controlled by the consecutive participial chain *growing up...picking up...living on*:

> John Dalton lived from 1766 to 1844, *growing up* in a part of England which saw the Industrial Revolution changing every man's life, *picking up* as his first science the vestiges of the 17TH-century scientific revolution, *living on* to see the beginning of the modern concern for science as a responsibility of the makers of public policy.
>   Frank Greenaway, *John Dalton and the Atom*, 1

It is perhaps simultaneity rather than continuity suggested by the present participles below as they participate in the rhythm of all of the actions described:

> I remember I could hear the sounds of the appliances turn-
> ing on and off, those gentle sounds, freezing this, heating
> that, whirring and spinning, clicking, starting, stopping.
> Elia Kazan, *The Arrangement*, 136

Accidental parallelism

Sometimes a writer through repetitions of similar sounds, words, or structures creates an unintended parallelism that is inappropriate to the subject matter. Novelist Martin Amis tells of "the only piece of lit-erary counsel" ever given to him by his father, novelist Kingsley Amis:

> "Things like 'Raging and cursing in the blazing heat...'
> It would have to be 'Raging and cursing in the
> intolerable heat.'"
>
> You couldn't have *ings* like that. And sometimes you
> couldn't even have two. The same went for *–ics, –ives,*
> *–lys,* and *–tions.* And the same went for all prefixes too.
> Martin Amis, *Experience: A Memoir*, 22

Repetition *and* variation constitute that dual essence of prose rhythm, as they do of form in music or in painting. Many types of par-allel arrangement, of balance and calculated imbalance in phrase and clause, of repetitions and ellipses, pairings, catalogings, contrasts and other groupings, assembled together into distinct prose textures, can contribute to the unique rhythms of almost any kind of prose. When the diverse shapes of parallelism are called into play, when careful struc-turing and more relaxed rhythms interchange and merge, writing can profit from a vast and fluid variety of patterns.

The aloneness many of us feel on this earth is assuaged, more or less effectively, by the deep and abiding relationships we have with other human beings—with our parents, our children, our brothers and sisters, our wives, husbands, sweethearts, lovers, closest friends. These relationships are not always as close as we would like them to be, and communication is often distressingly difficult. Yet there is always the hope that each man and woman who seeks this special warmth will eventually find it.

Albert Rosenfield

I always loved English because whatever human beings are, we are storytellers. It is our stories that give a light to the future. When I went to college I became a history major because history is such a wonderful story of who we think we are. English is much more a story of who we really are.

Nikki Giovanni

CHAPTER THIRTEEN

Cohesion

...when we talk about flow we're talking about the
variation of sentence structure and lengths; about the
"sequence of syntax" and its effects on the reader's
emotional response; about the rhythmic mimesis and
the way it contributes to those effects; and about the
rhythmic relation of the work's parts to the whole.
Thus, if we want to write fiction that flows, we need
to explore the syntax of our prose on all levels, from
the micro level of the sentence to the macro level of
the complete work.

> David Jauss, "What We Talk About When
> We Talk About Flow," 20

POET-NOVELIST David Jauss is writing about fiction but the techniques he describes apply as well to other kinds of writing. Cohesion in any kind of prose comes from making clear the relationship of one *idea* to another: natural-seeming movement results from integrity of meaning and the showing of relationships. These are realized on the page through the structures of presentation, namely syntax.

Repetition is an essential technique of cohesion. Repetition involves not just the semantic content of words but their syntactic identities and functions. Variety in syntax combines with repetition in contributing to sentence flow, especially the use of sentences of differing lengths and structures, and the fine-tuning that brings varied sentence openers and sentence endings. Imaginative writers–and those willing to experiment or to violate conventions–may introduce a persistent variation that unifies, as in the first two examples below showing unusual uses of conjunctions.

Conjunctions

The obvious way of joining two sentences is with a simple conjunction, making a direct connection and implying a specific relation. The excerpts below rely in large part on the novel use of conjunctions for their cohesion, within individual sentences and, just as importantly, between them.

The word *But* is a frequent opener for sentences and paragraphs. In the first example, it is followed by four sentences opening with *And* and one with *Yet*, creating an almost biblical cadence:

> *But* as he spoke, the phantom years scrolled up their vision, and only the eyes of Ben burned terribly in darkness, without an answer.
>
> *And* day came, and the song of waking birds, and the Square, bathed in the young pearl light of morning. *And* a wind stirred lightly in the Square, and, as he looked, Ben, like a fume of smoke, was melted into dawn.
>
> *And* the angels on Gant's porch were frozen in hard marble silence, and at a distance life awoke, and there was a rattle of lean wheels, a slow clangor of shod hoofs. *And* he heard the whistle wail along the river.
>
> *Yet*, as he stood for the last time by the angels of his father's porch, it seemed as if the square already were far and lost; or, should I say, he was like a man who stands upon a hill above the town he has left, yet does not say "The town is near," but turns his eyes upon the distant soaring ranges.
> Thomas Wolfe, *Look Homeward, Angel*, 521-522

The conjunction *and* contributes to cohesion in a highly different context below. This passage is quoted not because most of us will have occasion to imitate it, but because it displays pointedly a cohesion that depends largely on strategic repetition, especially of *and* through a series of paragraphs, with the unusual syntax and absence of punctuation making vivid the painful drama and emotional path:

> time passed *and* my grandfather threw my grandmother down the stairs *and* he put a gun to her head again *and* he threw her down the stairs *and* he put a gun to her head. *And* the girl in the back room she was a "vegetable" you know they said keep quiet they said shame the girl in the back room who cried *and* screamed all night was my

father's sister. *And* my grandmother tended her day *and*
night *and* then she died *and* the back room remained empty
as it still does today. *And* my grandfather ranted at the top of
his lungs for someone to bring him food his socks his his his
and my grandmother for fear for fear of for fear of being
slapped at the back of the head brought him his food *and* his
housecoat *and* his socks

and when I was born my grandfather said a girl throw her in
the river that's what girls are good for. In the old country we
throw them in the river. *And* my antie Joyce told my mother
we were like animals because we ran wild *and* made a lot of
noise up *and* down the place.
      Jennifer A. Khawaja, "The Queen, Carcasses, and Other
      Things," 43

As seen above, this means of moving from one sentence to the next can
produce prose that is highly emotive and mannered. But it can also
serve in more general settings. The following extract depends strongly
for its cohesion not only on the relationship of ideas, but on syntactic
choices including short conjunctions as sentence openers, among them
for, and, or, and *but.* Other cohesive devices include contrasts, adverbials of time and space, and pointer or transitional words such as *however, this, too, of course*:

More than a century went by, however, before this working-
man's garment attained the prominence and near-universal
recognition it possesses today. *For* it was not until the late
1960's that blue jeans, after several failed moves in previous
decades into a broader mass market, strikingly crossed
over nearly all class, gender, age, regional, national, and
ideological lines to become the universally worn and
widely accepted item of apparel they are today. *And* since
the crossover, enthusiasm for them has by no means been
confined to North America and Western Europe. In former
Soviet bloc countries and much of the Third World, too,
where they have generally been in short supply they remain
highly sought after and hotly bargained over.

A critical feature of this cultural breakthrough is, of course,
blue jeans' identity change from a garment associated exclu-
sively with work (and hard work, at that) to one invested
with many of the symbolic attributes of leisure: ease, com-

fort, casualness, sociability, and the outdoors. *Or,* as the costume historians Jasper and Roach-Higgins (1987) might put it, the garment underwent a process of cultural authentication that led to its acquiring meanings quite different from that with which it began. In bridging the work/leisure divide when it did, it tapped into the new, consumer-goods-oriented, postindustrial affluence of the West on a massive scale. Soon thereafter it penetrated those many other parts of the world that emulate the West.

But this still fails to answer the questions of why so rough-hewn, drably hued, and crudely tailored a piece of clothing should come to exercise the fascination it has to so many diverse societies and peoples, *or* why within a relatively short time of breaking out of its narrow occupational locus it spread so quickly throughout the world.

Fred Davis, "Blue Jeans," 87

At times, whether in fiction or nonfiction, using a conjunction as a sentence opener is like shifting gears, especially in the case of *yet* or *but.* The new sentence, sometimes the first in a new paragraph, is antithetical not just to the preceding clause or sentence but to a *group* of sentences, and it introduces its own group of sentences that contrast with the ideas of those preceding. Below, from a novel, an artful example:

Northern New Mexico was comparatively a rain forest; it looked as if an extremely choosy nutrient were coursing underground. Rocks burst with color. Rainbow striations shot across the walls of mesas, then disappeared into the ground. Dusky green succulents vividly dotted the tan hills, and the occasional saguaro stood in the distance with its hand raised in peace like a planetary alien.

But southern New Mexico was arid, eroded, and flat. As we drove, Clarissa liked to turn off the air-conditioning, roll down the window, and be dust-blown. I was beginning to sunburn on the right side of my face, and we screamed a conversation over the wind that ripped through the car.

Steve Martin, *The Pleasure of My Company,* 133

And twelve times, in the following paragraph, the conjunction *and* contributes to cohesion both as sentence opener and as connector of structures inside each of the sentences except the first. But the cohesion here has intricate and subtle syntactic patterning, including use of additional conjunctions—*so, but*—and more than a dozen pronouns, along with parallel designs of verbs and adjectives:

> Unoka was never happy when it came to wars. He was in fact a coward *and* could not bear the sight of blood. *And so* he changed the subject *and* talked about music, *and* his face beamed. He could hear in his mind's ear the blood-stirring *and* intricate rhythm of the *ekwe and* the *udu and* the *ogene*, *and* he could hear his own flute weaving in *and* out of them, decorating them with a colourful *and* plaintive tune. The total effect was gay *and* brisk, but if one picked out the flute as it went up *and* down *and* then broke up into short snatches, one saw that there was sorrow *and* grief there.
>
> Chinua Achebe, *Things Fall Apart*, 5

Moving in space, time, or method: where, when, or how

Just as conjunctions are used to gather a group of sentences into some sort of logical relation, single adverbs or adverbial connectors can also establish a unity of spatial or temporal order, or a pattern or method. Examples below compare directions or create an order across space and time with a now-then scheme:

> *In front of them* was the central valley. *Across the valley*, on the next mountain, dark belted pines climbed toward the sky. *To the right*, the clustered lights of the village spread thinner, becoming a line along the valley floor and finally disappearing in the distance. *Beyond* either end of the valley there was the faint, far glow of lights from larger towns.
>
> Timothy Houghton, *The First Season*, 75-76

> *Now*, as you watched, you saw another man come slipping through the green trees on the other bank, and *then* three more. *Then*, suddenly, as they were out of sight, came the sharp, sudden close clatter of machine guns. *With that sound*, all the walking around, all the dress rehearsal quality of before the battle, was gone. The boys who had dug shelters for their heads behind the railway bank were right, and, from *now* on, theirs was the business. *From where you stood*, you could see them, well protected, waiting stolidly. *Tomorrow* it would be their turn.
>
> Ernest Hemingway, *By-Line*, 288-289

Three –*ly* adverbs figure in the patterns of cohesion below, with contrasts of time and method linking the two sentences:

> *Traditionally*, ecologists have focused on local conditions
> when monitoring the effects of weather and climate
> on species distribution and population. *Paradoxically*,
> large-scale climatic indices such as the North Atlantic
> Oscillation have *recently* emerged as better predictors
> of ecological processes than local weather variables.
>   "This Issue, the Big Picture," *Nature*, ix

The relationship might have been clearer if *recently* had opened the second sentence in more specific contrast with *Traditionally*. The sentences as written, however, stress the paradox involving *local conditions* and *large-scale indices*.

Sentence connectors: words and phrases

In addition to conjunctions or adverbs of space, time, and method, there is an actual class of words existing for the purpose of cohesion and known as *conjunctive adverbs* or *sentence connectors*. Such words as *however, therefore, moreover, still, nevertheless*, if they are used with accuracy and restraint–as they so often are not–can give a sense of sturdy cohesion to a paragraph. There are also short phrases, almost stock phrases, that function in a similar way, expressing agreement, comparison, contrast, or some other relation. They can work well as sentence openers, but at times they are more effective if placed later in the sentence.

> *Still*, for all of these logistical details, few people would
> dispute that microfilm performs a valuable cultural service.
>   Nicholas A. Basbanes, *A Splendor of Letters*, 21

> There is no doubt, *however*, that the Etruscans developed
> a sophisticated means of documenting their thoughts.
>   Basbanes, 74

> *Less problematic*, but by no means simpler to organize, is
> the matter of rebuilding the library's collection of printed
> books.
>   Basbanes, 139

> *Of more immediate concern* is the desperate status of archival
> newspaper collections which have been routinely discarded
> by research libraries everywhere in favor of black-and-white
> microfilm copies.
>> Basbanes, 224

> The field of environmental aesthetics, *moreover,* is
> international in scope, as people from different countries,
> traditions, and cultures discover in it a common interest.
>> Arnold Berleant, *The Aesthetics of Environment,* xi

Other useful connectors include *on balance, on this subject, the question is, to summarize, to this end, put more generally, it is as if, this would suggest, for comparison, we now turn to...*

Tweaking of sentence openers, or adding one-word or short-phrase inserts, usually between sentences, can be useful if a writer is alert to over-use and triteness. A different class of cohesive devices has to do with the more integral linkage possible when like things are being joined. Devices of this kind range from simple repetition, synonymy, pronoun substitution, and demonstrative reference to complex patterns of parallelism. At the most obvious level, the link in the next example literally announces its own repetition and return:

> Much of the unhappiness, humiliation, misery, and waste of
> talent in our society is due to the great importance attached
> to "normal" intellectual brightness on the one hand and the
> great contempt felt for stupidity on the other. *The word
> "normal" in the preceding sentence* is important; its significance
> is spelled out in the sections later in this chapter on why
> the unorthodox bright are sometimes regarded as stupid.
>> Lewis Anthony Dexter, *The Tyranny of Schooling,* 18

A demonstrative, in the example that follows, replaces and carries forward the entire preceding idea:

> However cautiously, with whatever reservations, after what-
> soever purifications, we must come back to love. *That* alone
> raises us to the co-operation with the artist which is the sole
> reason for our aesthetic pilgrimage.
>> E. M. Forster, *Two Cheers for Democracy,* 123

Pronouns, determiners, demonstratives

Unobtrusive cohesion in the two following paragraphs is achieved in part by pronouns and determiners—*many, their, some, one, they, we, whose, another, other*. Also contributing to the unmannered cohesion in the passages are the phrase *for example*; the adverb *too*; the use of *center* in the first example and its repetition twice:

> During the last two decades, many scholars have been engaged in moving marginalized groups to the center of their fields of study. Their efforts have been both welcomed and challenged. Some feminist scholars, for example, have argued that one cannot simply add women into the knowledge mix, stir, and hope to adequately reconstruct history (or other disciplines). They call for new approaches. We too find the conceptual framework of centering women to be complex and ask, *how* are Asian/Pacific Islander American women being centered in history, and through whose eyes?
> Shirley Hune, *Asian/Pacific Islander American Women*, 5

> *One* study, conducted by a social anthropologist, collected basic information about the composition of the population moving into the city, *their* ways of life and *their* responses to the changes going on around them. *Another* social project set up a pilot program to help in-migrants build *their own* housing. *Other* investigations looked into the questions of health, nutrition and family-spending patterns. *Still others* surveyed migration characteristics, the attitude of the people towards authority and change and the relative importance *they* attached to various public services and physical improvements. *One of these* inquiries…
> Lloyd Rodwin, "Ciudad Guayana," 125

Below, first-person pronouns, along with demonstratives, help serve cohesion. The repeated *with* in the first sentence, and the initial *Yet* in the last sentence also contribute to a comfortable flow:

> The aloneness *many of us* feel on *this* earth is assuaged, more or less effectively, by the deep and abiding relationships *we* have with *other* human beings—with *our* parents,

our children, *our* brothers and sisters, *our* wives, husbands,
sweethearts, lovers, closest friends. *These* relationships
are not always as close as *we* would like *them* to be, and
communication is often distressingly difficult. Yet there is
always the hope that *each* man and woman who seeks this
special warmth will eventually find *it*.

    Albert Rosenfield, "Challenge to the Miracle of Life," 50

Syntactic placement through inversion, branching, apposition, and fragments

Along with different types of branchings, inversion is often used to
move materials into more obvious connection; here the pivotal inversion creates a pattern of chiasmus:

> But politics *was* now *peripheral*. *Closer* at home *was* an active
> social life.
>   Glyndon G. Van Deusen, *William Henry Seward*, 557

    Sentence fragments in a series sometimes serve to link sentences
to those that follow. Often, as in the passage below, the fragments
almost seem to be part of a series of free modifiers in the branching
sentence that precedes them:

> It was one of those pictures, the author at his desk. In an
> enactment of momentary interruption, the man was half-
> turned to the camera, left elbow on blotter, right hand
> splayed over knees. *Features fine and lined, light eyes, one eyelid
> drooping. A taut mouth. Forehead full, full crop of longish white
> hair. The torso broad but spare; the clothes unaffected, old and
> good.* As a boy, Leith had wondered how his father could
> always have good clothes so seldom renewed–a seeming
> impossibility, like having a perpetual two-days' growth of
> beard.
>   Shirley Hazzard, *The Great Fire*, 3-4

Parallelism

Well chosen parallel structures help make sentences cohere. Here the parallel material falls into a clear, coherent organization:

> *For the man, this meant* validating the religious vision of his favorite Christian authors by expressing that vision in the language and concepts of a new age, without committing himself to their religious literalism, their confusion of history and myth. *For the artist, it meant* transforming traditional allegory into a mythopoetic art sometimes close to Bunyan and Spenser, sometimes close to Faulkner, but at its best in an area all its own. *For both man and artist,* it meant devising a way of distinguishing false lights from true by observing their effects in the night. *It meant,* ultimately, correcting the dream in order to conserve it. *Both as man and as artist,* Hawthorne knew how to value the little circle of light in the darkness of human life.
>
> Hyatt H. Waggoner, "Arts and Belief," 195

> Coverdale can be equated with Hawthorne in many conspicuous ways. *Both* are bachelors and minor authors; *they* are reclusive and believe in a degree of solitude essential to them. *They* smoke cigars and drink wine occasionally, read Carlyle and Fourier, and have special fondness for fireplaces. *Their* routine activities are identical, as are their responses: *each* takes pride in the physical labor he does but grows weary of it, in part because it leaves no energy for literary work. *Each* first expects to live permanently in the community, but loses faith in its future and at times looks sardonically back on his earlier hopefulness.
>
> Arlin Turner, "Introduction," 13-14

The parallelism of like things said in like ways in the second example is related also to another important characteristic of the selection, for the parallelism seems, in a way, generated by the opening sentence and hangs together more convincingly perhaps, because of this common source. Much the same effect is achieved in the following example by moving out from the initial sentences of the paragraph and considering the developments step-by-step:

To turn a vegetable into a drug, scientists take a gene from the virus that causes a disease and insert it into a plant cell. The cell has to adopt the gene as part of its own DNA, the master molecule of the genetic code in every living thing. Each cell will pass on that inserted DNA when it divides into two new cells. The first task is finding the right gene. Scientists use enzymes to chop up the viral DNA into manageable fragments. Each fragment is then spliced into bacterial DNA. The modified bacteria are allowed to multiply into cell colonies. The new "recombinant" DNA sequences are transmitted to their offspring.
Diane Boudreau, "Swapping Genes," 19

Numbered lists link parallel ideas together and show relationships. Such a strategy can build a path through a murky landscape or at least set up guideposts. Below, the device makes clear a contrast between spontaneous personal expression and social communicative intentions:

No doubt this is pure conjecture, but the idea vividly suggests *two important points. First,* the smile has always been associated with restraint, with the limitations upon behavior that are imposed upon men and women by the rational forces of civilization, as much as it has been taken as a sign of spontaneity, or a mirror in which one may see reflected the personal happiness, delight, or good humor of the wearer. *Second,* although the verb *to smile* is most often used intransitively, without an object, the act of smiling itself is inevitably social and communicative, part of the complex nonverbal language with which our bodies are equipped. A decorous smile, a smile of restraint, is therefore an important ingredient of good manners, just as the lewd grin has to do with the bad. It can be a kind of mask.
Angus Trumble, *A Brief History of the Smile,* 3

Most writers want to consider with care whether or not a numbered or "bullet" list helps to clarify meaning or contribute to cohesion. Such lists may oversimplify, or sound authoritarian.

Questions and summary statements

Often a single question or a series of parallel questions sets an agenda for what is to follow, sometimes for a single paragraph, or more likely for an essay or book with no single answer but a group of parallel ideas as partial answers:

> How can we improve the lives and opportunities of migrant women engaged in legal occupations such as nannies and maids? How can we prevent trafficking and enslavement? More basically, can we find a way to counterbalance the systematic transfer of caring work from poor countries to rich, and the inevitable trauma of the children left behind? Our contributors do not have easy answers, but their essays, many based on recent and extensive fieldwork, do help us take that essential first step—to bring the world's most invisible women into the light.
>
> Barbara Ehrenreich and Arlie Russell Hochschild, *Global Woman*, 13

The cohering parallelism below returns to the topic sentence, reaffirming but qualifying it in a circular and unifying development:

> *Science is investigation. But* if it were only investigation, it would be without fruit, and useless. Henry Cavendish investigated for the mere fun of the thing, and left the world in ignorance of his most important discoveries. Our admiration for his genius is tempered by a certain disapproval; we feel that such a man is selfish and antisocial. *Science is investigation; yes. But* it is also, and no less essentially, communication. But all communication is literature. In one of its aspects, then, science is a branch of literature.
>
> Aldous Huxley, *The Olive Tree*, 56

Each of these two fragmentary parallel paragraphs expresses a negative, one preceding and one following a paragraph that gives details:

> *No letter. Nothing.*

> So he had to write to her. But all he remembered of that four days of paradise was stumbling off the ship into Daphne's arms—that is how it had seemed: a radiance of bliss. A wonderful spreading house on a hillside in a street of such houses, and a garden. A little verandah from where you

looked down at the sea, the murdering sea, and where he had danced with her, all night, cheek to cheek. Then that little house in the bushes that smelled of salt, and the waves crashing and thundering all around them.

But no address. Not a number, not the name of the street.
   Doris Lessing, *The Grandmothers*, 274

A more conversational cohesion is achieved below by word repetition (*story*), parallel structures, pronouns, and comparison and contrast:

I always loved English because whatever human beings are, we are *story*tellers. It is our *stories* that give a light to the future. When I went to college I became a history major because history is such a wonderful *story* of who we think we are. English is much more a *story* of who we really are.
   Nikki Giovanni, *Quilting the Black-Eyed Pea*, 108

Transitional words, comparison, contrast

Transitional words and phrases, repetition, parallelism, structures of comparison and contrast, and the other cohesive devices that operate between sentences also work for cohesion in longer passages:

Further, women's work-based networks reflect contradictory and simultaneous processes occurring in the factories. *On the one hand,* women's work is considered unskilled, and little formal training is provided. *Yet* there are many skills, especially social ones that are necessary to work effectively, so women socialize with each other regarding shop floor practices. *Although* Chicana cannery workers do not have the autonomy of nurses or sales clerks, their work-based networks function in a manner similar to the "sisterhoods" described by Susan Porter Benson and Barbara Melosh. *At the same time, although* all women were in the same position as line workers, ethnic cleavages among the work force were reflected in exclusive work-based networks. *In contrast to* Louise Lamphere's factory worker informants (see this issue), Chicana cannery workers formed their own networks and usually did not include their white ethnic compatriots. *Within the context of* working on the line, Chicanas established solidarity with their Chicana coworkers and maintained conflictive relations with other non-Chicana women.
   Patricia Zavella, "Abnormal Intimacy," 425-426

Below, in a different setting, the opening of Ernest Hemingway's introduction to *Men at War* shows many devices, including parallelism, at work over the space of three paragraphs. Only a few of the key cohesive structures are italicized:

> *This book will not tell you how to die.* Some cheer-leaders of war can always get out a pamphlet *telling* the best way to go through that small but unnecessary business at the end...

> No. *This book will not tell you how to die. This book will tell you,* though, how *all men* from the earliest times we know have fought and died. *So when you have read it* you will know that there are *no worse* things to be gone through than *men* have been through before.

> *When you read* the account of Saint Louis the IX's Crusade you will see that no expeditionary force can ever have to go through anything *as bad as those men* endured. *We* have only to fight *as well as the men* who stayed and fought at Shiloh. It is not necessary that *we* should fight *better.* There can be no such thing as *better*...
>
> Ernest Hemingway, *Men at War*, introduction

Variety in sentence length and cohesive flow

Contributing to the flow of the passage above is the great variety in the length of the sentences. Strands that are all the same length do not always make for a smooth weave, as is demonstrated by the series of sentences below, quoted from a newspaper's "Kids' Page." Two of the four sentences have twelve words, and the others eleven and thirteen, the similarity in length creating a lumpy rhythm:

> Only a portion of the painting is shown here, called a "detail." The actual painting is wider and includes more buildings and people.

> The artist Antonio Canal, also known as Canaletto, made this painting in 1763. In it, he included many of the buildings that surround the plaza.
>
> "California Classroom," E16

The article above continues with several more sentences of about the same length, perhaps in a mistaken effort to communicate at a level children would understand.

The way any piece of writing, from a pair of sentences to a much longer passage, makes us think of it as one piece is an important aspect of its style. The examples here have been chosen to emphasize the due place of syntactic structures in the techniques of such cohesion. Ideas and the words that carry them do not just accidentally fall together into a convincing procession. Cohesion that seems smooth and relaxed is sometimes quite hard to get and is always a matter, partly, of syntactic choices – from the straightforward use of connectors to the most ingenious patternings.

Somewhere a ponderous tower clock slowly dropped a dozen strokes into the gloom.
James Thurber

But I knew. I knew. I knew because he had been far away from me long before he went. He's gone away and he won't come back. He's gone away and he won't come back, he's gone away and he'll never come back. Listen to the wheels saying it, on and on and on. That's sentimental, I suppose. Wheels don't say anything. Wheels can't speak. But I hear them.
Dorothy Parker

Sun and moon, sun and moon, time goes.
John Updike

Space is all one space and thought is all one thought, but my mind divides its spaces into spaces into spaces and thoughts into thoughts into thoughts. Like a large condominium.
Andy Warhol

CHAPTER FOURTEEN

Syntactic Symbolism

THE birds in the sentence below may not symbolize anything, but the syntax used to record their flight seems to do more than just describe it in some arbitrary way. Rather, the syntax itself becomes a kind of simulation:

> He watched their flight: bird after bird: a dark flash, a swerve,
> a flash again, a dart aside, a curve, a flutter of wings.
> James Joyce, *A Portrait of the Artist as a Young Man*, 224

The abrupt, paratactic structure reflects the erratic motion of the birds in their darting, curving flight. A similar grammatical arrangement, another rapid, veering series, is used below to convey the successive jolts of a slight automobile accident in the following:

> They gripped...bump, jump, a swerve, two wheels lifted in
> the air, brakes on, bump with tree at edge of embankment,
> standstill.
> E. M. Forster, *A Passage to India*, 88

Although "a swerve" is written into both sentences, the actions are not as similar as the syntax used to describe them. Syntactic symbols do not persist. Syntax is by nature more limited than meaning, for it must carry many different meanings. A noun and a transitive verb and an object, for example, form a specific, single structure, of which there are millions of examples, all meaning different things. But now and then a skilled writer may use the same structure in a way that mimics the particular actions the sentence describes.

Out of the many unique phrasings and syntactic creations that follow as examples, familiar structures emerge. Here we will see the basic syntactic units and formulas discussed in earlier chapters applied with care and invention, combined and modified in many ways, often to excellent effect. Short basic sentences or left-, mid-, and right-branching ones are expanded with different kinds of free or bound modifiers, clauses, nominative absolutes, appositives, and set to various rhythms, some ordered by parallelism and some left irregular, suggesting now one thing, now–with a little change in the syntax–something quite different.

Syntactic symbols sometimes have the help of poetic diction, metrics, and sound symbolism. These techniques appear at times in prose, and word order is necessary to their effects. In the following sentence, the eight syllables of the two bulky, slow-moving words in italics themselves burden the line as if to prove its point; the syntax that permits this effect is no more special than the pairing of an adjective and a noun. The effect is mainly a matter of word length, but the words must be in the right order:

> That system, for all its *elephantine cumbersomeness*, is also,
> in the long run, wonderfully adaptable and flexible.
>   Stewart Alsop, *The Center*, 352

In the next sentence, thirteen stop consonants retard the progress of the sentence to produce an aural analogue for the announcement of the hour. The sentence is made symbolic primarily by its sounds, but the arrangement of the words helps to produce the intervals that contribute to the effect:

> Somewhere a *ponderous* tower *clock* slowly *dropped* a *dozen*
> *strokes into* the *gloom*.
>   James Thurber, *The Wonderful O*, 1

Repeated sibilants and liquid consonants in the example below suggest the lazy scene itself; they are helped along by the relaxed syntax of the fragment and the sentences that follow:

> A scene of somnolence and satisfaction. At tables all around
> under the great trees similarly blessed people lazed. The seas
> all around them, only a few feet below, sighed and hissed
> and lapped, and the voices were low and lazy.
>   Doris Lessing, *The Grandmothers*, 5

Next, sibilants are used to reproduce the very buzzing of the flies:

> The minute-winning days, like flies, buzz home to death.
> Thomas Wolfe, *Look Homeward, Angel*, 3

Although the sound-symbolism predominates, these effects rely on syntax as well for they result almost as much from getting the words in the right order as from any individual characteristics of the words themselves, their length, or sound. The onomatopoeia of the word *crunch* creates the verbal mimicry below, but even this poetic device operates along with a syntactic maneuver in which the monosyllable is tripled to imitate repeated footfalls:

> So Ella said, "Yes, ma'am," and hobbled down the gravel walk, *crunch crunch crunch* beneath the trees, and was gone.
> William Styron, *Lie Down in Darkness*, 121

Syntax alone accomplishes most of the symbolizing in the next sentence. Conjunctions are used to link the repetitions, re-creating the spaced effect of an echo:

> His echo, fugitive along the faces of the gorge, called pitifully *back and back and back* to us until it died in the distance.
> John Hersey, *A Single Pebble*, 66

And here, with varying repetitions, a novelist captures through syntax the shifting back-and-forth of a reiterated transaction:

> You have seen the rotting shell of the house with its sagging portico and scaling walls, its sagging blinds and plank-shuttered windows, set in the middle of the domain which had reverted to the state and had been *bought and sold and bought and sold again and again and again*.
> William Faulkner, *Absalom, Absalom!*, 213

A relentless syntax now travesties a weary orchestral drone:

> ...the din, already painful, went somehow up a notch, now almost completely covering the noise from the pit where the band went wearily on with *Over the Rainbow*, over and over, *Over the Rainbow*, over again.
> William Goldman, "Judy Floats," 78

Most artful syntax distinguishes this remarkable portrayal below. A woman riding in a taxicab hears repeated words in the turning of the wheels:

> But I knew. I knew. I knew because he had been far away from me long before he went. He's gone away and he won't come back. He's gone away and he won't come back, he's gone away and he'll never come back. Listen to the wheels saying it, on and on and on. That's sentimental, I suppose. Wheels don't say anything. Wheels can't speak. But I *hear* them.
> Dorothy Parker, "Sentiment," 355

Repetition is, naturally, one of the easiest symbolic effects to create, since it is also a quality of grammatical constructions when they are compounded and repeated, and needs no ingenious translation by the reader from symbol to sense, from syntax to meaning. Writing "this is repetitive and boring" a dozen times or so, for instance, tends to confirm its own accusation. This is unlikely and oversimplified, but it should be clear that such an effect, even much subtler, is not difficult to come by. A sense of the uneventful has very easily been infused into the next satiric statement:

> As long as he holds his breath, it will not rain, there will be no raindrops, no schizoid water wobbling, sideways, straight back, it will be an *even, even, even, even, even, even, even* world.
> Tom Wolfe, *The Kandy-Kolored Tangerine-Flake Streamline Baby*, 75

Below, in excerpts from closely textured fiction, repetitive structures are remembered and themselves repeated later with unusual effect:

> ...he was sharing Mr. Ramsay's evening walk *up and down, up and down* the terrace.
> Virginia Woolf, *To the Lighthouse*, 12

And two pages later, that:

> They knew what he liked best–to be for ever walking *up and down, up and down*, with Mr. Ramsay...
> Woolf, 14

A set of repeating alternations is recorded in the next example, and then, four pages later, used again in a new but analogous context. An imitative description of a roaring train in and out of a tunnel creates syntactic associations transferred to a metaphor for another monotonous routine, the alternation of school terms and vacations:

> He closed his eyes and the train went on, *roaring and then stopping; roaring again, stopping.* It was nice to hear it *roar and stop and then roar out of the tunnel again and stop.*
> James Joyce, *A Portrait of the Artist as a Young Man*, 13

> First came the *vacation and then the next term and then vacation again and then again another term and then again the vacation.* It was like a train going in and out of tunnels and that was like the noise of the boys eating in the refectory when you opened and closed the flaps of the ears. *Term, vacation; tunnel, out; noise, stop.*
> Joyce, 17

These repetitions create clear symbolic effects:

> Sun and moon, sun and moon, time goes.
> John Updike, *Rabbit, Run*, 114

> Bats, rats, birds, insects will as soon nest inside a house as out; it is to them a normal growth of the eternal jungle, which alternately produces *houses trees, houses trees.*
> E. M. Forster, *A Passage to India*, 35

> He was walking three steps backwards and three steps forwards along the gangway which connected the benches. *Three quick steps and turn and three quick steps and turn,* with his eyes on the ceiling.
> C. P. Snow, *The Search*, 38

> Two weeks later, the tape arrived of the race and I memorized it, especially those last hundred yards, Wowie alone, heading for the finish line, his body *rhythmically stretching and contracting* as his four legs *reached and folded, reached and folded.*
> Jane Smiley, *A Year at the Races*, 120

> They are not talking much, and the talk is quiet, *of nothing in particular, of nothing at all in particular, of nothing at all.*
> James Agee, *A Death in the Family*, 14

Another repetition of prepositional phrases, here artfully doubled, divides a sentence's spaces into spaces into spaces. This helps to imitate and dramatize an effective simile emphasized by its syntax as a fragment:

> Space is all one space and thought is all one thought, but my mind divides its *spaces into spaces into spaces and thoughts into thoughts into thoughts. Like a large condominium.* Occasionally I think about the one Space and the one Thought, but usually I don't. Usually I think about my condominium.
> Andy Warhol, *The Philosophy of Andy Warhol,* 143

Describing the beauty of Antigua, a novelist uses extravagantly duplicated syntactic patterns that suggest the layering of stage sets, as well as the lushness and lavishness of the island. The parallel syntax of this long sentence below continues for thirty repetitions of syntactic patterns with *real* or *unreal*:

> Antigua is beautiful. Antigua is too beautiful. Sometimes the beauty of it seems *unreal*. Sometimes the beauty of it seems as if it were stage sets for a play, for no *real* sunset could look like that; no *real* seawater could strike that many shades of blue at once; no *real* sky could be that shade of blue—another shade of blue, completely different from the shades of blue seen in the sea—and no *real* cloud could be that white and float just that way in that blue sky; no *real* day could be that sort of sunny and bright, making everything seem transparent and shallow; and no *real* night could be that sort of black, making everything seem thick and deep and bottomless.
> Jamaica Kincaid, *A Small Place,* 77ff

A more elaborate repetition, this time of a sentence, mimics the process of an assembly line in 1922. The same sentence is repeated four times in two pages, as the intervening steps are described by rhythms that track the actions themselves:

> Every fourteen seconds *Wierzbicki reams a bearing and Stephanides grinds a bearing and O'Malley attaches a bearing to a camshaft.* This camshaft travels away on a conveyor, curling around the factory, through its clouds of metal dust, its acid fogs, until another worker fifty yards on reaches up and removes the camshaft, fitting it onto the engine block (twenty seconds). Simultaneously, other men are unhooking parts from adjacent conveyors—the carburetor, the distribu-

tor, the intake manifold–and connecting them to the engine
block. Above their bent heads, huge spindles pound steam-
powered fists. No one says a word. *Wierzbicki reams a bearing
and Stephanides grinds a bearing and O'Malley attaches a bearing
to a camshaft.*
> Jeffrey Eugenides, *Middlesex*, 95-96

Parallel phrases of time and paired constructions, italicized below,
help a historian to show the importance colonial Americans attached
to the *movement* of the sun:

A typical example might begin: "as I was coming out of the
south field *about twilight...*"; "when my wife was suckling
her child *a little after daybreak...*"; "*about mid-day, when the
sun was high...*" By putting these fragments together (and
there are many more), we can begin to feel the importance
in these people's lives not just of the sun as such but of the
sun's movement, its regular *comings and goings* across the sky.
In fact, it seems entirely clear that *dawn and dusk, sunup and
sundown,* were the two most important markers in the overall scheme of their day.
> John Demos, *Circles and Lines*, 3

In the paragraph that follows the one quoted above, Demos continues
such pairings: "activity and experience," "sleep and wakefulness,"
"night and day."

Parallelism is used not to simulate repetition in the next two examples, but to suggest other kinds of movement and rhythm, rapid
motion and accelerated motion respectively:

Its tone changes with kaleidoscopic rapidity–from irony
to pathos to ridicule to poetry.
> Richard M. Kain, *Fabulous Voyager*, 240

The imagery is that of mobile, going things, increasingly
passionate and swift–first slow waves, then fitful music
leaping, then flames, then racing creatures.
> Dorothy Van Ghent, *The English Novel*, 273

Although syntactic symbolism is more often seen in fiction, essays,
or journalism, the writer of a book describing a computing process
here uses two noun phrases with like syntax to define *a string of bits,*

and, at the end of the sentence, a clause with an appropriate inversion of subject and predicate to portray the result that emerges at the conclusion of the process:

> Send a string of bits—*numbers to be added, words to be sorted*—into the circuitry and the bits will rattle through the gates until *out the other end comes the answer.*
> George Johnson, *A Shortcut Through Time,* 29

Parallel sentence structure combines with the action of –*ing* verbs to describe a pandemonium of enchanted fireworks:

> Dragons comprised entirely of green-and-gold sparks were soaring up and down the corridors, emitting loud fiery blasts and bangs as they went. Shocking-pink Catherine wheels five feet in diameter were whizzing lethally through the air like so many flying saucers. Rockets with long tails of brilliant silver stars were ricocheting off the walls. Sparklers were writing swearwords in midair of their own accord. Firecrackers were exploding like mines everywhere Harry looked, and instead of burning themselves out, fading from sight, or fizzling to a halt, these pyrotechnical miracles seemed to be gaining in energy and momentum the longer he watched.
> J. K. Rowling, *Harry Potter and the Order of the Phoenix,* 632

Again in fiction, we see –*ing* words setting up a symbolic series of actions, this time in a quieter scene. Onomatopoetic nouns contribute to the effect both through their sound and their syntactic arrangement. The actions wind down with the final passive:

> Later, as I lay in bed, I would try to imagine the Harts settling down for the night: each family member journeying to and from the bathroom—the swosh of toothbrushes, the shouts up and down the staircase, the yelps of laughter, and then the noise slowly dying out until the only sounds in the house were the murmur of bedsheets and the *flup flup* of book pages being turned.
> Zoë Heller, *What Was She Thinking?,* 130

Next, fragmentary syntax with repeated verbs as sentence openers helps to introduce the character who is speaking as well as the daughter she describes. The introductory predicates without subjects suggest the eagerness of the youngster to open her books and of the mother to tell about it:

> Sidda can't help herself. She just loves books. Loves the way they feel, the way they smell, loves those black letters marching across the white pages. When Sidda falls in love with a book, she is positive that she is the very first person in the world to have discovered it, poor child. Thinks that no one else anywhere, anytime, has ever heard of the book.
> Rebecca Wells, *Little Altars Everywhere*, 51

Verbs and verbals can reproduce several kinds of motion – smooth, continuous, or unpredictable – with the help of other syntactic features. The syntax below moves toward a kind of stoppage after a long mid-branch and toward the pivotal moment this provides, the sentence and the story turning on the verb in italics:

> Henry Levin, an ambitious, handsome thirty, who walked the floors in Macy's book department wearing a white flower in his lapel, having recently come into a small inheritance, *quit*, and went abroad seeking romance.
> Bernard Malamud, *The Magic Barrel*, 105

In the next example, the isolated adverb *again*, oddly set off by commas and then repeated, creates a syntactic pivot:

> Our voices, curving slowly around the woods, again, again swung back on silence.
> Truman Capote, *The Grass Harp*, 51

An abrupt interruption is next telescoped into a single sentence, closing it with an arresting, punctuated emphasis on the single last word, which inversion of the normal adjective-noun order has moved to the end:

> The pavements were slick with leavings, mainly cast-off, rotten leaves, flowers, fruit and vegetables which had met with disaster natural and slow, *or abrupt*.
> James Baldwin, *Giovanni's Room*, 70

Prose rhythm is also stopped short in this example:

> In a moment the vision had faded but she remembered
> where she was, *immobile*.
> Flannery O'Connor, *Everything That Rises Must Converge*,
> 218

The same syntactic format is used here, with its isolated terminal word,
a verbal appositive:

> Up the gangplank and the vision of the world adjusts itself,
> *narrows*.
> F. Scott Fitzgerald, *Tender Is the Night*, 205

A more complex syntactic narrowing, a kind of flickering out,
results from the careful juxtaposition in the first two sentences below
of words and phrases of decreasing length, and from the use, in the
third sentence, of those four stressed monosyllables that punctuate the
sense of utter extinction:

> One soul was lost; a tiny soul: his. It flickered once and
> went out, forgotten, lost. The end: black cold void waste.
> James Joyce, *A Portrait of the Artist as a Young Man*, 141

Similar techniques convey the ideas of the next three sentences
with a syntax that seems to match them. In the first, a verbal series
unfurls only to fall off at once. In the second, a compound-complex
sentence offers nine one-syllable verbs defining a series of actions that
itself illustrates the *routine* being described and tails off at the end. The
appositional list of the third appears to wither, diminish, and spend
itself grammatically:

> The bugle's voice unfurled, shivered, fell.
> Cynthia Ozick, *Trust*, 2

> My routine with the baby is that I leave the house at about
> four o'clock, stop by the post office to pick up the mail, go
> on to the park, let the baby play for a while, go around by
> the hardware store or the library, and head home in time for
> the show, which starts at 5:30.
> Lydia Davis, *Almost No Memory*, 159

> It was all dry: all withered: all spent.
> Virginia Woolf, *To the Lighthouse*, 224

A syntax of increase can be just as suggestive, here recounting the creation, growth, and reproduction of original life:

> The hundreds of millions of years passed and one day a special cell emerged in the pungent broths of the ocean or a lake. It had being; it ate food; it divided and so reproduced. It was alive and it was life.
> Philip Wylie, *The Magic Animal*, 22

Much of the success in the passages above is a matter of spacing, of grammatical pacing, of a writer's knowing where the sentence should end, and when, and how it should get there—by a process of increase or narrowing, or according to some definite and controlled rhythm, like repetition or acceleration. The compound predicates of the next two sentences add other obvious examples; the course of the writing takes form as a deliberate verbal sequence that ends appropriately, inevitably, just where it does:

> He is born, goes to school, marries, has children, quarrels with his fellows, suffers the same defeats which afflict his contemporaries, and dies.
> Robert Payne, *The Christian Centuries*, 391

> If Langer is right, then poetry of this kind (for her there is no other kind) presents human feelings as they are born, develop, gather momentum, branch, sub-divide, coalesce, dwindle, and die away.
> Donald Davie, *Articulate Energy*, 85

The next example awaits a sound that is finally heard in its second sentence, at the climax of an inverted syntax that delivers the capitalized and onomatopoetic ending only after a piling of adjectives to suspend and dramatize its arrival:

> He was straining his ears, waiting to hear some sound—a sound that he thought would surely stop the beating of his heart. Then he heard it; there came a distant, definite, soft, crushing yet pulpy: PLOP!
> Richard Wright, *Savage Holiday*, 51

Consider the next craftily paced sentence:

> And as it ended, as they sat up in the gloom and prepared to enter ordinary life, suddenly the long drawn strangeness of the morning snapped.
> E. M. Forster, *A Passage to India*, 16

Holding the verb–the telling of the action–until the very end, and prefacing the main clause with two parallel left-branches creates for the narrated act an analogous grammar of suspension, which subordinates, holds off, and then suddenly stops.

Another strategy involving verbs works in a different way. Especially in nonfiction, a verb is sometimes placed at the beginning of each item in a series that accumulates quickly. The first example, with nine items, dramatizes the multiple responsibilities facing a president-elect in an all-too-short transition period:

> There was so much to do: select the cabinet, important
> sub-cabinet officials, and the White House staff; work with
> the Bush people on the mechanics of the move; begin brief-
> ing on national security and talk to foreign leaders; reach
> out to congressional leaders; finalize the economic proposals
> I would present to Congress; develop a plan to implement
> my other campaign commitments; deal with a large number
> of requests for meetings and the desire of many of our
> campaign workers and major supporters to know as soon
> as possible whether they would be part of the new admin-
> istration; and respond to unfolding events.
> Bill Clinton, *My Life*, 447

The next example makes similar use of predicate verbs–*indicates, points to, designates, brings, introduces*–but interrupts them with modifiers forming a rhythm that mimics the picking and choosing of the chopsticks being described:

> First of all, a chopstick–as its shape sufficiently indicates–
> has a deictic function: it points to the food, designates the
> fragment, brings into existence by the very gesture of
> choice, which is the index; but thereby, instead of ingestion
> following a kind of mechanical sequence, in which one
> would be limited to swallowing little by little the parts of
> one and the same dish, the chopstick, designating what it
> selects (and thus selecting there and then *this* and not *that*),
> introduces into the use of food not an order but a caprice,
> a certain indolence: in any case, an intelligent and no
> longer mechanical operation.
> Roland Barthes, "Chopsticks," 41-42

The syntax of the following passage also is geared to the quick survey it provides, moving briskly through a summary and then plunging toward its close, as does the book under discussion:

> His too was a remarkable book, if only for its scope.
> Davidson starts with "The Rise of Intelligence" when
> "man first rose above the brute." Then he trots briskly
> through "ancient Turanian," Semitic, and Aryan
> education, picks up speed on "civic education" in Judaea,
> Greece, and Rome, gallops swiftly across Hellenistic,
> Alexandrian, Patristic, and Muslim education; leaps
> magnificently over the thorny barriers of scholasticism,
> the medieval universities, the Renaissance, Reformation,
> and Counter-Reformation; and then plunges wildly
> through the remaining five centuries in sixty-four
> pages flat.
>   Bernard Bailyn, *Education in the Forming of American
>   Society*, 6-7

Once again a sentence ends, symbolically, just where it should. In the preceding example, it is a main clause that moves toward this appropriate close, but the symbolic conclusion might just as well be reached later, with the main clause followed by loose or free material before the end of the sentence. The next selections work this way. They are cumulative or right-branching sentences whose symbolic effects are generated by the cadencing of the right-branch toward the fitting close. In the first two, it is clear how the cumulative grammar is able to depict, in order, things laid down and dropped-off:

> Keziah Dane was thinking of another kind of morning
> in another day, *finding peace again for all the anguish she had
> known, and pride for all the dreams long since laid down.*
>   Sue Grafton, *Keziah Dane*, 220

> The big studio audience is rapt, *silent as Barbra Streisand
> softens and rounds the long-held note, stripping the brass from
> it before she lets it fall, ever so gradually, into a throbbing,
> eyes-closed, roller-coaster drop-off.*
>   Diane Lurie, "The Tears of Barbra Streisand," 96

Varied parallelism sets the rhythm for the two right-branching examples that follow, one cadenced to recede, the other to descend:

> And I could see the great forward lunge of the horses and the crowd breaking and rolling *back* like a wave, *back,* and screaming and cursing, and some laughing—*back and around and out* into the avenue, stumbling and pushing, as the horses, heads high and bits froth-flecked, went over the curb to land stiff-legged and slide over the cleared walk as upon ice skates and past, carried by the force of the charge, sideways now, legs stiff, sparks flying, to where another crowd looted another store.
> Ralph Ellison, *Invisible Man*, 480

The dizzying backward rush is imaged grammatically above in a sentence that lunges forward by recapitulation, as *back* is carried from the main clause into the right-branch and repeated as part of the larger, driving accumulation. In the descending example below, the large right-branch starts rather emphatically with the strong, punctuated repetition of the prepositional objects, and then falls off in a slackened syntax that repeats the preposition and adds a new object loosely with a conjunction:

> And Giovanni fell—*back into the room, the streets, the world, into the presence and the shadow of death.*
> James Baldwin, *Giovanni's Room*, 230

In the following constructions, the symbolic effects are themselves patterns of expansion, gradation, or accumulation. In the first two, one both left- and right-branching, the other with only a cumulative addition, syntactic materials accrete to suggest successive geological deposition:

> *For nearly forty million years, from that extensive rupture in the ocean floor,* small amounts of liquid rock seeped out, *each forcing its way up through what had escaped before, each contributing some small portion to the accumulation that was building on the floor of the sea.*
> James Michener, *Hawaii*, 4

> The truth is there, *ready for you to catch with both mind and heart by contemplating the layers of compressed volcanic ash which alternate with the strata of lava belonging to different*

> *ecological areas, deposited by succeeding eruption, changing in*
> *texture as well as color, dipping into an inky sea to slake with*
> *salt and sulphur the thirst of millennia.*
>   H. C. Brewster, "Saint Philomena," 573

The next cumulative structure organizes the grammatical material beyond the base clause into sections set off by commas, each slightly longer than the previous section. The grammar is analogous to the graded rise of the water level:

> The water would rise inch by inch, covering the grass
> and shrubs, covering the trees and houses, covering the
> monuments and the mountain tops.
>   James Joyce, *A Portrait of the Artist as a Young Man,* 117

Describing the style of Virginia Woolf, a later writer uses unusual word order in the first sentence below to cast a striking metaphor. The cumulative structure of the second sentence elaborates.

> Hooked on a well-thrown line of words, is landed, a fine fat
> fish. She knows how to draw the world out, breaking the
> air with colour and the beat of life, and before we can truly
> admire it at our feet, the line is out on the water again, catch
> after catch, drawn from the under-depths, the shimmering
> world that slips through our hands.
>   Jeanette Winterson, *Art Objects,* 64

Below, we move even beyond the freedom of the loose or cumulative sentence. In different ways, the syntax of the next two examples is symbolically overloaded. The first joins the participial overflow of its left-branching opener to the conglomerated subject of its second huge sentence to parody Vassar's kaleidoscopic riches:

> Bucolically set in rolling orchard country just outside the
> town of Poughkeepsie, with the prospect of long walks and
> rides along curving back roads and cold red apples to bite;
> framed by two mirrorlike lakes, by a lively off-campus street
> full of dress shops, antique stores, inns, which were brim-
> ming now with parents, brothers, and fiancés, Vassar, still
> warm and summery, gave the impression of a cornucopia
> overflowing with promises. The bareheaded Yale boys in
> roadsters parked outside Taylor Gate; the tall, dazzling girls,
> upperclassmen, in pale sweaters and skirts, impeccable, with

pearls at the throat and stately walks, like goddesses; the
vaulted library; the catalogue already marked and starred for
courses like Psychology and Philosophy ("The Meaning of
Morals, Beauty, Truth, God–open only to freshmen by
special permission"); the trolley tracks running past the
spiked fence downtown to further shopping, adventure,
the railroad station, New York, plays, concerts, night clubs,
Fifth Avenue bus rides–all this seemed to foretell four years
of a Renaissance lavishness, in an academy that was a Forest
of Arden and a Fifth Avenue department store combined.
Mary McCarthy, *On the Contrary*, 197

In the second example, with frenzied variety, a grammatical dis-
array is paraded to mime and to mock the flood, fragmentation, and
artificiality of architectural research:

Coarse paper; rebellion; grease pencil; imaginative sketch,
weird perspectives; publication; exhibition; model; the great
architectural critic inventing cinemascopic epigrams; world-
wide recognition, lectures, disappearance of rebellion; inte-
gration into the system; publicity; books on architecture and
urbanism; publicity; radio, television; USA, USSR: FAIA, Bel-Air,
La glorie!

That is how ARCHITECTURAL RESEARCH nowadays is born,
lives, and dies!

Launched the wrong way; misunderstood; pursued incor-
rectly; non-existent; worse, some sympathetic ones but not
always very smart persuaded that it is successful research by
a pseudo-philosophical, half-mathematic and half-literary
(but not always shocking) jargon; with accents of simplicity
or intellectual supremacy; with a good stock of sophisti-
cated, barbaric and suggestive drawings...calling themselves
"searchers" or "researchers" forcing their way into the world
of worlds; far from the people, far from themselves...showing a frozen future in a few booklets and publicity meetings to which they invite some big wheels...who
happen also
to be purchasing agents...making their vision highly
commercial.

Hoopla! let's stop the charlatans of research! **STOP THE
FLOW OF SHINY PHOTOS TO THE ARCHITECTURAL
MAGAZINES!**
Ionel Schein, "A Phenomenology of Research," 31

Unpacked and examined, this rare kind of supersentence can be read as a cluttered repository of its syntactic opposite – the elliptical fragment. But such fragments, even when they come together with others in a single sentence, do not usually undergo such vast multiple collisions as the one above. Far simpler patterns are the rule. The syntactic format is usually parataxis, where independent units are run together without conjunctive material, sometimes punctuated, sometimes not. The paratactic series below symbolizes the quick shuttling of the passing scene:

> They were in town now. *Streets, houses, buildings* shuttled past.
> Ross Lockridge, Jr., *Raintree County*, 872

The fragmented grammar below reveals the events being described in a confusion of contact clauses and smaller grammatical units:

> Events unrolled themselves then, like a reel of film spinning backward in flickering confusion, Mrs. Rice, yes, and then this morning, the maid came, last night I drank, I was upset, yes, Mrs. Rice and what she said.
> Brian Moore, *The Lonely Passion of Judith Hearne*, 117

The contrasting examples below, from the closing lines of two novels, portray the exhilarating release of energy into action and, oppositely, the subsidence of action into rest and temporary silence:

> His hands lift of their own and he feels the wind on his ears even before, his heels hitting heavily on the pavement at first but with an effortless gathering out of a kind of sweet panic growing lighter and quicker and quieter, he runs. *Ah: runs. Runs.*
> John Updike, *Rabbit, Run*, closing lines

> As he stretched out, he took a long breath, and then he lay, looking at the mesh of the screen, pulled loose by vines, and listening to the steady scratching of Mrs. Tuttle's broom. He wanted to tell her to sprinkle the floor. She was raising too much dust. In a few minutes he would call down to her, "Damp it down, Mrs. Tuttle. There's water in the sink." But not just yet. At this time he had no messages for anyone. *Nothing. Not a single word.*
> Saul Bellow, *Herzog*, closing lines

In the following passage, a final catastrophe is postured by an abrupt syntactic interruption that substitutes *when* for *if* and, at the end, by a short sentence and two two-word fragments, dramatic in their rhythms after the longer sentences that precede:

> On average, objects greater than a hundred yards in diameter strike the planet once every five thousand years and asteroids half a mile across thunder down at intervals of three hundred thousand years. Three hundred thousand years is a long time in anybody's book. But if–when–such a collision occurs, the explosion will be in the million-megaton range and will cloak the atmosphere in dust, thrusting the entire planet into a deep freeze and effectively stifling all plant growth for a period of a year or more. There will be no crops. No forage. No sun.
>
> T. Coraghessan Boyle, "Chicxulub," 135

From highly different contexts, we see fragments, short sentences, interruptions, disconnections, combining with repeated first person pronouns to suggest the splintered, disjointed immediacy, of a terrible experience, in the first example, and an almost unfathomable realization in the second:

> *A dog, but not a dog.* It was bigger than a pariah, much bigger than a jackal, almost the size of a wolf.... It had picked me as its enemy. I wasn't ready to die.
>
> I let the dog inch so close I could feel a slimy vapor spray out of its muzzle. I let it crouch and growl its low, terrible, gullety growl. I took aim and waited for it to leap on me.
>
> The staff crushed the dog's snout while it was still in mid-leap. Spiny twigs hooked deep into its nostrils and split them open. I saw all this as I lay on the winter-hard ground.
>
> The women helped me up. One of them poked the wounded animal with a twig.... I'd never seen that much blood. The women dragged the body to the nullah and let it flow away.
>
> Bharati Mukherjee, *Jasmine*, 56-57

"We"– this "we" is everyone who has never experienced
anything like what they went through– don't understand.
We don't get it. We truly can't imagine what it was like.
We can't imagine how dreadful, how terrifying war is; and
how normal it becomes. *Can't understand, can't imagine.*
Susan Sontag, *Regarding the Pain of Others*, 125-126

Prose is linear. It is read and is said to move. It must by nature,
therefore, generate a symbolics of spatial or temporal movement
widened by its context beyond the limits of the actual sentence read
from left to right in so many seconds. In whatever context, the movement may resemble accumulation or attrition, progress or other
process, even stasis, or any one of these interrupted, turned, reversed.
In space or time or both, it can go in any direction as continuous or
repetitive, accelerated or retarded, smooth, halting, or halted. The variety is enormous.

The range of choices an author has is suggested by the evidence
of this last chapter. Here syntax as style has moved beyond the arbitrary, the sufficient, and is made so appropriate to content that, shar-
ing the very qualities of the content, it is carried to that point where it
seems not only right but inevitable. In its usual form, a syntactic symbol is a verbal, syntactic pattern intended to be read for a nonverbal
movement or development of some kind: language arranged to look
or sound like action.

To conclude, we turn to the closing paragraph of a book of literary criticism. Helen Vendler borrows the words *loosening* and *quicken-
ing* from Jorie Graham's poem "The Surface." These two words
combine with other *–ing* words in a rhythm that offers metaphoric
echoes of the effect being described:

In these knottings and loosenings, slowings and quickenings,
ending in, stopping on, a word, Graham finds the only
linguistic and imaginative equivalents for the self as she
now understands it. Because the phenomena of perception
are for the trilingual poet detached from any one language
of embodiment, they exist finally as metaphysical notions,
transiently embodied but never finally capturable in form.
Helen Vendler, *The Given and the Made*, 130

Writing is difficult. Whether a writer's sensitivities are informed by one or several languages, it is not easy to capture a unique perception or idea in poetry or prose. Professional writers, however, do the best they can in whatever circumstances they find themselves. That best is often eloquent and precise, artful but unpretentious enough to become a model for other writers.

A critic who reports on a syntactic habit of a certain author's style, or on some other verbal effect, by importing that very characteristic into her own style offers a nice sort of evidence for the conclusion of this chapter and the end of the book. One premise of this volume has been that syntax and style are reciprocal concerns—that it can make good sense, and help to make good prose, to think of syntax *as* style. The chapters have exhibited more than a thousand sentences on the assumption that good style is learned by emulation of authors who display it. As the examples show, although the syntactic means are relatively simple and few, the stylistic effects are countless.

This is the nature, the great beauty of approaching the art of the sentence through syntactic categories along with prolific displays of the splendid sentences good writers achieve. *Artful Sentences* shows specific skills, widely applicable, that a writer can learn. It offers models that can be imitated, organizing them in a way that makes them accessible and comprehensive. Forms that seem limited, and even limiting, in fact offer a range of opportunities to a writer in command of them—and one who knows how to transgress against them—to achieve undreamed of effectiveness, grace, and versatility.

Bibliography – Index of Authors & Editions Quoted

Quotations from books are identified by author, title of book, place, publisher, and date. In some cases, the date of *first* publication is added in parentheses. Quotations from periodicals are identified by author (if credited in the periodical), title of article, and name and date of the publication. At the end of all entries are the page numbers of *Artful Sentences* on which the quotations appear.

Achebe, Chinua, *Things Fall Apart*. Oxford: Heinemann, 1996 (1958), *241*

Ackerman, Diane, *Cultivating Delight: A Natural History of My Garden*. New York: HarperCollins, 2001, *190*

Ackmann, Martha, *The Mercury 13*. New York: Random House, 2003, *73*

Adams, Charles S., "Guest Column: The Real Small World(s)," PMLA 155, no. 2 (March 2000), *179*

Adichie, Chimamanda Ngozi, *Purple Hibiscus*. Chapel Hill, N.C.: Algonquin Books, 2003, *95*

Agee, James, *A Death in the Family*. New York: Avon, 1966 (1957), *19, 109, 198, 257*

Aiken, Conrad, *Ushant: An Essay*. Boston: Little, Brown, 1952, *45, 78*

Albee, Edward, *The American Dream and The Zoo Story: Two Plays by Edward Albee*. New York: New American Library (Signet), 1961 (1959), *175*

Alderson, Maggie, *Pants on Fire*. Victoria, Australia: Penguin Books, 2000, *194*

Alexander, Shana, *Life*, May 19, 1967, *74*

Alexie, Sherman, *The Toughest Indian in the World*. New York: Grove Press, 2000, *194*

Ali, Monica, *Brick Lane*. New York: Scribner, 2003, *150, 174*

Allen, Don Cameron, *The Ph.D. in English and American Literature*. New York: Holt, Rinehart and Winston, 1968, *77*

Allen, Fred, *Treadmill to Oblivion*. Boston: Little, Brown, 1954, *101*

Allen, Jerry, *The Thunder and the Sunshine: A Biography of Joseph Conrad*. New York: G. P. Putnam, 1958, *97, 166*

Alpert, Hollis, *The Claimant*. New York: Dial Press, 1968, *33*

Als, Hilton, "The Theatre," *The New Yorker,* August 23, 2004, *191*

Alsop, Stewart, *The Center.* New York: Harper & Row, 1968, *254*

Altick, Richard, *Preface to Critical Reading.* New York: Holt, Rinehart and Winston, 1963, *217*

Alvarez, Julia, *How the Garcia Girls Lost Their Accent.* New York: Penguin Books, 1992, *92*

Ambler, Eric, *Intrigue*. New York: Alfred Knopf, 1943, *11, 80*

The American Heritage Dictionary of the English Language, 4th ed. Boston: Houghton Mifflin, 2000, *60*

Amey, Ralph, *Wines of Baja California: Touring and Tasting Mexico's Undiscovered Treasures.* South San Francisco, Calif.: Wine Appreciation Guild, 2003, *211*

Amis, Kingsley, *The Anti-Death League.* New York: Harcourt Brace, 1966, *165*

— , *Lucky Jim.* New York: Viking, 1965, *18, 47, 108*

Amis, Martin, *Experience: A Memoir.* New York: Hyperion, 2000, *234*

Angelou, Maya, *Singin' and Swingin' and Gettin' Merry Like Christmas.* New York: Bantam Books, 1977 (1976), *12*

Angoff, Charles, *The Tone of the Twenties and Other Essays.* South Brunswick, N.J.: A. S. Barnes, 1966, *162*

Anzaldúa, Gloria, *Borderlands / La Frontera: The New Mestiza.* San Francisco: Aunt Lute Books, 1999 (1987), *30*

Applebaum, Anne, *Between East and West: Across the Borderlands of Europe.* New York: Pantheon Books, 1994, *159, 163*

Ardrey, Robert, *African Genesis.* New York: Atheneum, 1961, *210*

Armour, Richard, *American Lit Relit.* New York: McGraw-Hill, 1964, *80*

Arnold, Magda B., *Emotion and Personality.* New York: Columbia University Press, 1960, *223*

Asimov, Isaac, *From Earth to Heaven.* Garden City, N.Y.: Doubleday, 1960, *83, 84, 232*

Atkinson, Brooks, *Brief Chronicles.* New York: Coward-McCann, 1960, *11*

Atwan, Robert, ed., *The Best American Essays.* Boston: Houghton Mifflin, 2003, *108*

Atwood, Margaret, *The Blind Assassin.* New York: Random House, 2001, *190*

— , "Giving Birth," *We Are the Stories We Tell*, ed. Wendy Martin. New York: Random House, 1990, *22*

— , *Negotiating with the Dead: A Writer on Writing.* New York: Anchor Books, 2003 (2002), *53, 53, 53*

— , *Surfacing.* New York: Popular Library, 1976 (1972), *15, 17, 18, 69*

Auden, W. H., *The Dyer's Hand and Other Essays.* New York: Random House, 1962 (1945), *14*

Bach, Richard, *Stranger to the Ground.* New York: Harper & Row, 1963, *99*

Baez, Joan, *And a Voice to Sing With*. New York: Summit Books, 1987, *218*

— , "Foreword," *Long Time Coming and a Long Time Gone* by Richard Fariña. New York: Random House, 1969, *100*

Bailyn, Bernard, *Education in the Forming of American Society*. Chapel Hill: University of North Carolina Press, 1960, *265*

Bainton, Roland H., *Here I Stand: A Life of Martin Luther*. New York: New American Library (Mentor), 1950, *80, 81, 232*

Bajwa, Rupa, *The Sari Shop*. New York: W. W. Norton, 2004, *94*

Baker, Carlos, *Ernest Hemingway—A Life Story*. New York: Scribner's, 1969, *12*

Baldwin, James, *Another Country*. New York: Dell, 1969, *43*

— , *Giovanni's Room*. New York: Dial Press, 1963 (1956), *136, 210, 261, 266*

— , *Go Tell It on the Mountain*. New York: Grosset & Dunlap, 1952, *198, 199, 199*

— , *Tell Me How Long the Train's Been Gone*. New York: Dial Press, 1968, *15, 99*

Baldwin, Norman R., "Island Cottage," *The Countryman*, Summer 1966, *198*

Barnard, Mary, *The Mythmakers*. Athens: Ohio University Press, 1967, *99*

Barth, John, *The Floating Opera*. Garden City, N.Y.: Doubleday, 1967, *162*

— , *Giles Goat-Boy*. Garden City, N.Y.: Doubleday, 1966, *16, 98*

— , *Lost in the Funhouse*. Garden City, N.Y.: Doubleday, 1968 (1963), *71, 119, 166*

Barthes, Roland, "Chopsticks," in *A Slice of Life: Contemporary Writers on Food*, ed. Bonnie Maranca. New York: Overlook Press, 2003, *264*

Basbanes, Nicholas A., *A Splendor of Letters: The Permanence of Books in an Impermanent World*. New York: HarperCollins, 2003, *242, 242, 242, 243*

Bausch, Richard, "Requisite Kindness," in *Wives and Lovers: Three Short Novels*. New York: Harper Perennial, 2004, *140*

Baxandall, Michael, *Words for Pictures: Seven Papers on Renaissance Art and Criticism*. New Haven, Conn.: Yale University Press, 2003, *93*

Bayard, Louis, "I'm Maxed Out on Maxims," *Washington Post*, January 18, 2004, *54*

Beattie, Ann, "The Rabbit Hole as Likely Explanation," *The New Yorker*, April 12, 2004, *93*

Beckett, Samuel, *Murphy*. New York: Grove Press, 1957 (1938), *13*

Beebe, Mary Livingstone, "Introduction," *Landmarks: Sculpture Commissions for the Stuart Collection at the University of California, San Diego*, ed. Beebe, James Stuart DeSilva, and Robert Storr. New York: Rizzoli, 2001, *196*

Behan, Brendan, *Confessions of an Irish Rebel*. New York: Bernard Geis, 1965, *17*

Belenky, Mary, Blythe Clinchy, Nancy Goldberger and Jill Tarule, *Women's Ways of Knowing*. New York: Basic Books, 1986, *156*

Bellow, Saul, *Henderson the Rain King*. Greenwich, Conn.: Fawcett, 1958, *99*

— , *Herzog*. Greenwich, Conn.: Fawcett, 1965, *133, 178, 269*

— , *Humboldt's Gift*. New York: Viking, 1976 (1973), *67*

— , *Mosby's Memoirs and Other Stories*. New York: Viking, 1968 (1951), *45*

Benchley, Nathaniel, *Welcome to Xanadu*. New York: Atheneum, 1968, *41, 41*

Bender, Aimee, *An Invisible Sign of My Own*. New York: Anchor Books, 2000, *12, 14*

Benedict, Ruth, *Patterns of Culture*. New York: New American Library (Mentor), 1958 (1934), *231*

Benét, Stephen Vincent, *Thirteen O'Clock: Stories of Several Worlds*. New York: Farrar & Rinehart, 1937 (1932), *87*

Berger, Harry Jr., *The Allegorical Temper*. New Haven, Conn.: Yale University Press, 1957, *127*

Berleant, Arnold, *The Aesthetics of Environment*. Philadelphia: Temple University Press, 1992, *243*

Bernier, Olivier, *The World in 1800*. New York: John Wiley & Sons, 2000, *68*

Berry, Wendell, *Citizenship Papers*. Washington, D.C.: Shoemaker & Hoard, 2003, *40*

Bettelheim, Bruno, *The Uses of Enchantment: The Meaning and Importance of Fairy Tales*. New York: Vintage Books, 1989 (1975), *74*

Bittman, Mark, *How to Cook Everything*. New York: Macmillan, 1998, *230*

Blackmur, R. P., "*The Idiot*: A Rage of Goodness," *Eleven Essays in the European Novel*. New York: Harcourt Brace, 1948 (1943), *99*

Bolinger, Dwight, *Aspects of Language*. New York: Harcourt Brace, 1968, *155*

Boudreau, Diane, "Swapping Genes," *ASU Vision* (Arizona State University, Tempe) 7, no. 2 (Spring 2004), *247*

Bowen, Catherine Drinker, *Adventures of a Biographer*. Boston: Little, Brown, 1959 (1946), *87*

Boyd, Valerie, *Wrapped in Rainbows: The Life of Zora Neale Hurston*. New York: Scribner, 2003, *17*

Boyle, T. Coraghessan, "Chicxulub," in *Tooth and Claw*. New York: Viking, 2005, *193, 270*

— , *Drop City*. New York: Viking, 2003, *144*

— , "Filthy Things," in *Stories*. New York: Viking, 1998, *190*

Bradbury, Ray, "Any Friend of Trains Is a Friend of Mine," *Life*, August 2, 1968, *27*

Brand, Stewart, *The Clock of the Long Now: Time and Responsibility*. New York: Basic Books, 1999, *75, 207, 218*

Brewster, H. C., "Saint Philomena," *Sewanee Review*, Summer 1966, *267*

Brightman, Carol, "Character in Biography," *The Best of* The Nation, ed. Victor Navasky and Katrina Van den Heuvel. New York: Thunder's Mouth Press, 2000, *26*

Brooke, Rupert, *The Prose of Rupert Brooke*, ed. Christopher Hassal. London: Sidgwick & Jackson, 1956, *13*

Brookner, Anita, *Hotel du Lac*. London: Granada, 1985, *81*

Brooks, Van Wyck, *A Chilmark Miscellany*. New York: E. P. Dutton, 1948, *88*

Brown, Huntington, *Prose Styles: Five Primary Types*. Minneapolis: University of Minnesota Press, 1966, *127*

Buckley, Jerome H., *The Victorian Temper*. New York: Vintage Books, 1951, *142*

Buell, Lawrence, *Writing for an Endangered World: Literature, Culture, and Environment in the U.S. and Beyond*. Cambridge, Mass.: Belknap (Harvard University Press), 2001, *39*

Burgess, Anthony, *Enderby*. New York: W. W. Norton, 1963, *9*

Bush, Douglas, *Mythology and the Romantic Tradition in English Poetry*. New York: W. W. Norton, 1963 (1937), *181*

Butler, Connie, "Robert Smithson," *The Contemporary (MOCA)*, September-October-November 2004, *195*

Byatt, A. S., "The Pink Ribbon," in *Little Black Book of Stories*. New York: Alfred A. Knopf, 2004, *214*

Caldwell, Ian, and Dustin Thomason, *The Rule of Four*. New York: Dial Press, 2004, *140*

Campbell, Lily B., *Shakespeare's Histories*. San Marino, Calif.: Huntington Library, 1947, *86*

Capote, Truman, "A Christmas Memory," *Breakfast at Tiffany's*. New York: Random House, 1958 (1950), *118*

— , *The Grass Harp*. New York: New American Library (Signet), 1956 (1951), *261*

— , *In Cold Blood*. New York: Random House, 1965, *201*

— , *Local Color*. New York: Random House, 1950 (1946), *13, 128*

— , *Other Voices, Other Rooms*. New York: Random House, 1948, *169*

Carson, Elof Axel, *The Gene: A Critical History*. Ames: Iowa State University Press, 1966, *49*

Cary, Joyce, *Herself Surprised*. New York: Harper & Row, 1941, *133*

Cassady, Neil, *Collected Letters, 1944-1967*, ed. Dave Moore. New York: Penguin Books, 2004, *71*

Cather, Willa, *The Song of the Lark*, in *A Grammar of the English Language* by George O. Curme. Essex, Conn.: Verbatim, 1993 (1931), *76*

Cecil, Lord David, *The Fine Art of Reading*. Indianapolis: Bobbs-Merrill, 1956, *105*

Chabon, Michael, "Dust and Demons," *New York Review of Books*, March 25, 2004, *48*

Chang, Lan Samantha, *Hunger*. New York: Penguin Books, 2000, *148*

Chappell, Fred, *I Am One of You Forever*. Baton Rouge: Louisiana State University Press, 1985, *67, 155*

Chase, Mary Ellen, *The Bible and the Common Reader*. New York: Macmillan, 1945, *22*

Chase, Richard, *The American Novel and Its Tradition*. Garden City, N.Y.: Doubleday (Anchor Books), 1957, *229*

Chevalier, Tracy, *Girl with a Pearl Earring*. New York: Plume, 2001 (1999), *143*

Child, Julia, and Simone Beck, *Mastering the Art of French Cooking*, Vol. 2. New York: Alfred Knopf, 1983 (1970), *93*

Chomsky, Noam, *Aspects of the Theory of Syntax*. Cambridge, Mass.: Harvard University Press, 1965, *10*

— , *On Language*. New York: New Press, 1998, *16*

— , *Syntactic Structures*. The Hague: Mouton, 1957, *10*

Christensen, Francis, *Notes Toward a New Rhetoric*. New York: Harper & Row, 1967, *157*

Christian, Eugene, and Molly Griswold Christian, *250 Meatless Menus and Recipes*. New York: Molly Griswold Christian, 1910, *58*

Churchill, Winston, *A Roving Commission: My Early Life*. New York: Scribner's, 1930, *197*

Chute, Marchette, *Two Gentle Men: The Lives of George Herbert and Robert Herrick*. New York: E. P. Dutton, 1959, *163*

Cisneros, Sandra, *The House on Mango Street*. New York: Vintage Books, 1991, *45*

Clark, Sir Kenneth, *Ruskin Today*. London: John Murray, 1964, *206*

Clinton, Bill, *My Life*. New York: Alfred A. Knopf, 2004, *264*

Clinton, Hillary Rodham, *Living History*. New York: Scribner, 2003 (new edition), *179*

Coetzee, J. M., *Disgrace*. New York: Viking Penguin, 1999, *197*

Cohen, Ralph, "Do Postmodern Genres Exist?," *Postmodern Genres*, ed. Marjorie Perloff. Norman: University of Oklahoma Press, 1989, *226*

Consumer Reports, "How to be a Turned-on, Tuned-in Citizen," October 1968, *196*

Cooper, Alan, and Robert Reimann, *About Face 2.0: The Essentials of Interaction Design*. Hoboken, N.J.: John Wiley & Sons, 2003, *57, 57*

Cornford, F. M., *Before and After Socrates*. Cambridge: Cambridge University Press, 1966 (1932), *33*

Cozzens, James Gould, *Children and Others*. New York: Harcourt Brace, 1964 (1958), *135*

— , *Morning Noon and Night*. New York: Harcourt Brace, 1968, *71, 80*

Craig, Charmaine, *The Good Men: A Novel of Heresy*. New York: Penguin Putnam, 2002, *136*

Crews, Frederick C., *E. M. Forster: The Perils of Humanism*. Princeton, N.J.: Princeton University Press, 1962, *220*

Cronin, A. J., *The Green Years*. Boston: Little, Brown, 1944, *173*

— , *The Keys of the Kingdom*. Boston: Little, Brown, 1948 (1941), *33, 167, 182*

Crowther, Bosley, *The Great Films*. New York: G. P. Putnam, 1965, *228*

Cunningham, Michael, *The Hours*. New York: Farrar, Straus & Giroux, 1998, *38, 69, 114, 148*

Curme, George O., *A Grammar of the English Language: Syntax*, vol. 2. Essex, Conn.: Verbatim, 1993 (1931), *76*

Dahlberg, Edward, *Alms for Oblivion*. Minneapolis: University of Minnesota Press, 1964, *13*

Davie, Donald, *Articulate Energy: An Enquiry into the Syntax of English Poetry*. New York: Harcourt Brace, 1958 (1955), *13, 263*

Davis, Fred, "Blue Jeans," *Signs of Life in the USA*, ed. Sonia Maasik and Jack Solomon. Boston: St. Martin's Press, 2000, *240*

Davis, Lydia, "Glenn Gould," *Almost No Memory*. New York: Farrar, Straus & Giroux, 1997, *262*

Day, Donald, *Uncle Sam's Uncle Josh*. Boston: Little, Brown, 1953, *71*

Declaration of Independence, 65, 139

Deese, James, "Behavior and Fact," *American Psychologist*, May 1967, 120

DeLillo, Don, *Underworld*. New York: Simon & Schuster, 1997, 143

Demos, John, *Circles and Lines: The Shape of Life in Early America*. Cambridge, Mass.: Harvard University Press, 2004, 259

Dexter, Lewis Anthony, *The Tyranny of Schooling*. New York: Basic Books, 1964, 243

Dickey, James, *Spinning the Crystal Ball*. Washington, D.C.: Library of Congress, 1967, 192

Didion, Joan, *Where I Was From*. New York: Knopf, 2003, 16, 81, 202

Dillard, Annie, *The Writing Life*. New York: Harper & Row, 1989, 66

Dittmar, Trudy, *Fauna and Flora, Earth and Sky*. Iowa City: University of Iowa Press, 2003, 14, 44, 45

Dobson, Michael, and Nicola J. Watson, *England's Elizabeth*. Oxford: Oxford University Press, 2002, 100

Dolan, Joseph P., and Lloyd J. Holloway, *The Treatment and Prevention of Athletic Injuries*. Danville, Ill.: Interstate Printing, 1961, 49

Dorson, Richard M., *American Folklore*. Chicago: University of Chicago Press, 1959, 196

Draznin, Yaffa, ed., *My Other Self: The Letters of Olive Schreiner and Havelock Ellis 1884-1920*. New York: Peter Long, 1992, 191

Drinkwater, John, *Inheritance*. New York: Henry Holt, 1931, 20

Durrell, Lawrence, *Justine*. New York: E. P. Dutton, 1957, 18

Dylan, Bob, *Chronicles, Volume One*. New York: Simon & Schuster, 2004, 189

Eastman, Max, *Art and the Life of Action*. New York: Alfred A. Knopf, 1954, 88

Eckert, John E., and Frank R. Shaw, *Beekeeping*. New York: Macmillan, 1960, 49

Ehrenreich, Barbara, "Maid to Order," *Global Woman: Nannies, Maids, and Sex Workers in the New Economy*, ed. Barbara Ehrenreich and Arlie Russell Hochschild. New York: Henry Holt, 2002, 73, 248

Eliot, T. S., *On Poetry and Poets*. New York: Farrar, Straus & Cudahy, 1962 (1943), 220

Ellis, Havelock, *My Life*. Boston: Houghton Mifflin, 1939, 92

Ellison, Ralph, *Invisible Man*. New York: New American Library (Signet), 1952, 26, 43, 83, 172, 266

— , *Shadow and Act*. New York: Random House, 1964, 94, 97, 177

Empson, William, *Seven Types of Ambiguity*. New York: New Directions, [n.d.], 175, 211

— , *Some Versions of Pastoral*. New York: New Directions, 1960, 121

Ephron, Nora, *Heartburn*. New York: Alfred A. Knopf, 1983, 66

Espey, John, *The Anniversaries*. New York: Harcourt Brace, 1963, 114, 137

Esslin, Martin, *The Theatre of the Absurd*. Garden City, N.Y.: Doubleday (Anchor Books), 1961, 164, 164, 206, 225

Eugenides, Jeffrey, *Middlesex*. New York: Farrar, Straus & Giroux, 2002, *259*
Everett, Percival, "909," in *My California: Journeys by Great Writers*, ed. Donna Wares. Los Angeles: Angel City Press, 2004, *129*
— , *Erasure*. Hanover, N.H.: University Press of New England, 2001, *148*

Fasulo, Linda, *An Insider's Guide to the UN*. New Haven, Conn.: Yale University Press, 2004, *38, 38*
Faulkner, William, *Absalom, Absalom!* New York: Random House (Modern Library), 1951 (1936), *182, 255*
— , *Delta Autumn*, in *The Portable Faulkner*, ed. Malcolm Cowley. New York: Viking, 1961, *181, 182*
— , *The Hamlet*. New York: Vintage Books, 1964 (1931), *131*
— , *Sartoris*. New York: Harcourt Brace, 1929, *169*
Ferris, Timothy, *The Universe and Eye*. San Francisco: Chronicle Books, 1993, *218*
Finney, Jack, *The Woodrow Wilson Dime*. New York: Simon & Schuster, 1968, *32*
Fitzgerald, F. Scott, *The Crack-up*, ed. Edmund Wilson. New York: New Directions, 1945, *63, 192, 192*
— , *The Great Gatsby*. New York: Scribner's, 1953 (1925), *159*
— , *Tender Is the Night*. New York: Scribner's, 1962 (1933), *165, 202, 213, 223, 262*
— , *This Side of Paradise*. New York: Scribner's, 1960 (1920), *18, 23, 25*
Fitzgerald, Penelope, *The Blue Flower*. New York: Houghton Mifflin, 1995, *127, 229*
Flagg, Fannie, *Standing in the Rainbow*. New York: Random House, 2002, *50*
Fonda, Daren, "Revenge of the Bean Counters," *Time*, March 29, 2004, *17*
Forster, E. M., *A Passage to India*. New York: Harcourt Brace, 1924, *253, 257, 263*
— , *Two Cheers for Democracy*. New York: Harcourt Brace, 1951 (1938), *243*
Fowles, John, *The Magus*. Boston: Little, Brown, 1965, *42*
Frame, Janet, *The Reservoir: Stories and Sketches*. New York: George Braziller, 1963, *16, 25*
— , *Scented Gardens for the Blind*. New York: George Braziller, 1964, *17, 92*
Franzen, Jonathan, *The Corrections*. New York: Farrar, Straus & Giroux, 2001, *14, 99, 144, 150*
Frayn, Michael, *Against Entropy*. New York: Viking, 1967, *233*
Freedman, Ralph, *The Lyrical Novel: Studies in Herman Hesse, André Gide and Virginia Woolf*. Princeton, N.J.: Princeton University Press, 1963, *119*
Friedman, Mitchell, "Among Our Key People," *The Key Reporter* (Phi Beta Kappa) 69, no. 3 (Summer 2004), *184*
Fromm, Erich, *Sigmund Freud's Mission*. New York: Harper & Brothers, 1959, *221*
Frye, Northrop, *Fables of Identity*. New York: Harcourt Brace, 1963, *213*
Furedi, Frank, *Therapy Culture*. New York: Routledge, 2004, *38, 210*
Furman, Wendy, and Virginia James Tufte, "Metaphysical Tears: Carlotta Petrina's Re-Presentation of Paradise Lost, Book IX," *Milton Studies XXXVI*, ed. Albert C. Labriola. Pittsburgh: University of Pittsburgh Press, 1998, *102*

Kreiger, Murray, "Afterword," *Lord Jim* by Joseph Conrad. New York: New American Library (Signet), 1961, *212*

Kroll, Jack, "Theater of Crisis," *Newsweek*, May 5, 1969, *81*

Kunhardt, Philip B., Jr., *My Father's Country,* quoted in *Life* Magazine, July 4, 1970. New York: Random House, 1970, *203*

Lacayo, Richard, "Shakespeare: The Man Behind the Scenes," *TIME*, August 30, 2004, *207*

Lamott, Anne, *Bird by Bird: Some Instructions on Writing and Life.* New York: Anchor Books, 1995 (1994), *88, 144, 150, 150*

Land, Myrick, *The Fine Art of Literary Mayhem.* London: Hamish Hamilton, 1963 (1962), *224*

LaPolla, Randy J., and Robert D. Van Valin, *Syntax.* Cambridge: Cambridge University Press, 1997, *42, 95*

Laquer, Thomas, "Prelude," in *The Genius of the Language: Fifteen Writers Reflect on Their Mother Tongues,* ed. Wendy Lesser. New York: Pantheon, 2004, *116*

Lawrence, D. H., *Etruscan Places.* New York: Viking, 1957 (1932), *107*

— , *Sons and Lovers.* New York: New American Library (Signet), 1960 (1913), *109, 117, 119, 168, 231*

Lawson, Bruce, "Unifying Milton's Epics: Carlotta Petrina's Illustrations for Paradise Regained," *Milton Studies XXX,* ed. Albert C. Labriola. Pittsburgh: University of Pittsburgh Press, 1993, *166*

Lee, Carol, *Ballet in Western Culture: A History of Its Origins and Evolution.* Boston: Allyn and Bacon, 1999, *76*

Lee, Harper, *To Kill a Mockingbird.* Philadelphia: J. B. Lippincott, 1960, *136*

Lee, Hermione, *Virginia Woolf.* London: Random House, 1996, *101*

Lees, Francis Noel, "The Keys Are at the Palace," *College English*, November 1966, *227*

LeGuin, Ursula K., *The Wave in the Mind: Talks and Essays on the Writer, the Reader, and the Imagination.* Boston: Shambhala, 2004, *151*

Lekachman, Robert, *The Age of Keynes.* New York: Random House, 1966, *174*

Leslie, Mitch, ed., "Range of Newt and Name of Toad," *Netwatch, Science* 304, no. 5674 (21 May 2004), *196*

Lessing, Doris, *Children of Violence.* New York: Simon & Schuster, 1964 (1952), *165*

— , *The Grandmothers.* New York: HarperCollins, 2003, *40, 68, 192, 198, 249, 254*

— , *In Pursuit of the English.* London: MacGibbon & Kee, 1960, *105, 105*

Levin, Harry, *The Power of Blackness: Hawthorne, Poe, Melville.* New York: Alfred A. Knopf, 1958, *228*

Lewis, C. S., *Out of the Silent Planet.* New York: Macmillan, 1943, *103*

— , *That Hideous Strength.* London: Bodley Head, 1960 (1945), *15, 126*

Lewis, Sinclair, *Babbitt.* New York: New American Library (Signet), 1961 (1922), *131, 159, 169*

Lewis, Wyndham, *Blasting and Bombardiering.* Berkeley: University of California Press, 1967, *19, 48*

Martin, Steve, *The Pleasure of My Company*. New York: Hyperion, 2003, *10, 240*

Marx, Wesley, *The Frail Ocean*. New York: Ballantine Books, 1967, *27*

Masefield, John, *Live and Kicking Ned*. New York: Macmillan, 1939, *113*

Maugham, W. Somerset, *Of Human Bondage*. New York: Pocket Books, 1961 (1915), *117, 136, 159*

— , *The Razor's Edge*. Garden City, N.Y.: Doubleday, 1944, *222*

— , *The Summing Up*. New York: New American Library (Signet), 1964 (1938), *46*

McCarthy, Mary, *Cast a Cold Eye*. New York: Harcourt Brace, 1950 (1944), *166*

— , *On the Contrary*. New York: Farrar, Straus & Cudahy, 1961 (1946), *268*

McCartney, William, *Olfaction and Odours: An Ophrésiological Essay*. Berlin: Springer-Verlag, 1968, *84*

McCullers, Carson, *The Heart Is a Lonely Hunter*. New York: Bantam Books, 1958 (1940), *130*

— , *The Member of the Wedding*. New York: Bantam Doubleday Dell, 1973 (1946), *192*

— , *Reflections in a Golden Eye*. Boston: Houghton Mifflin, 1941, *79, 167*

McDonald, Forrest, *E Pluribus Unum: The Foundation of the American Republic*. Boston: Houghton Mifflin, 1965, *120*

McWhorter, John, *Doing Our Own Thing: The Degradation of Language and Music and Why We Should, Like, Care*. New York: Gotham, 2003, *59, 59*

Merton, Thomas, *The Behavior of Titans*. New York: New Directions, 1961, *21*

Michener, James, *Hawaii*. New York: Random House, 1959, *165, 266*

— , *The Source*. New York: Random House, 1965, *10*

Miller, Andrew, "Losing Their Religion," *The New York Times Book Review*, March 21, 2004, *105, 105*

Miller, Arthur, *Timebends: A Life*. New York: Penguin Books, 1995 (1971), *203*

Miller, Henry, *Henry Miller on Writing*, ed. Thomas H. Moore. New York: New Directions, 1964, *97*

Minich, Jerry, "A Small Garden," *A Place to Which We Belong*, ed. Dennis Boyer and Justin Isherwood. Madison, Wis.: The 1000 Friends of Wisconsin Land Use Institute, 1998, *125*

Moore, Brian, *The Emperor of Ice-Cream*. New York: Viking, 1965, *94*

— , *The Lonely Passion of Judith Hearne*. Boston: Little, Brown, 1955, *269*

— , *The Luck of Ginger Coffey*. Boston: Little, Brown, 1960, *18*

Moore, Lorrie, *Birds of America: Stories*. New York: Alfred A. Knopf, 1998, *180*

Moore, Marianne, *Predilections*. New York: Viking, 1955, *107*

Morris, William, *The Ideal Book*, ed. William S. Peterson. Berkeley: University of California Press, 1982, *74*

Morris, Wright, *The Field of Vision*. New York: Harcourt Brace, 1956, *41, 108, 118*

Morrison, Patt, "Flirting with Urbanismo," *My California: Journeys by Great Writers*, ed. Donna Wares. Los Angeles: Angel City Press, 2004, *200*

Morrison, Toni, *Beloved*. New York: Plume, 1988 (1987), *142, 149*

— , excerpt from *The Bluest Eye,* reprinted in *Blackeyed Susans, Midnight Birds*, ed. Mary Helen Washington. New York: Anchor Books, 1990, *194*

Mortimer, Penelope, *The Bright Prison*. New York: Harcourt Brace, 1956, *117*

— , *The Pumpkin Eater.* New York: McGraw-Hill, 1962, *206*

Morton, Charles W., *It Has Its Charms*. Philadelphia: J. B. Lippincott, 1966 (1960), *143*

Most, Mary, "Une Créature du Cinéma," *Cinema*, V, *24*

Mott, George Fox, *Transportation Century*. Baton Rouge: Louisiana State University Press, 1966, *228*

Mukherjee, Bharati, *Jasmine*. New York: Grove Press, 1989, *114, 270*

Munro, Alice, *Runaway: Stories*. New York: Alfred A. Knopf, 2004, *222*

Murdoch, Iris, *Bruno's Dream*. New York: Viking, 1969, *92, 128, 128*

— , *An Unofficial Rose*. New York: Viking, 1962, *25, 29, 74*

Muske-Dukes, Carol, *Married to the Icepick Killer: A Poet in Hollywood*. New York: Random House, 2002, *89*

Myerhoff, Barbara, *Number Our Days*. New York: E. P. Dutton, 1978, *174*

Nabokov, Vladimir, *Ada, or Ardor*. New York: McGraw-Hill, 1969, *13*

— , *Nabokov's Congeries*. New York: Viking, 1968, *79*

— , *Pnin*. New York: Atheneum, 1967 (1953), *46, 92, 122*

Naipaul, V. S., *Literary Occasions*. New York: Random House, 2003, *176*

Nash, Laura, and Howard Stevenson, "Success That Lasts," *Harvard Business Review*, February 2004, *31*

Naslund, Sena Jeter. *Four Spirits*. New York: William Morrow, 2003, *186*

National Commission on Terrorist Attacks Upon the United States, *The 9/11 Commission Report, Authorized Edition*. New York: W. W. Norton, 2004, *140*

National Endowment for the Arts, *Reading at Risk: A Study of Literary Reading in America*, Research Division Report 46, June 2004, Tom Bradshaw, Bonnie Nichols, and Mark Bauerlein, *132*

Nature, "This Issue, the Big Picture," July 1, 2004, *242*

Nevins, Allan, and Henry Steele Commager, *A Pocket History of the United States*. New York: Pocket Books, 1951 (1942), *221*

Nicholls, Henry, "One of a Kind," *Nature*, 3 June 2004, *187*

Noble, Frances Khirallah, *The Situe Stories*. New York: Syracuse University Press, 2000, *16*

Nodelman, Sheldon, "The Mastery of Matisse," *Art in America*, May 2004, *164*

Oates, Joyce Carol, *The Faith of a Writer: Life, Craft, Art*. New York: HarperCollins, 2003, *12, 215*

O'Conner, Patricia T., *Words Fail Me: What Everyone Who Writes Should Know About Writing*. New York: Harvest (Harcourt), 1999, *115, 115*

O'Connor, Flannery, *Everything That Rises Must Converge*. New York: Farrar, Straus & Giroux, 1965, *262*

— , *A Good Man Is Hard to Find*. New York: Harcourt Brace 1955 (1953), *98*

O'Connor, William Van, *Campus on the River*. New York: Thomas Y. Crowell, 1959, *99*

O'Faolain, Sean, *I Remember! I Remember!* Boston: Little, Brown, 1961 (1959), *126*

— , *The Vanishing Hero: Studies of the Hero in the Modern Novel.* New York: Grosset & Dunlap, 1957, *100*

O'Hara, John, *Assembly.* New York: Random House, 1960, *14*

Olsen, Leslie A. and Thomas Huckin, *Technical Writing and Professional Communication.* New York: McGraw-Hill, 1991, *211*

Orwell, George, *Animal Farm.* New York: New American Library (Signet), 1954 (1946), *115, 128, 132*

Osborne, John, *Look Back in Anger.* New York: Bantam Books, 1967 (1957), *159*

Ozick, Cynthia, *Trust.* New York: New American Library, 1966, *262*

Paley, Grace, *The Collected Stories.* New York: Farrar, Straus & Giroux, 1994, *10, 112*

Parker, Dorothy, *Here Lies: The Collected Stories of Dorothy Parker.* New York: Viking, 1939 (1930), *15*

— , "Sentiment," *The Portable Dorothy Parker.* New York: Penguin Books, 1976 (1944), *256*

Paterniti, Michael, *Driving Mr. Albert: A Trip Across America with Einstein's Brain.* New York: Random House, 2000, *103, 122*

Paton, Alan, *Cry, the Beloved Country.* New York: Scribner's, 1948, *135*

— , *Too Late the Phalarope.* New York: Scribner's, 1953, *94*

Payne, Robert, *The Christian Centuries.* New York: W. W. Norton, 1966, *263*

Pepper, Clement S., "Electronics Put to Sea," *Radio Electronics*, August 1966, *199*

Perloff, Marjorie, *The Futurist Movement.* Chicago: University of Chicago Press, 1986, *207*

Petrie, Sidney, in association with Robert B. Stone, *What Modern Hypnotism Can Do for You.* New York: Hawthorne Books, 1968, *97*

Philbrick, Nathaniel, "Waterworld," *The New York Times Book Review*, May 16, 2004, *189*

Phillips, J. B., *Ring of Truth: A Translator's Testimony.* New York: Macmillan, 1967, *42*

Pinter, Harold. Website. http://www.haroldpinter.org/home/index.shtml Accessed 4 September 2004, *152, 152*

Plotkin, Mark, *The Shaman's Apprentice: An Ethnobotanist's Search for New Medicines in the Amazon Rain Forest.* New York: Penguin Books, 1994, *11*

Pollitt, Katha, *Subject to Debate: Sense and Dissents on Women, Politics, and Culture.* New York: Modern Library, 2001, *11*

Porter, Katharine Anne, *Flowering Judas and Other Stories.* New York: Random House, 1953 (1930), *42, 183*

— , *Leaning Tower and Other Stories.* New York: Harcourt Brace, 1944 (1934), *180*

— , *Pale Horse, Pale Rider.* New York: New American Library (Signet), 1962 (1936), *70*

Postrel, Virginia, *The Substance of Style: How the Rise of Aesthetic Value is Remaking Commerce, Culture & Consciousness.* New York: HarperCollins, 2003, *31, 145, 152, 230*

Power, Eileen, *Medieval People*, rev. ed. New York: Barnes and Noble, 1964 (1963), *228*

Powers, J. F., *Morte d'Urban*. New York: Pocket Books, 1963 (1956), *17, 98, 102*

Prager, Emily, "Swedish Food," *A Slice of Life*, ed. Bonnie Maranca. New York: Overlook Press, 2003, *65*

Prelutsky, Burt, "At Home with Mae West," *West Magazine, Los Angeles Times*, July 14, 1968, *232*

Price, Lorna, *Masterpieces from the Los Angeles County Museum of Art Collection*. Los Angeles: Los Angeles County Museum of Art, 1988, *191*

Prose, Francine, *The Lives of the Muses: Nine Women and the Artists They Inspired*. New York: HarperCollins, 2002, *206*

Proulx, Annie, *The Shipping News*. New York: Simon & Schuster, 1993, *143, 149*

Quindlen, Anna, *How Reading Changed My Life*. New York: Library of Contemporary Art (Ballantine), 1998, *156*

— , *Loud and Clear*. New York: Random House, 2004, *89, 232*

Randall, Alice, *The Wind Done Gone*. Boston: Houghton Mifflin, 2001, *150*

Rashid, Karim, "What's Really Important," an interview by Francine Maroukian, *Town and Country*, p. 80, quoted in Virginia Postrel, *The Substance of Style*, New York: HarperCollins, 2003, *152*

Reagan, Ronald, "Squall," February 24, 1930. Pre-Presidential Papers, Special Collection, Ronald Reagan Presidential Library, *122*

Reynolds, Susan Salter, "Discoveries," *Los Angeles Times Book Review*, September 19, 2004, *116, 116*

Rich, Adrienne, *Arts of the Possible: Essays and Conversations*. New York: W. W. Norton, 2002, *66*

Ricks, Christopher, *Dylan's Visions of Sin*. New York: HarperCollins, 2004 (2003), *91, 146*

Rishel, Joseph J., "Paul Cezanne," *Great French Paintings from the Barnes Foundation: Impressionist, Post-Impressionist, and Early Modern*. New York: Alfred A. Knopf, 1993, *151*

Robinson, Marilynne, *Housekeeping*. New York: Picador, 1980, *111*

Rodwin, Lloyd, "Ciudad Guayana: A New City," *Scientific American*, September 1965, *244*

Roosevelt, Franklin Delano, Inaugural address, 1933, *139*

Rosen, Charles, *Piano Notes: The World of the Pianist*. New York: The Free Press, 2002, *58, 58*

Rosenfield, Albert, "Challenge to the Miracle of Life," *Life Magazine*, June 13, 1969, *245*

Rosenthal, M. L., ed., *Selected Poems and Two Plays of William Butler Yeats*. New York: Macmillan, 1962 (1931), *211*

Ross, Stephanie, *What Gardens Mean*. Chicago: University of Chicago Press, 1998, *122*

Roth, Gerard, "The Quest to Find Consciousness," *Scientific American: Mind*, *Special Edition* 14, no. 1, 2004, *56, 56*

Rowling, J. K., *Harry Potter and the Order of the Phoenix*. New York: Scholastic Press, 2003, *67, 103, 260*

Royce, Joseph R., *The Encapsulated Man*. Princeton, N.J.: Van Nostrand, 1964, *224*

Ruse, Michael, "The Darwin Industry: A Guide," *Victorian Studies 39*, no. 2 (Winter 1996), *69*

Rushdie, Salman, *Haroun and the Sea of Stories*. New York: Viking, 1990, *101*

Russell, Bertrand, *Why I Am Not a Christian*. New York: Simon & Schuster, 1957, *213*

Salinger, J. D., *Franny and Zooey*. New York: Bantam Books, 1961, *42, 46, 132*

— , "The Laughing Man," in *Nine Stories*. New York: New American Library (Signet), 1954 (1948), *160*

— , *Raise High the Roof Beam, Carpenters; Seymour—An Introduction*. New York: Bantam Books, 1965 (1955), *198, 212, 231*

Salonen, Esa-Pekka, "Variations and Traditions: Classical Music in the Twenty-first Century," in *Symphony: Frank Gehry's Walt Disney Concert Hall*. New York: Harry H. Abrams, 2003, *197*

Sanderson, Ivan, *Follow the Whale*. Boston: Little, Brown, 1956, *107*

Sandler, Irving, *Art of the Postmodern Era: From the Late 1960s to the Early 1990s*. Boulder, Colo.: Westview, 1998, *208*

Sarton, May, *From May Sarton's Well*, ed. Edith Royce Schade. Watsonville, Calif.: Papier-mache, 1994, *75, 163*

— , *Journal of a Solitude*. New York: W. W. Norton, 1973, *14*

— , *Writings on Writing*. Orono, Maine: Puckerbush, 1980, *190*

Schaffer, Talia, *The Forgotten Female Aesthetes: Literary Culture in Late-Victorian England*. Charlottesville: University of Virginia Press, 2000, *68*

Schein, Ionel, "A Phenomenology of Research," *Arts and Architecture*, August 1966, *268*

Schell, Orville, "Gray Lady and a Greek Tragedy," *Los Angeles Times Book Review*, January 23, 2005, *75*

Schwarz, Benjamin, "New and Noteworthy: What to Read This Month," *Atlantic Monthly*, June 2004, *219*

See, Carolyn, *The Handyman*. New York: Ballantine Books, 2000, *15, 19*

— , "Sisters of a Kind," *Los Angeles Times Book Review*, August 22, 2004, *207*

Sewell, Elizabeth, *The Human Metaphor*. Notre Dame, Ind.: University of Notre Dame Press, 1964, *130*

Sheckley, Robert, *Mindswap*. New York: Delacorte, 1966, *28*

Shute, Nevil, *Pastoral*. Cleveland: World Publishing, 1945, *33*

Simpson, George Gaylord, *The Meaning of Evolution*. New Haven, Conn.: Yale University Press, 1952 (1949), *71*

Smiley, Jane, *Good Faith*. New York: Alfred A. Knopf, 2003, *115*

— , *Horse Heaven*. New York: Knopf, 2000, *140*

— , *A Year at the Races*. New York: Knopf, 2004, *257*

Smith, Bradford, *A Dangerous Freedom*. Philadelphia: J. B. Lippincott, 1954, *222*

Smith, Jack. *How to Win a Pullet Surprise*. New York: Franklin Watts, 1982, *113*

Smith, Zadie, *White Teeth*. New York: Vintage Books, 2000, *141*

Snow, C. P., *The Search*. New York: New American Library (Signet), 1960 (1958), *257*

— , *Variety of Men*. New York: Scribner's, 1967, *68*

Sontag, Susan, *Regarding the Pain of Others*. New York: Farrar, Straus & Giroux, 2002, *271*

Spacks, Patricia Meyer, *Boredom: The Literary History of a State of Mind*. Chicago: University of Chicago Press, 1995, *76, 88*

Spark, Muriel, *Memento Mori*. Philadelphia: J. B. Lippincott, 1959 (1958), *184*

— , *The Prime of Miss Jean Brodie*. New York: Delta, 1964 (1961), *133, 181, 184*

Speiser, Jean, *River in the Dark*. New York: John Day, 1960, *162, 164*

Spender, Stephen, "September Journal," *The Partisan Reader*, ed. William Phillips and Philip Rahv. New York: Dial Press, 1946, *129*

Spivak, Gayatri, "French Feminism Revisited: Ethics and Politics," *Feminists Theorize the Political*, ed. Judith Butler and Joan W. Scott. New York: Routledge, 1992, *41*

Spooner, John D., *The Pheasant-lined Vest of Charlie Freedman: A Novel of Wall-street*. Boston: Little, Brown, 1967, *144*

Stasio, Marilyn, "Crime," *The New York Times Book Review*, April 11, 2004, *112*

Stein, Gertrude, *Lectures in America*. Boston: Beacon Press, 1957 (1935), *125*

— , "Sacred Emily," *Geography and Plays*. Mineola, N.Y.: Dover, 1999 (1922), *12*

— , *Selected Writings of Gertrude Stein*, ed. Carl Van Vechten. New York: Random House, 1946, *134*

Steinbeck, John, *The Moon Is Down*. New York: Viking, 1942, *81, 117, 135, 144*

— , *The Pearl*. New York: Viking, 1947 (1945), *137*

— , *Sweet Thursday*. New York: Bantam Books, 1963 (1954), *15, 220*

— , *The Winter of Our Discontent*. New York: Viking, 1961, *96, 115, 118, 127*

Steinem, Gloria, *Revolution from Within: A Book of Self-Esteem*. Boston: Little, Brown, 1993 (1992), *210*

Stern, Richard, *Honey and Wax: Pleasures and Powers of Narrative*. Chicago: University of Chicago Press, 1966, *47*

Stetson, Erlene, "Silence: Access and Aspiration," *Between Women: Biographers, Novelists, Critics, Teachers and Artists Write About Their Work on Women*, ed. Carol Ascher, Louise DeSalvo, Sara Ruddick. New York: Routledge, 1993 (1984), *18*

Stevenson, Robert Louis, "The Strange Case of Dr. Jekyll and Mr. Hyde," in *Fables and Other Stories*. New York: Scribner's, 1925 (1896), *205*

Stewart, Garrett, review of *Literary Impressionism and Modernist Aesthetics*, by Jesse Matz, *Modernism/Modernity* 10, no. 4 (November 2003), *161*

Stewart, Janice S., *The Folk Arts of Norway*. Madison: University of Wisconsin Press, 1953, *200*

Stockwell, Anne, "Salma Hayek," *Ms. Magazine*, Winter 2003/2004, *179*

Stokstad, Erik, "Asthma Linked to Indoor Dampness," *Science* 304, no. 5675 (28 May 2004), *161*

Strauss, Michael A., "Reading the Blueprints of Creation," *Scientific American*, February 2004, *55, 56*

Street, John, "Here's Flowers for You," *The Countryman*, Summer 1966, *202*

Styron, William, *Lie Down in Darkness*. Indianapolis: Bobbs-Merrill, 1951, *114, 255*

Sullivan, Robert, *Rats: Observations on the History and Habitat of the City's Most Unwanted Inhabitants*. New York: Bloomsbury, 2004, *183*

Tan, Amy, *The Opposite of Fate: A Book of Musings*. New York: G. P. Putnam, 2003, *27, 39, 39, 41, 146, 151*

Tannen, Deborah, *Gender and Discourse*. New York: Oxford University Press, 1994, *75*

— , *You Just Don't Understand*. New York: William Morrow, 1990, *144*

Taubman, William, *Krushchev: The Man and His Era*. New York: W. W. Norton, 2003, *76*

Thomas, Audrey Callahan, *Ten Green Bottles*. Indianapolis: Bobbs-Merrill, 1967, *145, 221*

Thomas, Dylan, *Adventures in the Skin Trade and Other Stories*. New York: New Directions, 1955, *104, 156*

— , *The Beach of Falseá*. New York: Ballantine Books, 1968 (1963), *201*

Thomson, David, *England in the Nineteenth Century*. Baltimore: Penguin Books, 1963 (1950), *229*

Thurber, James, *Let Your Mind Alone*. New York: Grosset & Dunlap, 1960 (1935), *23*

— , "Newspaperman," *The New Yorker*, January 5, 1952, *193*

— , *The Wonderful O*. New York: Simon & Schuster, 1957, *174, 254*

Time, "...And Now a Word About Commercials," July 12, 1968, *231*

— , September 2, 1966, *169*

Tolkein, J. R. R., *The Fellowship of the Ring*. New York: Quality Paperback Book Club, 2001 (1954), *103*

— , *The Hobbit*. New York: Ballantine Books, 1966, *162, 192*

Toynbee, Philip, *Prothalamium*. Garden City, N.Y.: Doubleday, 1947, *108*

Tremain, Rose, *The Way I Found Her*. New York: Farrar, Straus & Giroux, 1997, *94*

Trillin, Calvin, *Floater*. Boston: Houghton Mifflin, 1980, *96*

— , *With All Disrespect: More Uncivil Liberties*. New York: Tricknor & Fields, 1985, *55*

Trilling, Diana, *Claremont Essays*. New York: Harcourt Brace, 1964 (1943), *175, 209*

Trumble, Angus, *A Brief History of the Smile*. New York: Basic Books, 2004, *247*

Tufte, Edward, *Beautiful Evidence*. Cheshire, Conn.: Graphics Press, 2006, *152*

— , *Envisioning Information*. Cheshire, Conn.: Graphics Press, 1990, *74*

Tufte, Virginia, with the assistance of Garrett Stewart, *Grammar as Style*. New York: Holt, Rinehart and Winston, 1971, *5*

Turner, Arlin, "Introduction," *The Blithedale Romance* by Nathaniel Hawthorne. New York: W. W. Norton, 1958, *246*

Turner, A. Richard, "Reason to Smile," *Los Angeles Times*, January 16, 2005, *163*

Tuve, Rosemond, *Allegorical Imagery*. Princeton, N.J.: Princeton University Press, 1965, *206*

Tyler, Parker, *The Films of Greta Garbo*. New York: Citadel Press, 1963, *210*

Untermeyer, Louis, *Lives of the Poets*. New York: Simon & Schuster, 1963 (1959), *195, 195, 196*

Updike, John, *Assorted Prose*. New York: Alfred A. Knopf, 1965, *177, 229*

— , *The Centaur*. Greenwich, Conn.: Fawcett, 1958, *42, 181*

— , *Of the Farm*. New York: Alfred A. Knopf, 1965, *98*

— , *Olinger Stories*. New York: Vintage Books, 1964 (1954), *95*

— , *Rabbit, Run*. Greenwich, Conn.: Fawcett, 1967 (1960), *119, 169, 257, 269*

— , *The Same Door*. New York: Alfred A. Knopf, 1959, *145*

U. S. Selective Service System Form 223, "Order to Report for Armed Forces Physical Examination," *85*

Van Deusen, Glyndon G., *William Henry Seward*. New York: Oxford University Press, 1967, *245*

Van Doren, Mark, *Collected Stories*, Vol. 1. New York: Hill & Wang, 1962, *106*

Van Ghent, Dorothy, *The English Novel: Form and Function*. New York: Harper & Row, 1967 (1963), *207, 259*

Vendler, Helen, *The Given and the Made: Strategies of Poetic Redefinition*. Cambridge, Mass.: Harvard University Press, 1995, *271*

Vidal, Gore, *Washington, D.C.* Boston: Little, Brown, 1967, *28*

Viramontes, Helena María, "The Cariboo Cafe," *The Moths and Other Stories*. Houston: Arte Publico Press, University of Houston, 1985, *184*

Virbila, S. Irene, "Still ahead of the curve: Vibrant, sexy and relaxed, the new Patina at Disney Hall attracts a lively crowd before and after concerts," *Los Angeles Times*, March 24, 2004, *33*

Vroman, Leo, *Blood*. New York: Natural History Press, 1967, *220*

Waggoner, Hyatt H., "Arts and Belief," *Hawthorne Centenary Essays*, ed. Roy Harvey Pearce. Columbus: Ohio State University Press, 1964, *246*

Wagoner, David, *The Escape Artist*. New York: Farrar, Straus & Giroux, 1965, *128*

Wain, John, *Death of the Hind Legs and Other Stories*. New York: Viking, 1966 (1963), *94*

— , *A Travelling Woman*. New York: St. Martins Press, 1959, *107, 107*

Walder, David, *The Gift Bearers*. New York: Coward-McCann, 1967, *100*

Walker, Alice, *In Search of Our Mothers' Gardens: Womanist Prose*. New York: Harcourt Brace Jovanovich, 1983, *102, 147, 147, 147, 148*

— , "A Sudden Trip Home in the Spring," *Black-Eyed Susans, Midnight Birds*, ed. Mary Helen Washington. New York: Anchor Books (Doubleday), 1990 (1975 and 1980), *13*

Wallant, Edward Lewis, *The Pawnbroker*. New York: Harcourt Brace, 1961, *223*

Walser, Richard, *Thomas Wolfe*. New York: Barnes & Noble, 1961, *227*

Warhol, Andy, *The Philosophy of Andy Warhol (From A to B and Back Again)*. New York: Harcourt Brace, 1975, *79, 258*

Warner, Marina, *From the Beast to the Blonde: On Fairy Tales and Their Telling*. New York: Noonday, Farrar, Straus & Giroux, 1996, *72*

Warren, Robert Penn, *Flood*. New York: Random House, 1964, *20, 167*

— , "Pure and Impure Poetry," *Selected Essays*. New York: Random House, 1958 (1935), *48*

— , *Wilderness*. New York: Random House, 1961, *89, 225, 226*

— , *World Enough and Time*. New York: Random House, 1950, *133*

Waterman, David, "Four's a Crowd," *The Guardian*, January 17, 2004, *106*

Waugh, Auberon, *The Foxglove Saga*. New York: Simon & Schuster, 1961, *135*

Waugh, Evelyn, *The End of the Battle*. Boston: Little, Brown, 1961, *127*

— , *A Little Learning: An Autobiography*. Boston: Little, Brown, 1964, *22, 73*

— , *The Loved One*. New York: Dell, 1958 (1948), *82*

Weinberg, Steven, *Facing Up: Science and Its Cultural Adversaries*. Cambridge, Mass.: Harvard University Press, 2003 (2001), *40*

Wells, Evelyn Kendrick, *The Ballad Tree*. New York: Ronald Press, 1950, *194*

Wells, Rebecca, *Little Altars Everywhere*. New York: HarperCollins, 1996 (1992), *93, 261*

Wells, Rulon, "Comments on Meter," *Essays on the Language of Literature*, ed. Seymour Chatman and Samuel R. Levin. Boston: Houghton Mifflin, 1967, *120*

West, Cornel, *Prophetic Fragments: Illuminations of the Crisis in American Religion and Culture*. Trenton: Africa World Press, 1988, *104, 104*

West, Rebecca, *The Birds Fall Down*. New York: Viking, 1966, *32*

Whall, Hugh D., "A House Is Not a Hot Rod," *Sports Illustrated*, July 28, 1969, *200*

Wheeler, Sara, "The Highbrow Hijacker," *The New York Times Review of Books*, April 18, 2004, *149*

White, E. B., *The Points of My Compass*. New York: Harper & Row, 1962 (1954), *18*

— , *The Second Tree from the Corner*. New York: Harper & Brothers, 1956, *80*

White, T. H., *Mistress Masham's Repose*. New York: G. P. Putnam, 1946, *168*

— , *The Once and Future King*. New York: Dell, 1960 (1939), *202*

Wiggins, Marianne, *Evidence of Things Unseen*. New York: Simon & Schuster, 2003, *209*

Wilder, Thornton, *The Eighth Day*. Harper & Row, 1967, *87*

Wiley, Marcia, "Special Report: New England Yachting: The Vineyard," *Yachting*, July 1966, *200*

Williams, Kathleen, *Spenser's World of Glass*. Berkeley: University of California Press, 1966, *127*

Williams, Tennessee, *The Roman Spring of Mrs. Stone*. New York: New Directions, 1950, *17*

Williams, William Appleman, *The Contours of American History.* Chicago: Quadrangle Press, 1966 (1961), *233*

Wilson, Angus, *A Bit Off the Map and Other Stories.* New York: Viking, 1957, *119*

— , *No Laughing Matter.* New York: Viking, 1967, *34*

Wilson, Edmund, *Memoirs of Hecate County.* New York: L. C. Page, 1959, *166*

— , *Patriotic Gore: Studies in the Literature of the American Civil War.* New York: Oxford University Press, 1962, *98*

Wilson, Elizabeth, *Adorned in Dreams: Fashion and Modernity.* New Brunswick, N.J.: Rutgers University Press, 2003, *13*

Winter, Ellen, *Gifted Children.* New York: Basic Books, 1996, *12*

Winterson, Jeanette, *Art Objects: Essays on Ecstasy and Effrontery.* New York: Random House, 1995, *11, 158, 159, 267*

— , *The Passion.* New York: Random House, 1989 (1987), *126*

Wodehouse, P. G., "The Man Who Disliked Cats," *The Man Upstairs and Other Stories.* New York: Penguin Books, 1938 (1914), *17*

— , *In His Own Words,* ed. Harry Day and Tony Ring. New York: Overlook Press, 2001, *69*

Wolf, Naomi, *The Beauty Myth: How Images of Beauty Are Used Against Women.* New York: HarperCollins, 2002 (1991), *19*

Wolfe, Thomas, *Look Homeward Angel.* New York: Scribner's, 1969 (1929), *238, 255*

— , *You Can't Go Home Again.* New York: Harper & Brothers, 1940, *118, 130*

Wolfe, Tom, *The Kandy-Kolored Tangerine-Flake Streamline Baby.* New York: Farrar, Straus & Giroux, 1966 (1963), *256*

Wood, Dennis, "Two Maps of Boylan Heights," in *You Are Here: Personal Geographies and Other Maps of the Imagination,* Katharine Harmon. New York: Princeton Architectural Press, 2003, *231*

Woodcock, George, *The Crystal Spirit: A Study of George Orwell.* Boston: Little, Brown, 1966, *79*

Woodhouse, C. M., "Introduction," *Animal Farm* by George Orwell. New York: New American Library (Signet), 1946, *106*

Woodman, Jim, *Air Travel Bargains.* New York: Simon & Schuster, 1968, *75*

Woolf, Leonard, *Downhill All the Way: An Autobiography of the Years 1919–1939.* London: Hogarth Press, 1967, *145*

Woolf, Virginia, *The Common Reader.* New York: Harcourt Brace Jovanovich, 1984 (1925), *18, 66, 160*

— , *Flush: A Biography.* New York: Harcourt Brace Jovanovich, 1933, *103*

— , *Mrs. Dalloway.* New York: Harcourt Brace, 1953 (1925), *108*

— , *To the Lighthouse.* New York: Harcourt Brace, 1955 (1927), *213, 256, 256, 262*

— , *A Writer's Diary,* ed. Leonard Woolf. New York: Harvest (Harcourt), 1982 (1954), *68*

Wright, Frank Lloyd, *Frank Lloyd Wright: Writings and Buildings,* ed. E. Kaufman and B. Raeburn. New York: Meridian Books, 1960, *176, 212*

Wright, Richard, *Savage Holiday.* New York: Avon Library, 1954, *263*

Wylie, Philip, *The Answer.* New York: Holt, Reinhart and Winston, 1956, *94*
— , *The Magic Animal.* Garden City, N.Y.: Doubleday, 1968, *263*
Wyndham, John, *Out of the Deep.* New York: Ballantine Books, 1953, *17*

Yachting, "This Month in Yachting," July 1966, *199*
Yagoda, Ben, *The Sound on the Page: Style and Voice in Writing.* New York: HarperCollins, 2004, *65*

Zavella, Patricia, "'Abnormal Intimacy': The Varying Work Networks of Chicana Cannery Workers," *Latina Issues: Fragments of Historia (Ella) (Herstory),* ed. Antoinette Sedillo Lopez. New York: Garland, 1994, *249*
Zimmer, Carl, "Mind Over Machine," *Popular Science,* February 2004, *165*
Zinsser, William K., *The City-Dwellers.* New York: Harper & Row, 1962 (1959), *77*

Index of Terms

Composed in Monotype Dante
Printed by Hamilton Printing Company
Design by Dmitry Krasny / Deka Design, Inc.
Production by Elaine Morse, Graphics Press LLC